LAW DICTIONARY

FOR

NON – LAWYERS

By

DANIEL ORAN, J.D.

ST. PAUL, MINN.
WEST PUBLISHING CO.
1975

Oran Law Dictionary
3rd Reprint—1980

to my parents, Max and Minerva
and to my wife, Elaine

*

INTRODUCTION

This is a guidebook to a foreign language. The language of Law uses mostly English words, but they rarely mean what they seem. Many look like everyday English, but have technical definitions totally different from their ordinary uses. Some contain complex legal ideas compressed into small phrases. Others mean several different things, depending on the area of law, business or politics they come from. Also, the language of Law contains more "leftovers" than most languages. Hundreds of Latin, Old English and Old French words are still used in their original forms. And the law keeps more outdated English words than any other profession.

This dictionary has two main purposes. Like any specialized dictionary, it attempts to help the reader both understand and use a technical vocabulary. It also tries to do one more thing: help the reader recognize and discard the vague, fuzzy words that sound precise and that lawyers often use as if they were precise. Using this guidebook, you will be able to understand a contract, a law, a court decision, and, perhaps, even a lawyer.

*

ACKNOWLEDGMENTS

Over the years, many people have given me training, ideas and encouragement that led to this dictionary. There is no way that I could list everyone who was helpful, but the shortest list would have to include Edwin Barrett, David Brodsky, Edgar Cahn, Jean Cahn, Thomas Emerson, Robert Fracasso, William Fry, Carolyn Hunter, Richard Jackson, Judith Lhamon, Edward Mattison, David Oran, Victoria Powell, Charles Reich, Ruth Robinson, Fred Rodell, Kirsten Seligman, Martin Seligman, Jay Shafritz, John Stein, Charles Todd, Dorothy Weitzman and Thomas Willging. As for the book itself, I owe thanks to William Statsky for structural suggestions and a wealth of other information and to Elizabeth and Jay Boris for suggestions each step of the way. Finally, my wife, Elaine, read every word and made hundreds of suggestions. To appreciate the size of this task, try reading a dictionary from cover to cover.

*

TABLE OF CONTENTS

*

HOW TO USE THIS DICTIONARY

HOW TO FIND THE WORD

1. Skim the area near where the word should be. Many legal words come from common bases and not every variation of each word is printed under a separate heading. The word you want may be printed in the definition of a nearby word.

2. Look up both halves of a compound word. For example, if you do not know what "comprehensive insurance" is and "comprehensive" is not listed in the dictionary, look under "insurance" even if you know what that word means.

3. Look up abbreviations exactly as found. They are in alphabetical order in the regular dictionary, not in a separate section.

4. If you cannot find a word in this dictionary, look in Appendix A, "Where to go for more information."

5. If neither this dictionary, nor the materials in Appendix A help, ask someone. If possible, ask the person who used the word. Many legal words are not spelled like they sound, so no amount of visual research will lead to their definitions.

READING THE DEFINITION

This book uses a few shortcuts to make it compact and to help make the definitions useful. The definitions speak for themselves, but the book can

HOW TO USE THIS DICTIONARY

be used more efficiently by first learning how it is set up:

1. BOLDFACE

If a word in a definition is in **Boldface,** it is defined in the dictionary. You can look it up if you need it.

2. BOLDFACE plus "(see that word)"

If you are referred to another word, complete knowledge of the word you originally looked up requires understanding the word you are sent to.

3. Italics

Italics are used to emphasize a word or to illustrate its use.

4. Commas (,), semicolons (;) and separate definitions (1, 2, 3.)

When definitions are separated by commas, they have different shades of meaning. When they are separated by semicolons, they are different, but related definitions. When they are separately numbered, they are either totally different or come from different areas of the law.

5. Ordinary English definitions omitted

Everyday English definitions of legal words are omitted unless they are necessary for comparison or to avoid confusion.

6. "Person" and "ix"

The word "person" is used in this dictionary to mean "person," "man or woman," "human being," "corporation," or "party." Also, the old

HOW TO USE THIS DICTIONARY

feminine suffix "ix" (executor/executrix) is omitted from those words that used to have alternate masculine/feminine endings.

7. Pronunciation

Most words in this dictionary are easy to pronounce; these do not have a pronunciation given. Other words need only accent marks for the strong syllable. This is done by underlining the parts of the word that get emphasized. For example, "testimony" means that the "tes" is sounded more strongly than the rest of the word. For the pronunciation of difficult words and an explanation of Latin pronunciation, see Appendix B, "Pronunciation."

8. Basic words

There are forty legal words that are used frequently in definitions. They are among the most basic words used in the law. If possible, look up those you do not know before using the dictionary. These central words are:

Action	Deed
Agency	Defendant
Bill	Document
Binding	Duty
Case	Estate
Contract	Evidence
Corporation	Executive
Court	Goods
Creditor	Grounds
Debtor	Judge

HOW TO USE THIS DICTIONARY

8. **Basic words**—Continued

Judgment	Plaintiff
Judicial	Pleading
Jury	Property
Law	Right
Lawsuit	Statute
Legislature	Testimony
Negotiable Instrument	Title
Order	Trial
Party	Will
Person	Witness

†

LAW DICTIONARY
FOR
NON-LAWYERS

A

A. **1.** (Latin) From, for, with (when translated into smooth English, can also mean in, of, by, etc.). **2.** Atlantic Reporter (see **National Reporter System**).

A.A.L.S. Association of American Law Schools.

A.B.A. American Bar Association; the largest voluntary organization of lawyers in the country. Its committees and branches are involved in almost every area of legal practice and government activity.

A.C.L.U. American Civil Liberties Union; a group that supports basic Constitutional freedoms by going to court, supporting and fighting laws, and public education.

A.F.D.C. Aid to Families with Dependent Children; the largest type of Federally funded welfare aid.

A.L.I. American Law Institute; an organization that writes model laws and carries on an education program for lawyers and other law-related persons.

A.L.R. **American Law Reports** (see that word).

A.P.A. **Administrative Procedure Act** (see that word).

A coelo usque ad centrum. (Latin) From the heavens to the center of the earth (a landowner's supposed property right).

A fortiori. (Latin) With stronger reason; for example: if it is true that a twenty-one year old person is an adult, then, *a fortiori,* a twenty-five year old person is an adult.

A mensa et thoro. A type of legal separation or limited **divorce** (see that word).

A posteriori. (Latin) From the effect to the cause; a method of reasoning that starts with experiments or observations and attempts to discover general principles from them.

A priori. From the cause to the effect; a method of reasoning that starts with general principles and attempts to discover what specific facts or real-life observations will follow from them.

Ab. (Latin) See **A.**

Ab ante. (Latin) In advance; before.

Ab antiquo. (Latin) Since ancient times.

Ab inconvenienti. (Latin) "From inconvenience"; a weak argument, offered only because you are forced to put up some sort of argument in a difficult case.

Ab initio. (Latin) From the very beginning; entirely and completely since the start.

Abandon. Give up completely and finally (see **abandonment**).

Abandonment. **1.** Complete and final giving up of property or rights with no intention of reclaiming them and to no particular person; for example: throwing away a book is *abandonment,* but selling or giving it away is not. **2.** A lawsuit may be thrown out of court if it is *abandoned* by failure to take any action on it for too long a time. **3.** Children are *abandoned* if they are either deserted or no longer cared for or looked after. **4.** A husband or wife is *abandoned* if the other leaves with the intent to stay away permanently.

Abatable nuisance. A **nuisance** (see that word) that is easily or practically stopped or made harmless.

Abate. **1.** Destroy or completely end. **2.** Greatly lessen or reduce.

Abatement. **1.** Reduction or decrease. **2.** Proportional reduction; for example: if a pot of money does not have enough to pay everyone it owes, each person may have to be satisfied with an *abatement* of his or her share. **3.** Removal of a **nuisance.** **4.** An ending or delaying of a lawsuit for technical reasons such as a failure to include all necessary persons. **5.** The order of reduction or elimination; for example, if a person leaves "five hundred dollars to John and five hundred dollars to my heirs," John gets five hundred dollars and the heirs' share may *abate* to zero if there is only five hundred dollars.

Abdication. The act of giving up the throne (by a king or other monarch).

Abduction. **1.** The criminal offense of taking away a person who is in the care of another. **2.** **Kidnapping** (see that word).

Abet. Encourage, request, order, or help another person to commit a crime.

Abettor. A person who **abets** (see that word) a crime.

Abeyance. In suspension; waiting; unfilled.

Abide. 1. Accept the consequences (usually of a court's judgment). 2. Be satisfied with. 3. Wait for. 4. Obey; for example: most persons *abide* by the law.

Abjuration. Taking an oath to give up property, rights, or personal convictions and opinions; for example: when you become a citizen, you *abjure* allegiance to all foreign governments.

Abnegation. Denial or renunciation.

Abode. Home or dwelling place.

Above cited (or Above mentioned). A vague legal phrase meaning "appearing earlier in this document."

Abovesaid. Vague and unnecessary word meaning "mentioned before" or "named before."

Abrogation. The destruction, ending or **annulling** of a former law.

Abscond. Secretly leave the area or hide in order to avoid some type of legal process such as an arrest or a lawsuit.

Absolute. Complete, final, and unconditional.

Absolute nuisance. A **nuisance** (see that word) that involves no **negligent** conduct.

Absque. (Latin) Without.

Abstention doctrine. The principle that a Federal court should refuse to decide some cases even though it has the power to do so; for example:

when a case can be taken care of purely by applying state law.

Abstract. **1.** A summary; for example: an abstract of **title** is a condensed history of the ownership of a piece of land that includes transfers of ownership and any rights (such as **liens**) that persons other than the owner might have in the land. **2.** See **abstraction**.

Abstraction. Taking something (usually money) with the intent to commit **fraud**.

Abuse. **1.** Misuse. **2.** Sexually molesting a child. **3.** Regularly injuring a child. **4.** Insult forcefully. **5.** *Abuse of discretion* is the failure to use sound, reasonable judgment as a judge or as an administrator. **6.** *Abuse of process* is using the legal process unfairly; for example: prosecuting a person for writing a bad check simply to put on pressure to pay.

Abut. Touch on, join, be side-by-side.

Accede. **1.** Come into a job or public office. **2.** Agree to.

Acceleration. **1.** Shortening of the time before a future event will happen. **2.** An *acceleration clause* is a section of a contract that makes the entire debt come immediately due because of a failure to pay on time or because of some other failure.

Accept. Receive with approval, satisfaction, or the intention to keep (see **acceptance**).

Acceptance. **1.** Agreeing to an **offer** and becoming bound to the terms of a **contract**. **2.** Taking something offered by another person with the intention of keeping it. **3.** Paying off on a **nego-**

tiable instrument, or the willingness and readiness to pay off; for example: a bank cashing a check.

Access. 1. Opportunity to approach; for example: most city lots have *access* to the street. 2. Right to approach; for example: *access* to public records includes both their practical availability and the right to see them.

Accession. 1. The right to own things that become a part of something already owned; for example: if land builds up on a riverbank, the bank's owner will also own the new land by *accession.* 2. See **accede.**

Accessory. 1. A person who helps commit a crime without being present. 2. An *accessory before the fact* is a person who encourages, orders or helps another to commit a crime without being present. 3. An *accessory after the fact* is a person who knows that a crime has been committed and helps to conceal the crime or the criminal.

Accident. A general word for an unexpected event (usually with harmful effects); the word has no precise legal meaning.

Accidental death benefit. Payment of extra insurance to the family of a person who died in an accident; usually the same thing as **double indemnity** (see that word).

Accommodation. A favor done for another person, usually involving **co-signing** to help another person get a loan or credit.

Accommodation paper. A **bill** or **note** that is signed on by one person as a favor to help another person get a loan.

Accommodation party. A person who signs an **ac-commodation paper** (see that word) as a favor to another person.

Accommodation personnel. Dummy incorporators (see that word).

Accomplice. A person who knowingly and voluntarily helps another person to commit a crime.

Accord. 1. An agreement to pay (on one side) and to accept (on the other side) less than all a debt or obligation is worth as full payment for that obligation; for example: there is an *accord* if a person agrees to take one hundred dollars as payment in full for one hundred and fifty dollars worth of damages to an auto and the person who did the damage agrees to pay the one hundred dollars. 2. An *accord and satisfaction* is an accord that has been completed by payment and a full **release.**

Account. A detailed written statement of money owed and paid.

Account stated. An exact figure for money owed, calculated by the person to whom the money is owed, and accepted as accurate by the person who owes the money.

Accountant. A person who specializes in the accuracy of financial records. This includes setting up financial record keeping systems, filling them in, and checking up on them. These duties include **auditing,** bookkeeping, and preparing financial statements. Normally, persons who do just bookkeeping do not have accounting skills. The next level of skill is accountant. Some accountants are specially trained and passed as Certified Public Accountants.

Accounts receivable. Lists of money owed to a person or company, but not yet paid.

Accredit. To officially recognize or approve something.

Accretion. The gradual adding on of land by natural causes such as the deposit of dirt by a river on its bank.

Accrual basis. A method of **accounting** that shows expenses **incurred** and income earned in a given time period, whether or not cash payments have actually changed hands during that period.

Accrue. Become due and payable; for example: in tax law, income *accrues* to a taxpayer when the taxpayer has an unconditional right to it and a likelihood of actually receiving it.

Accumulated earnings tax. A Federal tax on corporations that pile up profits without either distributing them to stockholders in the form of **dividends** or plowing the money back into the business.

Accumulation trust. A **trust** that keeps its income during the trust period rather than paying it out regularly to a **beneficiary.**

Accumulative sentence (or Accumulative judgment). A criminal **conviction** that takes place while another one is still being served. It takes effect after the first one is finished.

Accusation. A formal charge, made to a court, that a person is guilty of a crime.

8

Accusatory instruments. Papers that charge a person with a crime; for example: an **indictment,** an **information,** etc. (see these words).

Accused. The person against whom an accusation is made; the **defendant** in a criminal case.

Acknowledgement. 1. An admission or declaration that something is genuine; for example: a father's statements that a child is his may be an *acknowledgement.* 2. Signing a formal paper and swearing to it as your act before a court official such as a **notary public.**

Acquiescence. Silent agreement; knowing about an action or occurrence and remaining quietly satisfied about it.

Acquisition charge. A charge for paying off a loan before it comes due. Also called a *"prepayment penalty."*

Acquit. Set free from an obligation or an accusation; see **acquittal.**

Acquittal. 1. Formal legal determination that a person who has been charged with a crime is innocent. 2. A release from an obligation.

Act. 1. Something done voluntarily that may have legal consequences. 2. A written law that has been formally passed by a **legislature** such as Congress.

Act of bankruptcy. Any one of several financial actions (defined by Federal law) a person may take that makes that person **liable** to be proceeded against as a **bankrupt** by **creditors.**

Act of God. An event caused entirely by nature alone.

9

Actio. (Latin) A **right** and also the legal proceedings taken to enforce the right; an "**action**" or lawsuit; for example: in Roman law, an "*actio damni injuria*" was a lawsuit for **damages.**

Action. 1. Conduct or behavior. 2. The formal legal demand of your rights from another person made in court. Types of lawsuits are often grouped under various types of "actions" such as "**civil** action," "**common law** action," "**real** action," etc. (see these words). Actions may overlap; for example: one lawsuit may be both a common law action and a real action.

Actionable. An act or occurrence is *actionable* if it provides legal reasons for a lawsuit; for example: "*actionable words*" are statements by one person that are serious enough to support a lawsuit (or "action") for **libel** or **slander** by another person.

Actual. Real, substantial, and presently existing as opposed to possible or theoretical.

Actual authority. In the law of **agency** (see that word), the right and power to act that a **principal** (often an employer) intentionally gives to an **agent** (often an employee) or at least allows the agent to believe has been given. This includes both **express** and **implied** authority (see these words).

Actual cash value. The fair, usual or reasonable cash price that something will bring on the open market; the same as "**fair market price.**"

Actuarial method. The way of accounting for finances in a record book; for example, the *actuarial method* mentioned in the **Uniform Consumer Credit Code** is the method of applying payments made by a consumer first to **interest** and finance charges, then to paying off **principal** (the basic debt).

Actuary. A person who specializes in the mathematics of **insurance**; for example: the possibility of a person dying by a certain age, the money that should be paid for a certain type of insurance, etc.

Actus. (Latin) An **act** (see that word).

Ad. (Latin) To; for (when translated into smooth English, it can also mean by, because, until, near, etc.).

Ad damnum. (Latin) "To the **damages**"; that part of a **plaintiff's** original court papers that sets out the money loss or "damages."

Ad hoc. (Latin) "For this"; for this special purpose; for this one time; for example: an *ad hoc* committee is a temporary one set up to do a specific job.

Ad hominem. (Latin) "To the person"; argument or statements made against an opponent personally, rather than against the opponent's argument or position.

Ad idem. (Latin) To the same point; proving the same thing.

Ad litem. (Latin) "For the suit"; for the purposes of this lawsuit; for example: a *guardian ad litem* is a person who is appointed to represent a child (or other person lacking legal **capacity**) in a lawsuit.

Ad valorem. (Latin) According to value; for example: an *ad valorem* tax is a tax on the value of an item, rather than a fixed tax on the type of item. An *ad valorem* tax might tax a ten dollar hat fifty cents and a twenty dollar hat one dollar, while a specific hat tax might tax all hats seventy-five cents regardless of price or value.

Addict. A person who regularly uses something (such as a drug) to the extent that he or she no longer has control over the use.

Additur. 1. The power of a trial court to increase the amount of money awarded by a **jury** to a **plaintiff**. 2. The power of an **appeals** court to deny a new trial to the **plaintiff** if the **defendant** agrees to pay the plaintiff a certain amount of extra money.

Add-on. More goods bought before old goods are paid for; often, the contract for the original goods is rewritten to include the new things.

Adduce. Present or bring forward evidence in a trial.

Adeem. "Take away" (see **ademption**).

Ademption. 1. Disposing of something left in a **will** before death with the effect that the person it was left to does not get it. 2. The gift, before death, of something left in a will to the person who was left it; for example: Ed leaves a chair to Joan in his will, but gives her the chair before he dies.

Adequate. A general word for "enough." It has no precise legal meaning.

Adhesion. "Stick to"; for example: a "*contract of adhesion*" is one in which all the bargaining power (and all the contract terms) are unfairly on one side. This often occurs when buyers have no choice among sellers of a particular item.

Adjective law. Procedural law: the rules by which courts and agencies operate as opposed to what is usually thought of as "the law" or **substantive** law (see that word).

Adjourn. Postpone or suspend business (see **adjournment**).

Adjournment. Putting off business or a session to another time or place; the decision of a court, legislature, or other meeting to stop meeting either temporarily or permanently.

Adjudicate. To judge (see **adjudication**).

Adjudicated form. A **form** may be called "*adjudicated*" if a court has called it legally binding or has interpreted it in a useful way.

Adjudication. The formal giving, pronouncing, or recording of a **judgment** (see that word) for one side or the other in a lawsuit.

Adjudicative facts. Facts about the persons who have a dispute before an **administrative agency.** These are the "who, what, where, etc." facts that are similar to the facts that would go to a jury in a court trial. They are different from **legislative facts** (see that word).

Adjunction. Permanent attachment; for example: a patch sewn onto a coat.

Adjuration. Swearing to something under oath.

Adjust. Settle or arrange; bring persons to agreement, especially as to amount of money owed; the process is called "*adjustment*."

Adjusted gross income. A technical Federal income tax word that means, in general, the money a person makes minus deductions such as certain travel, work, business, or moving expenses, etc. For most persons, it is the same as "gross" or total income. The word is used for personal taxes, not for businesses.

Adjuster. A person who either determines or settles the amount of a claim or debt; for example: an *insurance adjuster* acts for an insurance company to determine and settle claims.

Adjustment securities. Stocks, etc. that are issued during a **corporate reorganization** (see that word). The "adjustments" are usually changes that make the new stock worth less than the stock it replaced.

Administer. 1. Manage; take charge of business. 2. Settle and **distribute** the estate (property, money, etc.) of a dead person. 3. Give; for example: *administer* an **oath.**

Administration. 1. Managing or running a business, organization, or part of a government. 2. Supervision of the **estate** of a dead person. 3. The persons and political party currently running the government.

Administrative agency. A sub-branch of the government set up to carry out the laws; for example: the police department is a local *administrative agency* and the **Internal Revenue Service** is a national one.

Administrative board. A broad term which may sometimes mean "**administrative agency**" (see that word) and sometimes mean a courtlike body set up by an agency to hold hearings.

Administrative discretion. Acts and duties performed by officials that are not precisely "covered" by a law or rules and that require the use of professional judgment and common sense.

Administrative law. 1. Laws about the proper running of an **administrative agency** (see that word) that are handed to agencies by **legislatures** and courts. 2. **Rules** and **regulations** set out by administrative agencies.

Administrative Procedure Act. A law that describes how U.S. agencies must do business (hearings, procedures, etc.) and how disputes go from these Federal agencies into court. Some states also have an Administrative Procedure Act.

Administrative remedy. A means of enforcing a right by going to an **administrative agency** (see that word) either for help or for a decision. Persons are often required to "**exhaust** administrative remedies," which means to fully submit their problem to the proper agency before taking it to court.

Administrator. A person appointed by the court to supervise handing out the **estate** (property) of a dead person.

Admiralty. A court that handles most maritime (seagoing) matters, such as collisions between ships and shipping claims.

Admissible. Proper to be used in reaching a decision; evidence that should be "let in" or introduced in court; evidence that the jury may use.

Admission. 1. An "*admission*" is a voluntary statement that a fact or a state of events is true (see **admissions**). 2. "*Admission to the bar*" is the formal procedure in which a lawyer is permitted to practice law. 3. "*Admission to bail*" is the court's decision to allow a person accused of a crime to be released if bail money is put up. 4. "*Admission* *of evidence"* is a decision by a judge to allow **evidence** to be used by the jury (or, if no jury, by the judge).

Admissions. Confessions, concessions, or voluntary acknowledgements; statements made by a **party** to a lawsuit (or the party's representative) that a fact exists which helps the other side or that a point the other side is making is correct.

Admit. See **admission.**

Admonition. 1. A reprimand given by a judge in place of a jail sentence or other serious punishment. 2. Oral advice by a judge to a jury.

Admonitory tort. An **intentional tort** of the type in which punishing the wrongdoer is more important than compensating the person hurt.

Adopt. 1. Accept, choose, or take as your own property, acts, or ideas. 2. Pass a law and put it into effect. 3. Take a child of another as your own, with all of the rights and duties there would have been if it had been your own originally. (Note: in some states, it is possible to adopt an adult in order to make that person your **heir.**)

Adult. A person over the legal age a state has set for full rights (such as voting) to begin.

Adulteration. Mixing inferior, cheaper, or harmful things in with better ones (to increase volume, lower costs, etc.).

Adultery. Voluntary sexual intercourse between a married person and a person who is not the husband or wife.

Advance. 1. Pay money before it is due; loan money; supply something before it is paid for. 2. An increase in price. **3.** A *motion to advance* is a request for an immediate trial.

Advance sheets. "Hot off the press" unbound copies of cases that will later be sent in bound form.

Advancement. Money or property given by a parent to a child (or to another **heir**) that the parent intends to be deducted from the child's eventual share in the parent's **estate** when the parent dies.

Adversary proceeding. A **hearing** (see that word) with both sides represented.

Adversary system. System of law in America, where the judge acts as the decision maker between opposite sides (between two individuals, between the state and an individual, etc.) rather than acting as the person who also makes the state's case or independently seeks out evidence. This latter method is called the "*inquisitorial system.*"

Adverse. Opposed; having opposing interests; against.

Adverse interest. Having opposing needs and desires from a person with whom you are associated.

Adverse possession. A method of gaining legal **title** to land by occupying the land openly and continuously for a number of years set by state law and openly and aggressively claiming your right to both own and occupy the land.

Advice. **1.** View or opinion. **2.** The **counsel** given to clients by their lawyers.

Advisement. Consideration; a case "under advisement" means that the judge has heard the evidence or arguments and will delay a decision in the case until it has been thought over for a while.

Advisory jury. A jury that a Federal judge can call to help decide **questions of fact** even though the judge has the right to decide them alone.

Advisory opinion. A formal opinion by a judge or judges about a question of law submitted by the **legislature** or by an **executive** (administrative) officer, but not actually presented to the court in a concrete lawsuit.

Advocacy. Forceful persuasion; arguing a cause, right, or position.

Advocate. 1. A person who speaks for another person, for a "cause", or for an organization in order to persuade others. 2. A lawyer. 3. To speak in favor of something.

Affiant. A person who swears to a written statement; a person who makes an **affidavit** (see that word).

Affidavit. A written statement sworn to before a person officially permitted by law to administer an oath; for example: an *affidavit of service* is a sworn statement that a legal paper has been "served" (mailed, handed to, ect.) upon another person in a lawsuit.

Affiliation proceedings. Same as **paternity suit** (see that word).

Affinity. Relationship by marriage; for example: a wife is related by *affinity* to her husband's brother.

Affirm. 1. Make firm; repeat agreement; confirm. 2. When a higher court **declares** that a lower court's action was valid and right, it "*affirms*" the decision. 3. Reaccept and make solid a contract that is breakable. 4. State positively.

5. Make a formal declaration in place of an **oath** (if oath-taking is against your principles).

Affirmance. See **affirm.**

Affirmation. A solemn and formal declaration in place of an **oath** for those persons whose religious beliefs forbid oath-taking.

Affirmative action. The requirement that an organization take steps to remedy past discrimination in hiring, promotion, etc.; for example, by recruiting more minorities and women.

Affirmative defense. That part of a **defendant's answer** to a **complaint** (see these words) that goes beyond denying the facts and arguments of the complaint. It sets out new facts and arguments that might win for the defendant even if everything in the complaint is true.

Aforesaid. A vague legal word meaning "preceding" or "already mentioned."

Aforethought. Planned in advance; premeditated.

After-acquired property. Property received after a certain event, such as the date a person **mortgages** other property. Some mortgages have an "*after-acquired property clause*" which means that anything added to the mortgaged property is subject to the mortgage just as if it were mortgaged directly.

After-acquired title. The legal principle that if a person transfers ownership to land for which he or she has no good **title** (right of ownership) and then gets good title to it, the title automatically goes to the person to whom the property was transferred.

After-born child. A legal principle that if a child is born after a **will** is made, the will can not prevent that child from taking a child's share of any **estate.**

Agency. 1. A relationship in which one person acts for or represents another by the latter's authority. 2. Short for "**administrative agency**" (see that word).

Agent. A person authorized (requested or permitted) by another person to act for him or her; a person entrusted with another's business.

Aggravated assault. A general term (defined more specifically by some state laws) that means an **assault** that is more serious or dangerous than normal.

Aggravation. Actions or occurrences that increase the seriousness of a crime, but are not part of the legal definition of that crime.

Aggressive collection. Various means of collecting a debt, such as **attachment, execution, garnishment,** etc. (see these words).

Aggrieved party. A person whose personal or property rights have been violated by another person.

Agreement. 1. A "meeting of minds." 2. An intention of two or more persons to enter into a **contract** with one another combined with an attempt to form a valid contract. An *agreement* may include the language used plus background facts and circumstances. 3. A contract.

Aid and abet. Intentionally help another person to commit a crime.

Aid and comfort. 1. Help or encourage. 2. To "*aid and comfort the enemy*" is committing **treason** according to the U.S. Constitution.

Aider. The legal conclusion that once a jury gives a **verdict,** those facts that the jury logically needed to reach the verdict are assumed to be properly **alleged** and proved.

Air rights. The right to build above a piece of land; for example: the right to put a building over a sunken road.

Alderman. 1. A person elected to a city council or other local governing body. 2. A low-level local judge.

Aleatory contract. A **contract** with effects and results that depend on an uncertain event; for example: insurance agreements are *aleatory.*

Alia. (Latin) 1. Other things. 2. Other persons.

Alias. (Latin) 1. Short for "alias dictus" or "otherwise called"; a fictitious name used in place of a person's real name. 2. An *alias* **writ** or **summons** (see those words) is a second (or third, etc.) one put out through the court if the first one did not work.

Alibi. (Latin) "Elsewhere"; the excuse that at the time a crime was committed a person was somewhere else.

Alien. Any person who is not a U.S. **citizen,** whether or not that person lives here permanently.

Alienable. Subject to removal, taking away, transfer or denial.

Alienate. Transfer, **convey,** or otherwise dispose of property to another person; the process is called "*alienation*" when land is transferred.

Alienation clause. A part of an **insurance** policy that **voids** (ends) the policy if the property being insured is sold or otherwise transferred.

21

Alienation of affection. Taking away the love, companionship, or help of another person's husband or wife. (Note: this can no longer be the basis for a lawsuit in most states.)

Alimony. Court-ordered payments by a divorced husband to his ex-wife (or occasionally by wife to ex-husband) for ongoing personal support.

Aliquot. (Latin) A part; a fractional or proportional part.

Aliunde. (Latin) From another place; from outside this document.

All fours. Two cases or decisions are *on all fours* if they are generally similar and are exactly alike in all legally important ways.

Allegation. A statement in a **pleading** that sets out a fact that one side expects to prove.

Allege. State; assert; charge; make an **allegation**; for example: "*alleged*" often means "*merely* stated" or "*only* charged."

Allocation. Putting something in one place rather than in another; for example: crediting all of a payment to one account when it is not specifically marked and the customer has two accounts at the store.

Allocution. The formality in which a judge asks a prisoner whether he or she has any way to show that judgment should not be **pronounced** against him or her or has any last words to say before a sentence is given out.

Allodial. Old word describing land that was owned freely and completely.

Allograph. A document written or signed by one person for another person.

Allonge. A piece of paper attached to a **negotiable instrument** (see that word) to provide space for **endorsements** (signatures).

Alteration. 1. Making a thing different from what it was before without destroying its identity; a change or modification. 2. Writing or erasing on a document that changes its language or meaning.

Alternative pleading. Asserting facts that are mutually exclusive (that cannot logically, physically, etc. exist at the same time) in the same **pleading** (see that word).

Alternative relief. Asking the court, in a **pleading**, for help in ways that might contradict one another; for example: asking for either the return of a borrowed book or for payment of its value. Most courts allow this type of request.

Alternative writ. See **show cause order**.

Am.Jur. *American Jurisprudence*, a legal encyclopedia.

Ambiguity. Uncertainness; the possibility that something (usually a document) can be interpreted in more than one way.

Ambit. Boundary line; limit; border.

Ambulance chaser. 1. A lawyer or a person working for a lawyer who follows up on street accidents to try to get the legal business involved. 2. A lawyer who improperly solicits business or tries to get others to bring lawsuits.

Ambulatory. Movable; capable of being changed; **revocable**.

Amend. Improve; correct; change or review.

Amendment. 1. A change, usually for the better. 2. A change in a **bill** during its passage through a

legislature or in a law already passed. **3.** One of the provisions of the U.S. Constitution enacted since the original Constitution became law. **4.** The correction of a **pleading** that is already before a court.

American Digest System. A giant collection of summaries of every **reported** case (written **opinion**) in America since the sixteen hundreds. The years up to 1896 are in a *Century Digest*, each ten year period after that is in a *Decennial Digest* and the latest few years are in a *General Digest*. Each Digest has many volumes. The cases are organized by subjects according to the **Key Number System** (see that word).

American Jurisprudence. A legal encyclopedia that is cross-referenced with **American Law Reports** (see that word).

American Law Reports. A large series of books that selects important cases, prints them in full, and gives an **annotation** (a commentary) that is often long and that brings in a whole area of the law.

Amicable action. A lawsuit (involving a real, not a made-up problem) that is started by agreement of the two sides.

Amicus curiae. (Latin) "Friend of the court"; a person who is allowed to appear in a lawsuit (usually to file arguments in the form of a **brief,** but sometimes to take an active part) even though the person has no right to appear otherwise.

Amnesty. A wiping out, by the government, of guilt for persons guilty of a crime; a governmental forgiving.

Amortization. Paying off a debt in regular and equal payments. To *amortize* a loan, figure out the total interest for the whole time until the loan is paid off, add that total to the amount of the loan, and divide the total by the number of payments.

Analogy. Reasoning or arguing by similarities; for example: when there is no previous case on a subject (a "**precedent**"), lawyers will argue from cases that are similar or are decided by the same general principles.

Anarchy. Absence of government; absence of law.

Ancient lights. Windows that have had outside light for over a certain length of time (usually twenty years) cannot be blocked off by an adjoining landowner in some states.

Ancient writings. Documents over a certain age (usually thirty years) that are **presumed** to be genuine if they come from proper **custody** (keeping).

Ancillary. Aiding; a proceeding "on the side" that helps a main proceeding.

Ancillary administration. A proceeding in a state where a dead person had property, but which is different from the state where that person lived and has his or her main **estate administered.**

And/or. A vague term, best replaced by words that say exactly what you mean. For example: "I like ham and/or eggs" could be "I like ham; I like eggs; and I like them served together."

Animo. (Latin) With intention; for example: *animo furandi* (with intention to steal), *animo testan-*

di (with intention to make a will) or *animo rever-tandi* (with intention to return).

Animus. (Latin) Mind or intention (see **animo**).

Annex. Attach (usually something small to something large); for example: attaching a small piece of land to a large one or a small school district to large one; it can also mean attaching a side document to the main one or putting a permanent light fixture on a wall.

Annotated statutes. A set of books containing the laws plus commentary (history, explanations, cases discussing each law, etc.); for example: Connecticut General Statutes Annotated.

Annotation. 1. A note or commentary on a passage in a book or document intended to explain its meaning. 2. A legal *annotation* is usually an explanation of a **case** and a description of other similar cases. It usually follows the text of the **decision** in a collection of cases.

Annual percentage rate. The true cost of borrowing money, expressed in a standardized, yearly way to make it easier to understand **credit** terms and to "shop" for credit.

Annuity. A fixed sum of money paid to a person at fixed times for a fixed time period or for life.

Annul. Make void; wipe out; see **annulment**.

Annulment. 1. The act of making something **void** or wiping it out completely. 2. The *annulment* of a marriage wipes the entire past and past validity of the marriage off the books as opposed to a divorce, which only ends the marriage. A marriage will not usually be *annulled* by a court

26

unless it was **invalid** in some way from the beginning.

Anomalous. Unusual; an exception to a rule; abnormal.

Anon. Anonymous (author unknown).

Answer. The first **pleading** by the **defendant** in a lawsuit. This pleading responds to the charges and demands of the **plaintiff's complaint.** The defendant denies the plaintiff's charges and presents new facts to defeat them.

Ante. (Latin) Before.

Antenuptial. Before a marriage.

Anticipation. 1. The act of doing a thing before its proper time or simply to do it "before" something else. 2. The right to pay off a mortgage before it comes due without paying a "prepayment penalty."

Anticipatory breach. Breaking a contract by refusing to go through with it once it is entered into but before it is time to actually **perform** (do your side or share).

Antinomy. An inconsistency between ideas, authorities, laws, or provisions in a law.

Anti-trust acts. Laws to protect trade from **monopolies.**

Apparent. Easily seen; superficially true; for example: "*apparent authority*" is the **authority** an agent (such as an employee) seems to have, judged by the words and actions of the person who gave the authority and by the **agent's** own words and actions.

Appeal. 1. Ask a higher court to review the actions of a lower court in order to correct mistakes or injustice.   **2.** The process in no. 1 is called "*an appeal.*"

Appearance.   **1.** The coming into court as a **party** (**plaintiff** or **defendant**) to a lawsuit.   A person who does this "*appears.*"   **2.** The formal coming into court as a lawyer in a specific lawsuit; often also called "**entering**" the case.

Appellant.   The person who **appeals** a case to a higher court.

Appellate.   A higher court that can hear **appeals** from a lower court.

Appellate jurisdiction.   The power and authority of a higher court to take up cases that have already been in a lower court for trial and the power to make decisions about these cases without holding a trial.

Appellee.   The **party** in a case against whom an **appeal** is taken (usually, but not always, the winner in the lower court).

Appoint.   **1.** Give a person a job or duty; for example: to *appoint* a person to serve on a committee.   **2.** Give a **power of appointment** (see that word).

Apportionment.   Dividing something up by fair shares; for example: "one person—one vote" is the rule for the *apportionment* of voters to each **Congressional District** in a state so that each person is fairly represented.

Appose.   Examine the keeper of written records about those records.

Appraisal (or Appraisement).   **1.** Estimating the value of something by an impartial expert.   This is not the same as an **assessment** (see that word).   **2.** Fixing the fair value of **stock** by a court when stockholders in a **corporation** quarrel and some must be bought out.

Appreciation. The increase in value of a piece of property excluding increases due to improvements.

Apprehension. 1. The capture or arrest of a person on a criminal charge. 2. Fear.

Appropriation. 1. A **legislature's** setting aside for a specific purpose a portion of the money raised by the government; for example: a "*highway appropriation.*" 2. A governmental taking of land or property for public use. 3. Taking something wrongfully; for example: using a person's picture and name in an advertisement without permission.

Approval. A sale "*on approval*" means that the buyer may return the goods if they are unsatisfactory even if they are all the seller claims they are.

Appurtenance. Something that belongs to or is attached to something else; for example: both a right of way and a barn may be an appurtenance to land.

Appurtenant. Belonging to or added onto (see **appurtenance**).

Arbiter. A person who is chosen to decide a disagreement.

Arbitrage. Buying stocks or other financial papers in one market and selling them in another for the profit from price differences.

Arbitrary. Action taken according to a person's own desires; without supervision, general principles or rules to decide by.

Arbitration. Formally submitting a dispute to a person other than a judge whose decision is binding. This person is called an *arbitrator.*

29

Arbitrator. A person who conducts an **arbitration** (see that word).

Area-wide agreement. One union making the same labor agreement with many companies in one geographical area.

Arguendo. (Latin) Assume something as true (whether true or false) for the sake of argument.

Argument. 1. Persuasion by laying out facts, law and the reasoning that connects them. 2. The oral, in-court presentation of no. 1.

Argumentative. Stating not only facts, but conclusions.

Arms length. Not on close terms; not an "inside deal"; not done by a lawyer, **trustee,** or other person especially responsible to a person for faithfulness.

Arraign. To bring a **defendant** before a judge to hear the charges and to enter a **plea** (guilty, not guilty, etc.).

Arraignment. See **arraign**.

Array. The entire jury **panel**; a "challenge to the array" is an objection to the procedures by which the panel was chosen.

Arrears (or arrearages). Money owed that is overdue and unpaid.

Arrest. The official taking of a person to answer criminal charges. This involves at least temporarily depriving the person of liberty and may involve the use of force.

Arrest of judgment. A judge's temporary stopping of the court's **judgment** because of some apparent defect in the proceedings.

Arrogation. Claiming something or taking something without having any right to it.

Arson. The **malicious** and unlawful burning of a building.

Article. A separate and distinct part of a document.

Articles. 1. The separate parts of a document, book, set of rules, etc. 2. A law with several parts. 3. A system of rules; for example: "*articles of the navy*". 4. Certain types of contracts; for example: "*articles of partnership*," which set up a partnership or "*articles of association*," which set up non-**stock** (often non-profit) organizations.

Articles of incorporation. The document that sets up a **corporation**.

Artificial person. A being or "thing" that the law gives some of the legal rights and duties of a person; for example: a **corporation**.

As is. A thing sold "*as is*" is sold in a possibly defective condition and the buyer must take it with no promises other than that it is as seen and described.

As per. A general phrase used for "in accordance with" or "with reference to."

Asportation. Taking things and carrying them away illegally.

Assault. An intentional show of force or a movement that could reasonably make the person approached feel in danger of physical attack or harmful physical contact.

Assembly. 1. A large meeting. 2. The lower **house** of many state **legislatures**.

Assent. Approval; demonstrated agreement.

Assess. **1.** Set the value of something. **2.** Set the value of property for the purpose of taxing it. **3.** Charge part of the cost of a public improvement (such as a sidewalk) to each person or property directly benefiting from it.

Assessed valuation. The value placed on real estate for tax purposes by the government. It is usually less than "**market value.**"

Assessment. **1.** Deciding on the amount to be paid by each of several persons into a common fund. **2.** The process of listing and evaluating the worth of property for taxing it. This is not "**appraisal**" (see that word).

Assets. All money, property, and money-related rights (such as money owed) owned by a person or an organization. In a business, "*capital assets*" or "*fixed assets*" are those things that cannot be turned into cash easily (such as buildings); "*current assets*" or "*liquid assets*" are those things that can be turned into cash easily (such as cash or goods for sale); and "*frozen assets*" are those things that are tied up because of a lawsuit.

Assign. **1.** To appoint or select for a particular purpose or duty. **2.** To transfer or make over formally; for example: to **deed** over land to another person. **3.** To point out, set forth, or specify; for example: to "*assign errors*" is to specify them in a legal document.

Assigned account. Money owed by a customer to a business that is promised by the business to a bank as **security** for a debt owed to the bank by the business.

Assigned risk. A type of insurance (such as automobile accident insurance for a person who has had many accidents) that insurance companies handle only because state law requires it. These persons pay extra for insurance and are often assigned to each insurance company by a list.

Assignment. 1. The transfer of property or rights in property to another person. 2. See **assign.**

Assigns. Old word for persons to whom property is or will be transferred.

Assise (or Assize). Old word with various meanings including: certain English courts, laws, and **writs.**

Associate justice. The title of each judge (other than the chief justice) on an **appeals** court.

Association. General word meaning a group of persons joined together for a particular purpose.

Assumpsit. "He promised"; an old word meaning a promise to do or pay something. Certain types of lawsuits had this name; for example: "*indebitatis assumpsit*" was "he promised to pay the debt."

Assumption. The assumption of a **mortgage** is the taking over of a mortgage debt (for example, on a house) when buying the property.

Assumption of risk. If you expose yourself or your property to certain kinds of known dangers, you cannot collect **damages** if harmed. This is a legal rule in some states.

At large. 1. Unlimited, fully, in detail, everywhere. 2. Free, unrestrained, uncontrolled. 3. See **statutes at large.** 4. An *at large* election is one where everyone votes for a choice of all the candidates, rather than just candidates from one area.

Attachment. 1. The act of taking or seizing property or persons in order to bring them under the control of the court. For example: a bank account may sometimes be *"attached"* in order to make sure that a person pays a debt that might result from a successful lawsuit. 2. A document added onto another document. 3. A **security interest** (see that word), such as a **mortgage,** *attaches* if it is valid and can be enforced by the person who has it against the person who holds the attached property.

Attainder. The wiping out of **civil rights** that occurs when a person receives a death sentence. It usually includes the government's taking of all the person's property. This is no longer done in America. A *bill of attainder* was a **legislative** act pronouncing a person guilty (usually of **treason**) without a trial and sentencing the person to death and *attainder.* This is now prohibited by the Constitution.

Attempt. 1. An act that goes beyond preparation, but which is not completed. 2. An effort to commit a crime that goes beyond preparation, and which would have succeeded if it had not been prevented.

Attenuation. The breaking of a connection; for example: if many things happen between two events, the connection between these two events becomes *"attenuated"* or broken.

Attest. Swear to; act as a witness to; **certify** formally, usually in writing.

Attestation. The act of witnessing the signing of a document and signing that you have witnessed it.

Attorn. An old word that means: to agree to pay rent and be a tenant to a new landlord who buys the land.

Attorney. 1. Lawyer ("*attorney at law*"). 2. Any person who acts formally for another person ("*attorney in fact*").

Attorney General. The chief law officer of each state and also of the United States; the U.S. Attorney General is also the head of the Department of Justice and a Cabinet member.

Attorney's lien. The right of lawyers, in some circumstances, to hold a client's money already in the lawyer's hands or to get at a client's money in the court's hands, to pay for attorney's fees.

Attractive nuisance. A legal principle used in some states, that says if a person keeps dangerous property in a way that children might be attracted to it and be able to get at it, then that person is responsible even if the children are at fault when they get hurt.

Att'y. Attorney.

Audit. An official examination of an account or of a person's or an organization's financial situation.

Auditor. An official who examines **accounts** and decides whether they are accurate.

Authentication. A formal act **certifying** that a public document (a law, a record of **deeds,** etc.) is official and correct, so that it may be **admitted** as **evidence.**

Authorities. **Citations** or references taken from laws, decisions, texts, etc., in support of a legal position argued by an advocate, a decision maker, or a scholar.

Authority. 1. Permission to act. 2. Power to act. 3. See **authorities.**

Authorize. Give the right to act; *"authorized"* means officially permitted.

Autopsy. Examination of a dead body to find out the cause of death. Evidence from an autopsy is called "autoptic evidence."

Autre (or Auter). (French) Another; for example: *"Autre vie"* means "during another person's lifetime."

Auxiliary. Aiding, **subsidiary, ancillary.**

Avails. Profits or **proceeds.**

Aver. Declare, assert, **allege,** set out clearly and formally.

Averment. Statement of facts.

Avoidance. 1. Escaping or evading. 2. In pleading, avoidance is a statement admitting the facts in a pleading by the other side, but showing why these facts should not have their ordinary legal effect. 3. **Annulling** or cancelling.

Avowal. An offer of **proof** (made out of the jury's hearing) in order to have it just in case an **appeals** court says that the witness should have been allowed to testify before the jury.

Avulsion. The sudden loss of land, such as a storm tearing away part of a riverbank.

Award. 1. To give or grant by formal process; for example: a jury *awards* **damages** and a company awards a contract to a bidder. 2. The decision of an **arbitrator** or other non-judge in a dispute submitted to him or her.

B

B.F. Old abbreviation for the Latin "bona fides" (good faith).

B.I.A. Bureau of Indian Affairs: the branch of the U.S. **Interior** Department that acts as **trustee** for Indian lands and handles Indian problems.

B.J. Bar Journal.

B.N.A. Bureau of National Affairs; a publisher of **loose-leaf services** in specialty areas of the law.

Bad faith. Dishonesty in dealing with another person whether or not actual **fraud** is involved.

Badge of fraud. Strong suspicion of **fraud.**

Bail. 1. Persons who put up money or property to allow the release of a person in jail until time of trial. **2.** The money or property put up by the person in no. 1. This money, often in the form of a bail **bond,** may be lost if the person released does not appear in court.

Bail bond. A written statement of debt that is put up by an arrested person and others who back it up. It promises that the arrested person will show up in court or risk losing the amount of the bond.

Bailee. A person to whom property is loaned or otherwise entrusted.

Bailiff. 1. A **sheriff's** deputy or a low-level court official who keeps the peace in court. **2.** A low-level official; a superintendent or steward.

Bailment. A delivery of property by the owner to another person. It is for temporary care, as a loan, for repair, etc. A *bailment for term* is a delivery of property for a set length of time, such as a month.

Bailor. Person who entrusts property to another.

Bait and switch. Advertising one item to get people to come into a store and then persuading them to buy a different item. This may be illegal if the original item was never really available or if it was not really as advertised.

Balance sheet. A complete summary of the financial worth of a company, broken down by **assets** and **liabilities** (see these words).

Balloon payment (or Balloon loan). A loan in which the last payment is much larger than any of the other regular payments. This gives the customer a feeling that low payments will pay off a debt, but the *balloon payment* at the end is rarely noticed and must often be **refinanced.** The Federal Truth-in-Lending law requires the clear disclosure of a balloon payment and many state laws prohibit them entirely.

Banc. (French) Bench; place where the court normally does business. A court "sitting in banc" (or "en banc") is a session of all the judges together.

Bank. 1. A commercial business that the laws allow to receive deposits, make loans, and perform other money-related functions. 2. See **Banc.**

Banker's lien. A bank's right to take for its own the money or property left in its care by a customer if the customer owes an overdue debt to the bank and if the money, to the bank's knowledge, belongs fully to the customer.

Bankruptcy. The procedure, under the Federal Bankruptcy Act, by which a person is relieved of all debts once the person has placed all property and money in the court's care; or by which an organization in financial trouble is either restructured by the court or ended and turned into cash to pay **creditors** and owners. *Bankruptcy* is a legal word and, while triggered by **insolvency,** (see that word) does not mean the same thing.

Bar. 1. The entire group of lawyers permitted to practice law before a particular court. 2. The part of some courtrooms where prisoners stand. 3. A barrier or prohibition.

Bar act. State law that sets up what a lawyer may and may not do.

Bar association. A voluntary group of lawyers as opposed to a group of lawyers who are required to be members of a court's **"integrated bar"** (see that word).

Bar examination. The written test that a new lawyer must pass in order to practice law. Some states use the "Multi-state" exam and some rely entirely on their own tests.

Bargain. A mutual understanding, **contract** or agreement.

Bargaining agent. A union that has the exclusive right to represent all the employees of a certain type at a company.

Bargaining unit. Those employees in a company who are best suited to be treated as one group for purposes of being represented by a union.

Barratry. The offense of stirring up quarrels or lawsuits; usually applied to a laywer's trying to stir up a lawsuit from which the lawyer can profit.

Barrister. 1. An English lawyer who argues in actual court trials. 2. A lawyer.

Barter. An exchange of things for things as opposed to a sale of things for money.

Basis. The amount that property is assumed to be worth for tax purposes at the time you receive it.

Bastardy action. Same as **paternity suit** (see that word).

Battery. Any intentional, unwanted, unprovoked, harmful physical contact by one person (or an object controlled by that person) with another person.

Bearer. A person in possession of a **negotiable instrument** (for example, a check) that is made out "payable to bearer" or that is indorsed in blank (signed, but no name filled in on the "payable to" line).

Behoof. Old word for use or benefit.

Belief. A sense of firmness about the truth of an idea that lies somewhere between "suspicion" and "knowledge."

Below. A lower court.

Bench. 1. The place where judges sit in court. 2. Judges collectively are "the bench."

Bench warrant. A paper issued directly by a judge to the police or other **peace officers** to permit the arrest of a person.

Beneficial. Giving a profit or advantage.

Beneficial interest. Right to profits resulting from a contract, **estate,** or property as opposed to the legal ownership of these things.

Beneficiary. 1. A person (or organization, etc.) for whose benefit a **trust** is created. 2. A person to whom an **insurance** policy is payable. **3.** A person who inherits under a **will**.

Benefit. Any advantage, profit, or privilege.

Benefit of clergy. The right that clergymen had in old England to avoid trial by all non-church courts.

Benevolent corporation (or Benevolent association). Non-profit charitable organization that may receive certain tax advantages.

Bequeath. **1.** Give **personal property** or money (as opposed to real estate) by **will**. **2.** Give anything by will.

Bequest. **1.** A gift by will of personal property. **2.** Any gift by will.

Best evidence. A rule of **evidence** that requires that the most reliable available proof of a fact must be produced; for example: if a painting is available as evidence, a photograph of the painting will not do.

Bestiality. Sexual intercourse between a human and an animal; a crime in most states.

Beyond a reasonable doubt. The level of proof required to convict a person of a crime. For a jury to be convinced "beyond a reasonable doubt," it must be fully satisfied that the person is guilty. This is the highest level of proof required in any type of trial. It does not mean "convinced one hundred percent," but it comes close to that meaning.

Bias. **1.** Preconceived opinion that makes it difficult to be impartial. **2.** Preconceived opinion by the judge about one or more of the persons in-

41

volved in a lawsuit as opposed to an opinion about the subject matter.

Bicameral. Two chambers; a legislature with two "houses," such as the U.S. Senate and House of Representatives.

Bigamy. The crime of having two husbands or wives at the same time.

Bilateral contract. A deal that involves promises, **rights,** and **duties** on both sides; for example: a **contract** to sell a car is *bilateral* because one person promises to turn over the car and the other person promises to pay for it.

Bill. **1.** A formal written statement sent to a higher court either to inform it of certain facts or to request certain actions; for example: a *bill of exceptions* is a list of objections to the rulings and actions of the trial judge by one side. **2.** A **draft** of a law proposed to a **legislature** or working its way through the legislature. **3.** A law passed by a legislature when it proceeds like a court; for example: a *bill of impeachment.* **4.** An unusually important declaration; for example: the *Bill of Rights* (see that word). **5.** A list of debts, contract terms or items; for example: a *bill of lading* (list of goods shipped). **6.** A type of **negotiable instrument** (see that word), promising the payment of money; for example: a *bill of exchange* (a written **order** from A. to B., telling B. to pay C. a certain sum of money). **7.** A statement of details in court; for example: a *bill of particulars* (a breakdown of one side's demands against the other in a lawsuit) or a *bill of indictment* (the formal accusation of a crime presented to a grand jury.

Bill of attainder. See **attainder.**

Bill of lading. A document given by a railroad, shipping company, or other **carrier** that lists the goods accepted for transport and sometimes lists the terms of the shipping agreement.

Bill of particulars. A detailed statement of charges or claims by a **plaintiff** or the **prosecutor** (given upon the **defendant's** request).

Bill of review. Request that a court set aside a prior **decree.** It is a new suit, not a reopening of the old one.

Bill of Rights. The first Ten Amendments (changes) to the U.S. Constitution that provide for: **1. Freedom of speech,** religion, press, assembly and to petition the government. **2.** Right to keep weapons. **3.** Freedom from being forced to give room or board to soldiers. **4.** Freedom from unreasonable searches and seizures and the requirement that **warrants** be supported by **probable cause. 5.** The requirement that crimes be **indicted,** the prohibition against **double jeopardy,** the freedom from being a witness against yourself in a criminal trial, and the requirement that no rights or property be taken away without **due process of law** and just compensation. **6.** The rights to a speedy criminal trial, an impartial jury, knowledge of the charges, **confrontation** of adverse witnesses, **compulsory process** of witnesses, and the help of a lawyer. **7.** The right to a jury trial. **8.** The prohibition against excessive **bail,** excessive fines, and cruel and unusual punishment. **9.** The fact that some rights are spelled out in the Constitution does not mean that these are all the rights the people have. **10.** Any powers not kept solely for the U.S. belong to the states and to the people.

Bind. 1. Hold by legal obligation. **2.** To "*bind over*" is to transfer or send a **defendant** to the court that will hear the case.

Binder. Temporary, preliminary **insurance** contract.

Binding authority. Sources of law that *must* be taken into account by a judge in deciding a case; for example: **statutes** from the same state or decisions by a higher court of the same state.

Binding over. 1. Act by which the court requires a **bond** or **bail** money. **2.** Act by which a court transfers a defendant to another court in the same system.

Black Acre. A made-up name for a piece of real estate for use in teaching law; often used together with "*White Acre*."

Black Letter Law. Important legal principles that are accepted by most judges in most states.

Blackmail. Illegal pressure or **extortion** of money by threatening to expose a person's illegal act or threatening to destroy a person's reputation; some states require this to be in writing for it to be the crime of blackmail and not just extortion.

Blackstone. *Blackstone's Commentaries on the Common Law*; an influential treatise on the law of England, written in the eighteenth century.

Blank. 1. A space left in a written or printed document. **2.** A printed document (a "form") with spaces to be filled in; a model document.

Blank indorsement. Signing a **negotiable instrument**, such as a check, without specifying to whom it is being signed over (leaving a blank in that space) and thus not limiting who can cash it.

Blanket. Covering most (or many) things.

Blotter. The police record form for **booking** (see that word) a **defendant**.

Blue book. 1. A book showing the proper form of case **citations.** 2. A book that gives the organization of and lists the persons in a state government.

Blue law. A state law that forbids selling or other activities on Sunday; originally, any law based on religious restrictions.

Blue ribbon jury. A **jury** specially chosen to try important or complex cases. This practice is rarely permitted.

Blue sky law. A law **regulating** and supervising sales of **stock** and other activities of investment companies to protect the public from fly-by-night or **fraudulent** stock deals.

Board of directors. Governing group of a **corporation.**

Body. 1. A person or an organization such as a "*body corporate*" (a corporation). 2. The main or most important part of a document. 3. A collection of laws.

Body execution. Legal authority to deprive a person of freedom and to take that person to jail.

Boiler plate. A form for a document, usually sold by a stationery store; the word implies standardization or lack of tailoring to the individual legal problem.

Bona fide. (Latin) Honest; in good faith; real.

Bond. A document that is evidence of a debt. The debt may be money owed (such as a U.S. *savings bond*) or money owed only if a certain act is not done (such as *a bail bond*).

Book value. 1. **Net worth** (see that word); clearly proven **assets** minus **liabilities.** 2. The worth of something as recorded on a company's **financial statement.**

Booking. 1. The police writing down facts about a person's arrest and charges along with identification and background information. This is recorded on the police **blotter** in the police station. 2. The process in no. 1 plus questioning the person, setting bail, etc. "Booking," if this extensive, may take place in a courthouse, jail, etc.

Bookkeeping. Writing down the financial transactions of a business in a systematic way.

Boot. Something extra thrown into a bargain.

Bottomry. A loan to repair or equip a ship.

Boycott. The refusal to do business with and the attempt to stop others from doing business with a company. In labor law, a *primary boycott* involves a union and an employer while a *secondary boycott* involves companies that do business with (usually by buying from) the union's employer.

Bracket. See **tax rate.**

Breach. Breaking a law or failing to perform a duty.

Breach of contract. Failure, without legal excuse, to **perform** any promise or to carry out any of the terms of a **contract.**

Breach of peace. A vague term for a disturbance of public order. It is defined and enforced differently in different states.

Breach of promise. Short for "breach of promise to marry."

Breaking. Using force or some kind of destruction of property (including things that do not permanently destroy, such as picking a lock), usually to illegally get into a building.

Bribery. The offering, giving, receiving, or soliciting of anything of value in order to influence the actions of a public official.

Brief. 1. A written summary or condensed statement of a series of ideas or of a document. 2. A written statement prepared by one side in a lawsuit to explain its case to the judge. It usually contains a fact summary, law summary, and an argument about how the law applies to the facts. 3. A summary of a published opinion in a case prepared for studying the case.

Bring suit (or Bring an action). Start a lawsuit, usually by filing the first papers.

Broker. An **agent** who is employed by different persons to buy, sell, make bargains or enter into **contracts.**

Brother. Old expression for "fellow lawyer."

Budget. 1. Money allowed for a particular purpose. 2. An estimate of money that will be spent in a particular time period.

Buggery. **Sodomy** or **bestiality** (see those words).

Building line. A certain distance inside the border of a lot, outside of which no building may extend.

Bulk transfer. According to the **Uniform Commercial Code,** a *"bulk transfer"* is "not in the ordinary course of business" and of "a major part of materials, supplies or other inventories." Rules against "bulk sales" "bulk mortgages" or "bulk transfers" are to protect a merchant's **creditors** from being cheated.

Bulletin. Name for many different types of legal publications such as pamphlets with **agency** rules or **law journals.**

Burden of going forward (or Burden of proceeding). The requirement to come forward with evidence on a particular question in a lawsuit, rather than wait for the other side to do it.

Burden of proof. The requirement that to win a point or have an issue decided in your favor in a lawsuit you must show that the weight of evidence is on your side, rather than "in the balance" on that question.

Bureaucracy. An organization, such as an administrative agency or the army, with the following general traits: a chain of command with fewer people at the top than at the bottom; well defined positions and responsibilities; fairly inflexible rules and procedures; "red tape"; many forms to be filled out; and **delegation** of authority downward from level to level.

Burglary. Breaking and entering the house of another person at night with the intention of committing a **felony** (usually theft). Some states do not require a "breaking" or that the building be a house or that it be at night for the entry to be called a *burglary*.

Business judgment rule. The principle that if persons running a **corporation** make honest, careful decisions within their corporate powers, no court will interfere with these decisions even if the results are bad.

Business record exception. An exception to the "hearsay exclusion rule" that allows original, routine records (whether or not part of a "business") to be used as **evidence** in a trial even though they are **hearsay** (see that word).

Business trust. A company set up in the form of a **trust** (see that word) that is similar to a **corporation** (see that word) in most ways. One difference is that the **trustees** are permanent, but a corporation's **directors** are usually elected for a year or a few years.

"But for" rule. Negligence alone will not make a person responsible for damage unless *"but for"* that negligence the damage would not have happened; for example: a failure to signal a turn may be negligent, but if the other driver was looking the other way, the failure to give a turn signal was not the cause of the accident.

By-laws. **Rules** or **regulations** adopted by an organization such as a **corporation,** club, or town.

C

C. Old abbreviation for the Latin "cum" (with).

C.A. Court of Appeals.

C.A.B. Civil Aeronautics Board: a U.S. agency that **regulates** all non-military flying.

C.C.A. Circuit Court of Appeals.

C.C.H. Commerce Clearing House; a publisher of **loose-leaf services.**

Cf. (Latin abbreviation) "Compare"; "cf. *Black's*" means "look at Black's for a comparison with or explanation of what is being discussed."

C.F. & I. (or C.I.F.) The price includes cost, freight and insurance (all paid by seller).

C.F.R. Code of Federal Regulations; the place where all Federal **administrative** rules are collected.

C.I.A. Central Intelligence Agency: the U.S. international spying department.

C.J. Chief judge or chief justice.

C.O.G.S.A. Carriage of Goods by Sea Act.

C.P. **Common Pleas** (see that word).

C.P.A. **Certified** Public Accountant (see **accountant**).

C.S.C. Civil Service Commission: **regulates** Federal employment (job classification, merit-system examinations, etc.).

C.T.A. **Cum testamento annexo** (see that word).

Cabinet. A group of persons who advise the U.S. President. It is made up of the heads of the major agencies such as the State and Treasury Departments. State governors may also have a cabinet.

Calendar. The trial list or **docket** of lawsuits ready for the court.

Call. 1. Public announcement (usually of a list). 2. A formal demand for payment according to the terms of a contract.

Call numbers. A way of finding books by using a combination of letters and numbers to identify the book. The first letter is the first letter of the last name of the author. No two authors share the same set of letters and numbers. Each library has its own setup under this system.

Camera. Chamber; see **in camera.**

Cancel. 1. Wipe out, cross out, or destroy the effect of a document by defacing it (by drawing lines across it, stamping it "cancelled," etc.). **2.** Destroy, **annul,** set aside or end; the process is called "*cancellation.*"

Cancellation. Under the **Uniform Commercial Code,** "*cancellation*" means ending a **contract** because the other side has **breached** (broken) the agreement.

Canon. A law, rule or principle.

Canon law. English religious law.

Canons of construction. Principles to guide the **interpretation** or **construction** of written documents to decide their legal effect.

Canons of Ethics. Old form (until 1969) for the **Code of Professional Responsibility** (see that word); the rules governing the legal profession.

Canons of Judicial Ethics. Old rules for judges' conduct, still used by many states, but gradually being replaced by the **Code of Judicial Conduct.**

Capacity. 1. Ability to do something. **2.** Legal right to do something.

Capias. (Latin) "That you take"; a **writ** from a judge to the **sheriff** or the police commanding them to take a **defendant** into **custody.**

Capital. 1. Head; chief; major; for example: *capital crimes* are those punishable by death and *capital punishment* is the death penalty. **2.** Relating to wealth; for example: *capital stock* is the stock put out by a corporation in exchange for the money invested in the company. **3.** Assets or worth.

Capital asset. Almost all property owned other than things held for sale. Examples of personal *capital assets* are personally owned stocks, land, trademarks, jewelry, etc. Business capital assets are described under **assets.**

Capital gains tax. A tax on the profit made on the increase in value of a *capital asset* (stocks, bonds, etc.) when it is sold.

Capitalize. 1. Treat the cost of something (a purchase, an improvement, etc.) as a **capital asset** (see that word). **2.** Issue **stocks** or **bonds** to cover an investment. **3.** Figure out the **net worth** or **principal** on which an investment is based.

Capitation tax. A tax on a person at a fixed rate, regardless of income, assets, etc.; a "head tax."

Caption. The heading or introductory section of a legal paper that has, for example, the names of the **parties,** the court, the case number, etc.

Care. 1. Safekeeping or **custody. 2.** Attention, heed or caution. There are various types of *care,* each defined in many ways, that apply to different situations; for example: in a normal driving situation, a person must act with "*reasonable care.*" One definition of reasonable care is "ordinary or due care . . . what may be expected from a normal person under the circumstances."

Carnal knowledge. Sexual intercourse.

Carrier. A person or organization that transports persons or property. A *common carrier* does this for the general public.

Carrier's lien. The right of a shipping company or other mover of property to hold the things shipped until the shipping costs have been paid.

Carry back (and Carry over). A tax rule that allows a person or company to use losses to reduce taxes in the year prior to (or the year following) the loss.

Carrying charges. 1. Costs of owning property, such as land taxes, mortgage payments, etc. **2. Interest.**

Cartel. A close association of companies carrying on the same or similar businesses.

Case. 1. Lawsuit; a dispute that goes to court. **2.** Short for *trespass on the case*, an old form of lawsuit that became **contract** law.

Case method (or Case system). The way most law schools teach law: by studying **cases** (judicial opinions) in each subject of the law historically and drawing general legal principles from them.

Casebook. A collection of written court opinions, usually by appeals judges. It is used for law school teaching.

Case-in-chief. The main **evidence** offered by one side in a lawsuit. This does not include evidence offered to oppose the other side's case.

Caselaw. All reported judicial decisions; the law that comes from reading judges' opinions in lawsuits.

Cases and controversies. The U.S. Constitution gives to the courts the power to decide "*cases or* *controversies.*" These are real (not hypothetical or faked) disputes that turn into lawsuits.

Cash basis. A system of bookkeeping that shows a profit or loss when the money actually comes in or goes out.

Cash surrender value. The amount of money an insurance policy will bring if cashed in with the company.

Casual. Accidental, by chance, unexpected, unintentional.

Casual ejector. See **ejectment.**

Casualty. Accident; unexpected accident; inevitable accident.

Categorical assistance. Financial help programs that have requirements in addition to financial need; for example: "Aid to the Blind."

Causa. (Latin) Cause, reason or motive.

Causa causans. (Latin) See **proximate cause.**

Causa mortis. (Latin) "In thinking about approaching death,"; for example: a gift *causa mortis* may be treated by the law as an attempt to avoid a tax on property given by **will** if the gift comes too close to death.

Causa proxima. (Latin) See **proximate cause.**

Cause. 1. That which produces an effect. 2. Motive or reason. 3. Lawsuit or legal action. 4. Short for "*just cause*" in the removal of a person from office or dismissal of a person from a job.

Cause of action. Facts sufficient to support a valid lawsuit; for example: a *cause of action* for **battery** (see that word) must include facts to prove an intentional, unwanted physical contact.

Caveat. 1. (Latin) "Let him or her beware"; usually used with another word, for example: *caveat emptor* (let the buyer beware), a rule of law that has been greatly weakened by recent laws and judicial decisions. 2. Warning.

Cease and desist order. A command from an **administrative agency** that is similar to a court's **injunction.**

Cede. 1. Assign, grant, or give up. 2. The transfer of land from one government to another.

Celebration. Formal ceremony.

Censorship. The denial of **freedom of speech** or freedom of the press.

Century Digest. (Abbreviated Cent. Dig.) See **American Digest System.**

Certificate. Written assurance that something has been done or some formal requirement has been met.

Certification proceeding. A procedure taken by the National Labor Relations Board to find out if the employees of a company want a particular union to represent them.

Certified. Officially passed, "checked out" or approved.

Certified check. A check that a bank has marked as "guaranteed cashable" for its customer before it goes out.

Certiorari. (Latin) "To make sure"; a request for *certiorari* (or "cert." for short) is like an **appeal,** but one which the higher court is not required to take for decision.

Cession. A giving up of something; see **cede.**

Cestui que. (French) "He or she who"; used in combination with another word; for example: "cestui qui trust", he or she who has a right to the property, money, and **proceeds** being managed by another. The modern phrase is "**beneficiary** of a **trust.**"

Chain of title. List of the consecutive passing of the legal right to a piece of land.

Chain referral. See **pyramid sales scheme.**

Challenge. An objection; for example: an objection to the right of a **juror** or a judge to hear a case.

Chambers. Judge's private office; business that takes place here is "*in chambers.*"

Champerty. Taking over a lawsuit being brought by another person either by buying the other person's claim or by sharing any "winnings" of the suit. This practice is illegal.

Chancery. An old court that handled **equitable actions.** The **equity** power is now part of regular courts in most states.

Chapter Eleven. A plan in which the **bankruptcy** court helps a debtor to make arrangements to pay off his or her bills.

Chapter Ten. See **reorganization.**

Chapter Thirteen. See **wage earner's plan.**

Character evidence. **Testimony** about a person's personal traits and habits that is drawn from the opinions of close associates.

Charge. 1. A **claim, obligation, burden** or **liability.** 2. The judge's final summary of the case and instructions to the jury. 3. A formal accusation of a crime. 4. Paying for something "on time."

Charge-off. Lowering the value of something in a company's records; for example: when a debt becomes too difficult to collect, it may be charged off (also called *write-off*).

Charitable trust. A **trust** set up for a public purpose such as a school, church, charity, etc.

Charter. 1. An organization's basic starting document; for example: a corporation's **articles of incorporation** combined with the law that gives the right to **incorporate.** 2. Renting a ship or other large means of transportation.

Chattel. Personal property or animals; any property other than land.

Chattel mortgage. A **mortgage** (see that word) on **personal property.**

Chattel paper. A document that shows both a debt and the fact that the debt is **secured** (see that word) by specific goods.

Check. 1. A document in which a person tells his or her bank to pay a certain amount of money to another person. It is a type of **negotiable instrument** (see that word). 2. A restraint; for example: each branch of the Federal government "*checks and balances*" the others so that no one branch can take over running the country.

Check-off. A system in which union dues are collected directly from a worker's pay for the union by the company.

Choate. Complete; valid against all later claims; opposite of **inchoate** (see that word).

Chose. (French) A thing; a piece of personal property.

57

Chose in action. (French) A right to recover a debt or to get **damages** that can be enforced in court. These words also apply to the thing itself that is being sued on; for example: an accident, a contract, stocks, etc.

Circuit. A division of the U.S. or of a state into areas which different sets of judges serve.

Circuit court. Name given to different types and levels of courts in different states. Named originally because judges "rode circuit" to serve outlying areas. Often abbreviated "Cir. Ct."

Circuit court of appeals. See U.S. Court of Appeals.

Circumstantial evidence. Proof of facts that *indirectly* prove a main fact in question; for example: **testimony** that a person was seen walking in the rain is **direct evidence** that the person walked in the rain, but testimony that the person was seen indoors with wet shoes is *circumstantial evidence* that the person had walked in the rain. Another example of circumstantial, or indirect evidence: a live dodo-louse offered to prove that dodos are not extinct.

Citation. 1. A notice to appear in court or risk losing a right; for example: to inherit money. 2. A reference to a legal authority and where it is found; for example: 17 U.Dl.L.R. 247 is the citation to an article that begins on page 247 of volume 17 of the University of Dull Law Review. 3. A notice of a violation of law; for example; a *traffic citation.*

Citator. A set of books that tells what happened to a case or statute after it came out. It will tell, for example, if a case has been **overruled, distinguished,** or **followed** (see these words). This is done by looking up the case by its **citation** (see that word) and checking whether there are citations to other cases listed under it. If there are, it means that the case was mentioned in these later cases. Some of these citations will be preceded by letters such as "d" (which means that the later case shows why the earlier one was different). The most used citator is called *Shepard's Citations.* It lists almost every case and law printed in the U.S. "Shepardizing" now means the same thing as "using a citator" because most citators are printed by that company.

Cite. 1. Summon a person to court. 2. Refer to specific legal references or authorities. 3. Short for "**citation.**"

Citizen. 1. A person born in or **naturalized** in the U.S. 2. A person is a citizen of the state where he or she has permanent residence and a corporation is a citizen of the state where it was legally created.

Civil action. Every lawsuit other than a criminal proceeding; a lawsuit that is brought to enforce a right or gain payment for a wrong, rather than a court action involving the government trying to punish a crime; in general, a lawsuit brought by one person against another.

Civil law. 1. Law handed down from the Romans. 2. Law that is based on one elaborate document or "**code,**" rather than a combination of many laws and judicial opinions. 3. Government by civilians as opposed to government by the military.

Civil rights. The rights of all citizens that are guaranteed by the Constitution; for example: freedom of speech.

Civil service. Government employment. All government employees (except for elected officials and judges) who are chosen by a standardized, supervised method rather than by political appointment are "civil servants."

Civilian. 1. Not a member of the armed forces. 2. Not a member of the police department.

Claim. 1. Demand as your own; assert; urge; insist. 2. One side's case in a lawsuit.

Claim for relief. The core of a modern **complaint** (first **pleading** in a lawsuit). It may be a short, clear statement of the claim being made that shows that if the facts **alleged** can be proved, the **plaintiff** should get help from the court in enforcing the claim against the **defendant**.

Class action. A lawsuit brought for yourself and all other persons in the same situation.

Classified. 1. Secret. 2. Put into a special category or "class."

Clause. A single paragraph, sentence or phrase.

Clayton Act. A Federal law, passed in 1914, that extended the **Sherman Act's** prohibition against **monopolies** and price discrimination.

Clean hands. Acting fairly and honestly in all matters connected with a lawsuit you are bringing, especially in a request for **equitable relief.**

Clear. 1. Final payment on a check by the bank on which it was **drawn.** 2. Free from doubt or restrictions.

Clear and convincing proof. Stronger **evidence** than simply better than fifty-fifty (what is required in normal **civil** cases), but not necessarily as strong as "*beyond a reasonable doubt*" (what is required in criminal cases).

Clear and present danger. A test of whether or not speech may be punished. According to this standard, it may be punished if it will probably lead to violence soon or if it presents a serious, immediate weakening of national safety and security.

Clear title. Legal ownership that is free from all restrictions and doubt.

Clemency. 1. Lenient treatment of a criminal. 2. Reducing the punishment of a criminal.

Clerical error. A mistake made while copying something or writing it down as opposed to a mistake in judgment or decision-making.

Clerk. Court official who keeps court records, official files, etc.

Client. A person who employs a lawyer; for some purposes, a person who merely discusses a possible attorney-client relationship with a lawyer.

Clifford trust. A **trust** that is set up to give the income to someone else, keep the **principal** (original money put in) for yourself, and get tax benefits.

Close. 1. Old word for an enclosed or well-marked piece of land. 2. See **closing.**

Closed corporation (or Close corporation). A corporation with total ownership in a few hands.

Closed shop. A company where only members of a particular union may work in certain jobs.

Closely held   Stock, or a company, that is owned by a family or by another company.

Closing.   The final meeting for the sale of land in which all payments are made, the property is formally transferred, and the **mortgage** is fully set up by filling out all necessary papers for the mortgage lender.   "Closing costs" are all charges for finishing the deal, such as transfer taxes, mortgage fees, credit reports, etc.   These costs are all set down on a "closing statement" also known as a "**settlement sheet.**"

Cloture.   A formal process of ending debate in a meeting.

Cloud on title.   A **claim** or **encumbrance** against property which, if valid, would lower the value or add difficulties to its legal ownership.

Co.   A prefix meaning with, together, or unitedly; for example: a *co-defendant* is a person who is a full defendant along with another person in a trial.

Co-buyer.   A vague term that includes both persons with and without an ownership right in the thing purchased.

Code.   1. A collection of laws.   2. A complete, interrelated and exclusive set of laws.

Code of Hammurabi.   The first full scale set of laws, written four thousand years ago in Babylon; it was remarkably complete and was "modern" in many of its provisions.

Code of Judicial Conduct.   New rules for judges' conduct adopted by the American Bar Association and in use in many states.

Code of Professional Responsibility. The rules that govern the legal profession. It contains both general ethical guidelines and specific rules prohibiting things that may be punished. It was written by the American Bar Association and adopted by the states.

Codicil. A supplement or addition to a **will** that adds to it or changes it.

Codification. Process of collecting and arranging the laws of an area into one complete system approved in one piece by the **legislature**; to *codify* in this way includes arranging the laws by subject.

Coercion. Compulsion or force; making a person act against free will.

Cognizance. Judicial power to decide a matter; judicial decision to "take notice" of a matter and accept it for decision.

Cognovit note. Written statement that a debtor owes money and *"confesses judgment"* or allows the creditor to get a **judgment** in court for the money whenever the creditor wants to or whenever a particular event takes place (such as a failure to make a payment).

Cohabitation. 1. Living together. 2. Living together as husband and wife. 3. Living together and having sexual intercourse. 4. Having sexual intercourse.

Coinsurance. A division of risk between an insurance company and its customer on all losses less than one hundred percent if the amount of insurance is less than the amount of the loss; for example: if a watch worth one hundred dollars is insured for fifty dollars and suffers fifty dollars worth of damage, the company will pay only twenty-five dollars.

Collateral. 1. "On the side"; for example: "*collateral ancestors*" include uncles, aunts, and all persons similarly related, but not direct ancestors such as grandparents. 2. Money or property put up to back a person's word when taking out a loan.

Collateral attack. An attempt to avoid the effect of a court's action or decision by taking action in a different court proceeding.

Collateral estoppel. Being stopped from making a claim in one court proceeding that has already been disproved by the facts raised in a prior, different proceeding.

Collateral warranty. A guarantee about land or buildings that was made by an ancestor.

Collective bargaining. 1. The requirement that under certain circumstances employers must bargain with official union representatives about wages, hours and other employment conditions. 2. The process of negotiating described in no. 1.

Collective bargaining agreement. The contract between a union and its employer that results from negotiation between the employer and union representatives.

Collusion. 1. Secret action taken by two or more persons together to cheat another or to commit **fraud**; for example: it is *collusion* if two persons agree that one should sue the other because the second person is covered by insurance. 2. An agreement between husband and wife that one of them will commit (or appear to commit) an act that will allow the other one to get a divorce.

Color. Appearance or semblance; looking real or true on the surface, but actually false; for example: acting *under color of law* is taking an action that looks official or backed by law, but which is not.

Color of title. Apparent **title,** based on a document such as a **deed,** a court **decree,** etc.; probably not a real or valid title.

Colorable. False; counterfeit; having the appearance, but not the reality.

Co-maker. A second (or third or more) person who signs a **negotiable instrument,** such as a check, and by doing so promises to pay on it in full.

Combination. 1. A group of persons working together for an unlawful purpose. 2. A putting together of inventions, each of which might be already **patented,** but which by working together produce a new, useful result. This *combination* might get a patent.

Comity. Courtesy and respect; a willingness to do something official, not as a matter of right, but out of goodwill and tradition; for example: nations often give effect to the laws of other nations out of *comity* and state and Federal courts depend on comity to keep many of their results in line with one another.

Commerce. Department of Commerce: the Cabinet department that promotes U.S. trade, economic development and technology; includes the **patent** office and many scientific and business-development branches.

Commerce clause. The part of the U.S. Constitution that allows Congress to control trade with foreign countries and from state to state. This is called the *"commerce power."* (Article One, Section Eight of the Constitution).

Commercial code. See **Uniform Commercial Code.**

Commercial paper. All **negotiable instruments** (see that word) related to business; for example: **bills of exchange.**

Commingling. Mixing together; for example, putting two different persons' money into one bank account.

Commission. **1.** Written grant of authority to do a particular thing given by the government to one of its branches or to an individual or organization. **2.** A group of persons like one mentioned in no. 1. **3.** Payment (to a salesman or other agent) based on the amount of sales or on a percentage of the profit. **4.** Doing a criminal act.

Commissioner. The name for the heads of many government **boards** or **agencies.**

Commitment. The formal process of putting a person into the official care of another person, such as the warden of a prison or the head of a psychiatric hospital.

Committee. **1.** A sub-group that a larger group appoints to do specialized work; for example: the Agriculture Committee of the House of Representatives. **2.** A person or group of persons appointed by a court to take care of the money and property of a person who is legally **incompetent**; a type of **trustee.**

Commodity. 1. Anything produced, bought, or sold. 2. Raw or partially processed materials. 3. Farm products such as corn.

Common. 1. A piece of land used by many persons. 2. Usual; ordinary; regular; applying to many persons or things.

Common carrier. See **carrier.**

Common council. A local (town or city) **legislature.**

Common count. See **count.**

Common law. 1. Judge-made law (as opposed to **legislature**-made law). 2. Law that has its origins in England and grows from ever-changing custom and tradition.

Common law action. A civil lawsuit (as opposed to criminal) that is between private individuals or organizations and contains a request for money **damages.**

Common law marriage. A marriage created by a couple publically holding themselves out as married and living together as married in a way and for a time period sufficient to create a legal marriage.

Common law trust. **Business trust** (see that word).

Common pleas. The name for several different types of **civil** trial courts.

Common scheme (Common plan). 1. Two or more different crimes planned together. 2. Dividing a piece of land into lots with identical restrictions on land use.

Common stock. **Shares** in a **corporation** that depend for their value on the value of the company. These shares usually have voting rights (which other types of company stock lack). However, they earn a **dividend** (profit) only after all other types of the company' obligations and stocks have been paid.

Community property. Property owned in *common* (both persons owning it all) by a husband and wife. *"Community property states"* are those states that call all property acquired during the marriage the property of both partners no matter whose name it is in.

Commutation. Changing a criminal punishment to one less severe.

Compact. An agreement or contract (usually between governments).

Company. Any organization set up to do business.

Comparative negligence. A legal rule, used in some states, by which the amount of "fault" on each side of an accident is measured and the side with less fault is given money **damages** depending on the difference between the seriousness of each side's fault (the more usual rule is that any **negligence** at all stops that side from getting any damages in most situations).

Comparative rectitude. Legal rule by which a divorce is given to the person in a marriage who the judge decides has behaved the best. Also called "least fault" divorce.

Compelling state interest. A reason for a state law, rule, policy or action that is strong enough to justify limiting a person's **constitutional rights.**

Compensation. Payment for loss, injury, or damages.

Compensatory damages. The actual loss suffered by a **plaintiff,** as opposed to **punitive damages** (see that word).

Competent. Properly qualified, adequate, having the right natural or legal qualifications; for example: a person may be *competent* to make a **will** if he or she understands what making a will is, knows that he or she is making a will, and knows generally how making the will affects persons named in the will and affects relatives.

Competent evidence. **Evidence** that is both relevant to the point in question and the proper type of evidence to prove the point; evidence that is not kept out by any **exclusionary rule** (see that word).

Complainant. **1.** Person who makes an official complaint. **2.** Person who starts a lawsuit (see **plaintiff**).

Complaint. The first main paper filed in a **civil** lawsuit. It includes, among other things, a statement of the wrong or harm done to the **plaintiff** by the **defendant** and a request for specific help from the court.

Compliance. Acting in a way that does not violate a law; for example: when a state gets Federal money for a state project, the project must be in *compliance* with the Federal law that allows the money and, sometimes, with the **regulations** of the Federal agency that gives it out.

Composition. A formal agreement involving a **debtor** and several creditors that each **creditor** will take less than the whole amount owed as full payment.

69

Composition in bankruptcy. A **composition** (see that word) under the Federal Bankruptcy laws with or without the consent of the creditors.

Compound interest. Interest on interest; adding interest to the **principal** (the main debt) at regular intervals and then computing the interest on the last principal plus interest.

Compounding a felony. Taking money or other gain in exchange for not prosecuting a major crime committed against you.

Comprises. Made up of; includes.

Comptroller. Top financial officer.

Compulsory process. Official action to force a person to appear in court.

Compurgator. See **wager of law.**

Con. Short for *"contra"*; against; on the other hand.

Conciliation. The process of voluntarily bringing together two sides to agree to a compromise.

Conclusion of law. An argument or answer arrived at by not only drawing a conclusion from facts, but also by applying law to the facts; for example: it is only a **conclusion of fact** to say that a person hit another person with a car, but it is a *conclusion of law* to say that the accident was the driver's fault.

Conclusive. Beyond dispute; ending inquiry or debate; clear; for example: a *conclusive presumption* is a legal conclusion that cannot be overturned by any facts.

Concur. Agree; for example: a *concurring opinion* is one in which a judge agrees with the result reached in an **opinion** by another judge, but not necessarily with the reasoning that the other judge used to reach the conclusion.

Concurrent. "Running together"; having the same authority; at the same time; for example: courts have *concurrent jurisdiction* when each one has the power to deal with the same subjects and cases and *concurrent sentences* are prison terms that run at the same time.

Condemn. 1. Find guilty of a criminal charge. 2. Governmental taking of private property with payment, but not necessarily with consent. 3. A court's decision that the government may seize a ship owned privately or by a foreign government. 4. Official ruling that a building is unfit for use. This process (and the process involved in definitions nos. 1, 2 and 3) is called *condemnation:*

Condition. A future, uncertain event that creates or destroys rights and obligations; for example: a **contract** may have a *condition* in it that if one person should die, the contract is ended. Conditions may be **express** or **implied** (see these words). Also, they may be **precedent** (if a certain future event happens, a right or obligation is created) or **subsequent** (if a certain future event happens, a right or obligation ends).

Conditional. Depending on a **condition** (see that word); unsure; depending on a future event; for example: a *conditional sale* is a sale in which the buyer must wait for full ownership of the thing bought until it is fully paid for.

Condominium. Several persons owning individual pieces of a building (usually an apartment house) and managing it together.

Condonation. Willing forgiveness by a wife or husband of the other's actions that is enough to stop those actions from being **grounds** for a **divorce.**

Confederacy. 1. A general word for persons who band together to do an illegal act. A more usual word for this is "**conspiracy**" (see that word). 2. A loose union of independent governments. A more usual word for this is "**confederation.**"

Confession. 1. A voluntary statement by a person that he or she is guilty of a crime. 2. Any admission of wrongdoing.

Confession and avoidance. Same as **affirmative defense** (see that word).

Confession of judgment. See **judgment** and **cognovit;** a process in which a person who borrows money or buys on credit signs in advance to allow the lawyer for the lender to get a court judgment without even telling the borrower.

Confidential relation. Any relationship where one person has a right to expect a higher than usual level of care and faithfulness from another person; for example: client and attorney, child and parent; employee and employer. Another name for these relationships, if a strong duty exists, is a **fiduciary relationship** (see that word).

Confidentiality. 1. The requirement that a lawyer, or anyone working for a lawyer, not disclose information received from a client. There are exceptions to this requirement; for example: if the lawyer is told that the client is about to commit a crime. 2. The requirement that certain other persons (such as clergy, physicians, husbands, wives, etc.) not disclose information received under certain circumstances. This is called **privileged communication.**

Confiscate. The government's taking of private property without payment.

Conflict of interest. Being in a position where your own needs and desires could possibly lead you to violate your duty to those persons who have a right to depend on you. A conflict need not even be intentional; for example: a judge who holds XYZ stock may be unconsciously influenced in a case concerning the XYZ Company.

Conflict of laws. The choice between laws that a judge must make when the laws of more than one state or country may apply to a case.

Conformed copy. An exact copy of a document on which has been written explanations of things that could not be copied; for example: the handwritten signature and date might be replaced on the copy by the notation "signed by John Jones on Oct. 3, 1975."

Confrontation. The right of a criminal **defendant** to see and **cross-examine** all witnesses against him or her.

Confusion. Mixing or blending together; for example: *confusion of goods* is a mixing together of the property of two or more persons with the effect that it is not possible to tell which goods belong to which person.

Conglomerate. A company that owns, or is made up of, companies in many different industries.

Congress. 1. The **legislature** of the United States (the House of Representatives plus the Senate);

73

often abbreviated "Cong." **2.** A meeting of officials (often of different countries).

Congressional Record. A daily printed record of proceedings in Congress. It tells how each **bill** was voted upon, which bills were sent to and from each committee, etc.

Conjugal. Having to do with marriage; for example: *conjugal rights* are a husband and wife's rights to companionship, love and sex from the other.

Connecting up. A thing may be put into **evidence** subject to "connecting up" with later evidence that will show its **relevance,** etc.

Connivance. The consent or help of a husband or wife to the other's acts in order to obtain a divorce.

Consanguinity. Blood relationship; kinship.

Consecutive sentence. See **cumulative sentence.**

Consent. Voluntary and active agreement; for example: a *consent decree* is a **divorce** that is granted against a person who is in court or represented by a lawyer in court and who does not oppose the divorce.

Consequential damages. Indirect losses or injuries; results of a wrongful act that do not show up immediately or upon superficial examination; for example: the loss of business a taxi-driver suffers from an accident that damages the taxi.

Conservator. Guardian or preserver of property appointed for a person who cannot legally manage it.

Consideration. The reason or main cause for a person to make a **contract**; something of value received or promised to **induce** (convince) a person to make a deal. Without "*consideration*" a contract is not valid; for example: if Ann and Sue make a deal for Ann to buy a car from Sue, Ann's promise to pay a thousand dollars is *consideration* for Sue's promise to hand over the car and vice versa.

Consignment. Handing over things for transportation or for sale, but keeping ownership.

Consolidation. 1. The trying together of different lawsuits that are on the same general subject and between the same persons and treating them as only one lawsuit. 2. Generally, bringing together separate things and making them into one thing; often abbreviated "consol." 3. Two **corporations** joining together to form a third, new one.

Consortium. The right of a husband or wife to the other's love and services. "*Loss of consortium*" might be sued for by, for example, the husband of a woman who was badly injured in an accident.

Conspiracy. Two or more persons joining together to do an unlawful act; sometimes, the joining together itself is unlawful, even if the act planned is not.

Constable. Low level peace officer who does court-related work.

Constitute. Make up; for example: "duly *constituted*" means properly put together and formally valid and correct.

Constitution. 1. The basic first document of a country, state, or organization that sets out its basic principles and most general laws. 2. The U.S. Constitution is the basic law of the country, from which most other laws are drawn and to which all other laws must yield. Often abbreviated "Const."

Constitutional. **1.** Consistent with the Constitution; not in conflict with the fundamental law of the state or country. **2.** Depending on the Constitution; for example: a *constitutional court* is one set up by the Constitution.

Constitutional law. The study of the law that applies to the organization, structure, and functions of the government, the basic principles of government, and the validity (or *constitutionality*) of laws and actions when tested against the requirements of the Constitution.

Constitutional right. A right guaranteed to the people by the Constitution (and, thus, safe from **legislative** or other attempts to limit or end the right).

Construction. Deciding (usually by a judge) the meaning and legal effect of ambiguous or doubtful words by looking at not only the words themselves, but also at surrounding circumstances, relevant laws and writings, etc. (Looking at just the words is called "**interpretation.**")

Constructive. True legally even if not factually; "just as if"; established by legal interpretation; inferred; implied; for example: a *constructive eviction* might occur when a landlord fails to provide heat in winter. This means that the tenant might be able to treat the legal relationship between landlord and tenant as if the landlord had tried to throw the tenant out without good reason and give the tenant the right to stop paying the rent.

Constructive desertion. Forcing a husband or wife to leave; for example: when Mary is forced to leave because conditions at home are so bad that it amounts to John forcing her out of the house, John has "constructively deserted" Mary and Mary may get a divorce based on this in some states.

Constructive trust. A situation in which a person holds legal **title** to property, but the property should, in fairness, actually belong to another person (because the title was gained by **fraud,** by a clerical error, etc.). In this case, the property may be treated by a court as if the legal owner holds it in **trust** for the real owner.

Consular court. A court held by the *consuls* (representatives) of one country inside another country.

Consumer. Person who buys (or rents, travels on, etc.) something for personal, rather than business use.

Consumer credit. Money, property, or services offered to a person for personal, family or household purposes "on time." It is "*consumer credit*" if there is a finance charge or if there are more than four **installment** payments.

Consummate. Finish; complete what was intended.

Consummation. 1. Completion of a thing; carrying out an agreement. 2. "Completing" a marriage by having sexual intercourse.

Contemner. A person who commits **contempt of court** (see that word).

Contemplation of death. An act taken "*in contemplation of death*" is one caused by or influenced

77

strongly by thinking about your own probable imminent death (see "**causa mortis**").

Contempt. 1. An act designed to obstruct a court's work or lessen the dignity of the court. 2. A willful disobeying of a judge's command or official court order. 3. It is also possible to be in *contempt* of a **legislature** or an **administrative agency.**

Contest. 1. Oppose or defend against a lawsuit or other action. 2. Oppose the validity of a **will.**

Context. Surrounding words.

Contingent. Possible, but not assured; depending on some future events or actions that may or may not happen; for example: a *contingent estate* is a right to own or use property that depends on an uncertain future event for it to take effect.

Contingent fee. A method of paying a lawyer a percentage of the possible "winnings" from a lawsuit rather than a flat amount of money.

Continuance. The postponement of a lawsuit to a later day or session of court.

Contra. (Latin) Against; on the other hand; opposing.

Contraband. Things that are illegal to import or export or that are illegal to possess.

Contract. An agreement that affects the legal relationships between two or more persons. To be a *contract*, an agreement must involve: at least one promise, **consideration** (something of value promised or given), persons legally capable of making binding agreements, and a reasonable amount of agreement between the persons as to what the contract means. A contract is called **bilateral** if

78

both sides **expressly** make promises (such as the promise to deliver a book on one side and a promise to pay for it on the other) or **unilateral** if the promises are on one side only (usually because the other side has already done its part). According to the **Uniform Commercial Code,** a contract is the "total legal obligation which results from the parties' agreement . . ." and according to the Restatement of the Law of Contracts, it is "a promise or set of promises for the breach of which the law in some way recognizes a duty."

Contravention. Something done in breaking a legal obligation; for example: speeding in a downtown area is usually in *contravention* of the traffic laws.

Contribution. 1. The sharing of payment for a debt among persons who are all **liable** for the debt. 2. The right of a person who has paid an entire debt to get back a fair share of the payment from another person who is also responsible for the debt.

Contributory negligence. Negligent (see that word) conduct by a person who was harmed by another person's negligence; a **plaintiff's** failure to be careful that is a part of the cause of his or her injury.

Controller. Top financial officer.

Controversy. Any **civil** lawsuit.

Controvert. Dispute, deny, or oppose.

Contumacy. The refusal to appear in court when required to by the law.

Contumely. Rudeness; scornful treatment.

Convention. 1. A meeting of representatives for a special purpose, such as to draw up a **constitution**

or to nominate a candidate for an election. **2.** An agreement between countries on non-political and non-financial matters; for example: fishing rights.

Conventional. 1. Usual or ordinary. **2.** Caused by an agreement between persons rather than by the effect of a law; for example: *a conventional mortgage* is one that involves just a person lending and a person borrowing money on a house as opposed to a mortgage involving a government subsidy or guarantee.

Conversion. 1. Any act that deprives an owner of property without that owner's permission and without just cause; for example: it is *conversion* to refuse to return a borrowed book. **2.** The exchange of one type of property for another; for example: turning in one type of **stock** to a company and getting another in return.

Conveyance. 1. A transfer of **title** to land. **2.** Any transfer of title.

Convict. 1. Find a person guilty of a criminal charge. **2.** A person in prison.

Conviction. The result of a criminal trial in which a person is found guilty.

Cooling off period. 1. A period of time in which no action of a particular sort may be taken by either side in a dispute; for example: a period of a month after a union or a company files a **grievance** against the other. During this period, the union may not strike and the company may not **lock out** the employees. **2.** A period of time in which a buyer may cancel a purchase; many states require a three-day cancellation period for door-to-door sales. **3.** An automatic delay in some states, in addition to ordinary court delays, between the filing of **divorce** papers and the divorce **hearing.**

Co-partnership. Partnership (see that word).

Copyright. The author's (or other originator's) right to control the copying and distributing of books, articles, movies, etc. This right is created, **regulated,** and limited by Federal statute. The symbol for copyright is ©.

Coram. (Latin) Before; in the presence of; for example: *coram nobis* (before us) is the name for a type of **appeal.**

Corbin. *Corbin on Contracts*; a treatise on the law of contracts.

Co-respondent. The "other man" or "other woman" in a divorce suit based on **adultery.** Sometimes spelled "corespondent." Also see "correspondent."

Corner. Owning enough of some stock or **commodity** to have control over the selling price in the general marketplace.

Corollary. A secondary or "side" deduction or inference in logic or argument.

Coroner. Official who conducts inquiries into the cause of any violent or suspicious death. If the case is serious, there is a *coroner's inquest* or *hearing.*

Corporal punishment. Physical punishment (beating, etc.).

Corporate. Belonging to a **corporation.**

Corporate veil. The legal assumption that actions taken by a **corporation** are not the actions of its owners and that these owners cannot usually be held responsible for corporate actions.

Corporation. An organization that is formed under state or Federal law and exists, for legal purposes, as a separate being or an "**artificial person.**" It may be public (set up by the government) or private (set up by individuals) and it may be set up to carry on a business or to perform almost any function. It may be owned by the government, by a few persons, or by the general public through purchases of stock. Abbreviated "corp."

Corporeal. Having body or substance; visible and tangible.

Corpus. (Latin) "Body"; main body of a thing as opposed to attachments; for example: "*corpus juris*" means "a body of law" or a major collection of laws. It is also the name for one major legal encyclopedia.

Corpus delicti. (Latin) "The body of the crime." **1.** The material substance upon which a crime has been committed; for example: a dead body or a house burned down. **2.** The fact that proves that a crime has been committed.

Corpus Juris. A legal encyclopedia that also ties in with the **American Digest System.** *Corpus Juris Secundum* is its most recent update.

Corpus juris civilis. "The body of the civil law"; the main writings of Roman law.

Correlative. Ideas that have a mutual relationship and depend on one another to exist; for example: "parent" and "child" are *correlative* terms as are "right" and "duty."

Correspondent. Person who collects **mortgage** loan payments for the lender. Also see "co-respondent."

Corroborate. Strengthen or add weight by additional confirming facts or evidence.

Corruption of blood. An old punishment for a crime by which a person was deprived of the right to pass on property to **heirs** at death.

Co-signer. A general term for a person who signs a document along with another person. Depending on the situation and on the state, the person may or may not have a primary responsibility (for example, for a debt) and may or may not have rights in any property involved.

Costs. Expenses of one side in a lawsuit that the judge orders the other side to pay or reimburse.

Council. A local or city legislature, sometimes called "*common council.*"

Counsel. 1. A lawyer for a client. 2. Advice (usually professional advice). 3. "*Of counsel*" usually means not the primary lawyer in court, but an assistant lawyer on the case.

Counsellor. Lawyer.

Count. 1. Each separate part of a **civil complaint** or a **criminal indictment** (see these words). Each *count* must be able to stand alone as a separate and independent **claim** or **charge.** The "*common counts*" were the various **forms of action** (see that word) for money owed (for example, **assumpsit**).

Counterclaim. A claim made by a defendant in a **civil** lawsuit that, in effect, sues the **plaintiff** for money. It can be based on entirely different things from the plaintiff's **complaint** and may even be for more money than the plaintiff is asking.

Counterfeit. Forge, copy or imitate without authority or right, with the purpose of passing off the copy as the original.

Counteroffer. A rejection of an offer and a new offer made back.

Countersign. Sign a document in addition to the primary or original signature in order to approve the validity of the document.

County. Division of a state.

Course of dealing. The prior history of business between two persons.

Course of employment. Directly related to employment, during work hours, or in the place of work.

Court. 1. The place where judges work. 2. A judge at work; for example: a judge might say "the court (meaning he or she) will consider this matter." 3. All the judges in a particular area.

Court hand. An old system of Latin shorthand once used in England for legal documents.

Court martial. A military court for trying offenses by members of the armed forces.

Court of appeals. A court that decides appeals from a trial court. In most states, it is a middle level court (like the U.S. Court of Appeals), but in some states, it is the name for the highest court.

Court of claims. A specialized Federal court that handles money claims against the U.S.

Court of probate. A court that handles **wills** and **estates,** and sometimes handles the problems of **minors** or other legally **incompetent** persons.

Covenant. A written promise, agreement or restriction, usually in a **deed**; for example: a *covenant for quiet enjoyment* is a promise that the seller of land will protect the buyer against a defective **title** to the land and against anyone who claims the land; and a "*covenant running with the land*" is any agreement in a deed that is binding for or against all future buyers of the land.

Cover. 1. Make good. 2. Protect (for example, insurance "**coverage**"). 3. Protect yourself from the effects of a business deal that falls through or isn't made good on; for example: buy what you need from a new company when the original one can't make good on a sale.

Coverage. Amount and type of insurance.

Coverture. The status that married women used to have; the special rights and legal limitations of a married woman.

Craft union. A labor union whose members all do the same kind of work (plumbing, carpentry, etc.) for different types of industries and employers.

Credibility. The believability of a **witness** and of the **testimony** that the witness gives.

Credit. 1. The right to delay payment for things bought or used. 2. Money loaned. 3. See **credits**. 4. Deduction from what is owed.

Credit bureau. A place that keeps records on the credit used by persons and on their financial reliability.

Credit line. See **line of credit**.

Credit union. A financial setup that uses money deposited by a closed group of persons and lends it out again to persons in the same group.

Creditor. A person to whom a debt is owed.

Credits. Records in an account book of money owed to you or money you have paid out. (The opposite of **debits.**)

Crime. Any violation of the government's **penal** laws; an illegal act or failure to act.

Criminal. 1. Having to do with the law of crimes and illegal conduct. 2. Illegal. 3. A person who has committed a crime.

Criminal action. The procedure by which a person accused of a crime is brought to trial and given punishment.

Criminal conversation. **Adultery.**

Criminal forfeiture. The loss of property to the government because it was involved in a crime; for example: an automobile used to smuggle narcotics.

Criminology. The study of the causes, prevention and punishment of crime.

Cross-claim. A claim brought by a **defendant** against a **plaintiff** or a **co-defendant.** It must be based on the same subject matter as the plaintiff's lawsuit.

Cross-complaint (or Cross-action or Cross-demand). Other words for either a **counterclaim** or a **cross-claim** (see these words).

Cross-examination. The questioning of an opposing witness during a trial or **hearing.**

Cruel and unusual punishment. Punishment, by the government, that is prohibited by the Constitution. Recently, the courts have decided that many more types of punishment should be discon-

86

tinued as *"cruel and unusual"* because they shock the moral sense of the community.

Cruelty. In the law of **divorce,** *cruelty* is that treatment by a husband or wife that gives the other **grounds** for a divorce. Its definition is different in each state. Each state's official phrase for *cruelty* varies widely and has no strong connection to what it actually takes to get a divorce based on it. Some states' words for cruelty are: *"extreme cruelty,"* *"intolerable cruelty,"* *"cruelty,"* *"willful cruelty,"* and *"intolerable severity."*

Culpable. Blamable; at fault; a person who has done a wrongful act (whether criminal or civil) is called *culpable.*

Culprit. A person who has committed a crime, but has not yet been tried. This is not a technical legal word.

Cum. (Latin) With.

Cum testamento annexo. (Latin) "With the **will** attached"; an **administrator** who is appointed by a court to supervise handing out the property of a dead person whose will does not name **executors** (persons to hand out property) or whose executors cannot or will not serve.

Cumulative evidence. Evidence that is offered to prove what has already been proved by other evidence.

Cumulative sentence. An additional prison term given to a person who is already convicted of a crime, the additional term to be served after the first one is finished.

Cumulative voting. The type of voting in which each person (or each share of **stock,** in the case of a **corporation**) has as many votes as there are positions to be filled. Votes can be either concentrated on one or a few candidates or spread around.

Cure. It is a *cure* when a seller delivers goods, the buyer rejects them because of some defect, and the seller then delivers the proper goods.

Curia. (Latin) Old European word for court.

Curtesy. A husband's right to all or part of his dead wife's property. This right is now defined by state law and varies from state to state, but is the same within each state for either husband or wife. (See **dower**).

Curtilage. An area of household use immediately surrounding a home. It is usually fenced in.

Custody. A general term meaning various types of care and keeping; for example: parents normally have legal *custody* of their children, a warden has *custody* of prisoners, and a person has *custody* of a book loaned by another.

Custom. Regular behavior of persons in a geographical area or in a particular type of business that gradually takes on legal importance so that it will strongly influence a court's decision; "*unwritten law*."

Customs. 1. Taxes payable on goods brought into or sent out of a country. (Also called "**duty**.") 2. The branch of government that oversees and taxes goods brought in and out of a country.

Cy-pres. (French) "As near as possible"; When a dead person's **will** can no longer legally or practically be carried out, a court may (but is not obligated to) order that the dead person's **estate**

be used in a way that most nearly does what the person would have wanted. If the court does not use its *cy-pres powers*, the will may be held **void** and no longer binding.

D

D.B.N. **De Bonis Non** (see that word).

D.E.A. Drug Enforcement Administration: the branch of the U.S. Department of **Justice** that enforces narcotic and drug laws.

D.O.D. Department of Defense: the U.S. Cabinet department that runs the Army, Navy, etc.; also called "the Pentagon."

D.O.T. Department of Transportation: the U.S. Cabinet department that **regulates** interstate transportation through agencies such as the Federal Aviation Administration, Federal Highway Administration, etc. It also supervises the Coast Guard in peacetime.

Damages. **1.** Money that a court orders paid to a person who has suffered a loss or injury by the person whose fault caused it. **2.** A **plaintiff's** claim in a legal **pleading** for the money defined in no. 1. *Damages* may be **actual** and **compensatory** (directly related to the amount of the loss) or they may be, in addition, **exemplary** and **punitive** (extra money given to help keep a particularly bad act from happening again). Also, merely **nominal** damages may be given (a small sum when the loss suffered is either very small or of unproved amount).

Damnum. (Latin) Damages; for example: "*damnum absque injuria*" means a loss without a legal injury or without any way of suing for it in court.

Dangerous instrumentality. Things that are supposedly harmful in and of themselves or are designed to be harmful, such as guns.

Davis. *Davis on Administrative Law*; a treatise on that subject.

Day certain. A specific future date.

Day in court. The right to be notified of a court proceeding involving your interests and the right to be heard when the case comes up in court.

De. (Latin) Of, by, from, affecting, concerning, etc. Often the first word of an old English **statute** or **writ**.

De bonis non. (Latin) "Of the goods not already (taken care of)"; an **administrator** appointed to hand out the property of a dead person whose **executor** (person chosen to hand it out) has died.

De facto. In fact; actual; a situation that exists in fact whether or not it is lawful; for example: a *de facto corporation* is a company that has failed to follow some of the technical legal requirements to become a legal **corporation,** but carries on business as one in good faith.

De jure. Of right; legitimate; lawful, whether or not true in actual fact; for example: a president may still be the *de jure* head of a government even if the army takes actual power by force.

De minimus. Small, unimportant; also short for "*de minimus non curat lex*" (the law does not bother with trifles).

De novo. New; completely new from the start; for example: a *trial de novo* is a completely new trial ordered by the judge or by an **appeals** court.

De son tort. "Of his or her own wrong"; someone who takes on a responsibility he or she has no right to assume or meddles with affairs in which he or she has no right to get involved becomes responsible for all harm done as a result of those actions.

Dead man's acts. Laws, now mostly abolished, that prevented a person from **testifying** in a civil lawsuit against a dead person's representative about things that the dead person might have testified to.

Death. The end of life. The medical definition of the exact moment of death is not agreed upon. *Civil death* is the loss of **civil rights** (to marry, own property, etc.) that occurs in some states when a person is sentenced to life in prison. *Presumptive death* is "legal" death resulting from an unexplained absence for a length of time set by state law.

Debenture. A corporation's obligation to pay money (usually in the form of a **note** or **bond**) that is not **secured** (backed up) by any specific property.

Debits. Records in an account book of money you owe or money paid to you. (The opposite of **credits**.)

Debt. 1. A sum of money owed because of an agreement (such as a sale or loan). 2. Any money owed.

Debt poolers (or Debt adjusters or Debt consolidators). Persons or organizations who take a person's money and pay it out to **creditors** by getting the creditors to accept lower monthly payments. Unless these services are non-profit credit counselling organizations, the chances are that a person will wind up paying much more than by making the arrangements him or herself.

Debt service. Regular payments of **principal,** interest, and other costs such as insurance made to pay off a **mortgage** loan.

Debtor. A person who owes money.

Decedent. A person who has recently died.

Deceit. An intentionally false statement that fools another person and causes that person harm.

Decennial Digest. Abbreviated "Dec. Dig." (see **American Digest System**).

Decision. 1. Any formal deciding of a dispute, such as a judge's resolution of a lawsuit.

Decision on the merits. A final decision that reaches and fully decides the subject matter of a case with the effect that other lawsuits may not be brought by the same person on the same subject.

Declaration. 1. An unsworn statement made out of court; for example: a *dying declaration* about how a person was killed may be admitted as good **evidence** as may a *declaration against interest* (a statement that proves a fact that hurts the person speaking). 2. A formal statement of fact; for example: a *declaration of intention* is a preliminary statement made by a person who wants to become a U.S. **citizen.** 3. A public proclamation; for example: the Declaration of Independence.

Declaration of trust. A written statement by a person owning property that is held for another person. This is one way of setting up a **trust.**

Declaratory judgment. A judicial action that states the rights of the **parties** or answers a legal question without awarding any **damages** or ordering that anything be done. A person may ask a court for a *declaratory judgment* only if there is a real, not theoretical, problem that involves real legal consequences.

Decree. A **judgment** (see that word) of a court that announces the legal consequences of the facts found in a case and orders that the court's decision be carried out; for example: a *divorce decree.* Specialized types of decrees include a *consent decree* (agreed to by the parties) and a *decree nisi* (one that takes effect only after a certain time and only if no person shows the court a good reason why it should not take effect). Decrees are given by a court under its **equity** (see that word) powers.

Dedication. An owner's giving of land to the government for a specific public use, such as a park, and accepted for that use by the government.

Deductible. That which may be taken away or subtracted; something that may be subtracted from income for tax purposes.

Deduction. 1. Things subtracted from income for tax purposes; for example: a person may take a *deduction* of a certain amount of money from the amount of money he or she is taxed on for money given to charity, and thus reduce his or her income tax. **2.** A conclusion drawn from principles or facts already proved.

Deed. A document by which one person transfers the legal ownership of land and what is on the land to another person.

Deed of trust. A document by which a person transfers the legal ownership of land to independent **trustees** to be held until a debt on the land (a **mortgage**) is paid off.

Deem. **1.** Treat as if; for example: if a fact is "*deemed true*," it will be treated as true unless proven otherwise. **2.** Held to be; determined to be; for example: if a statute says that certain acts are "deemed to be a crime," they are a crime.

Defalcation. Failure of a person to account for money trusted to his or her care. There is the assumption that the money was misused.

Defamation. Injuring a person's character or reputation by false and **malicious** statements. This includes both **libel** and **slander.**

Default. **1.** A failure to perform a legal duty, observe a promise, or take care of an obligation: for example: the word is often used for the failure to make a payment on a debt once it is due. **2.** Failure to take a required step in a lawsuit: for example: to file a paper on time. This *default* leads to a **default judgment** against the side failing to file the paper.

Defeasance clause. The part of a **mortgage contract** that says that the mortgage is ended once all payments have been made.

Defeasible. Subject to being defeated, ended, or undone by a future event or action.

Defect. The absence of some legal requirement that makes a thing legally insufficient or nonbinding; for example: a *defective title* is one that is improperly drawn up, inaccurate, fails to comply with a law, or is obtained by unlawful means.

Defendant. The person against whom a legal action is brought. This legal action may be **civil** or **criminal.**

Defense. The sum of the facts, law, and arguments presented by the side against whom legal action is brought.

Deficiency. A lack or shortage; for example: a *deficiency* in a legal paper means that it lacks something to make it proper or able to take legal effect. Also, the difference between a tax owed and a tax paid is a *deficiency.*

Deficiency judgment. A court's decision that a person must pay more money owed than the amount **secured** by property; for example: when an auto dealer **repossesses** (takes back) a car for failure to make payments and then sells the car for eight hundred dollars, if the debt owed is one thousand dollars, some states will allow the car dealer to sue for a two hundred dollar *deficiency judgment.*

Deficit. Something missing or lacking; less than what should be; a "minus" balance; for example: if a city takes in less money than it must pay out in the same time period, it is called "*deficit financing*" or "*deficit spending.*"

Definitive. Capable of finally and completely settling a legal question or a lawsuit.

Deforcement. Old word for holding on to land or buildings and keeping out persons who now have a right to them.

Defraud. To cheat.

Degree. A step, grade, or division; for example: a "step removed" between two relatives (brothers are related in the first degree, grandparent and grandchild in the second). Also, a *degree* is a division of a crime into different levels of severity (first degree murder carries a more severe maximum punishment than second degree murder).

Del credere. (Italian) An **agent** who sells goods for a person and also **guarantees** to that person that the buyer will pay in full for the goods.

Delectus personae. (Latin) "Choice of person"; the right of a partner to choose, approve and disapprove of other partners.

Delegate. 1. A person who is chosen to represent another person or group of persons. 2. To choose a person to represent you or to do a job for you.

Delegation. 1. The giving of authority by one person to another; for example: a boss often *delegates* responsibility to employees. 2. An entire group of **delegates** or representatives.

Deliberate. 1. To carefully consider, discuss and work towards forming an opinion or making a decision. 2. Well advised; carefully considered; planned and thought out slowly enough. 3. Planned in advance; **premeditated**; intentional.

Delictum. (Latin) A crime, **tort,** or wrong ("delict" also means criminal or wrong).

Delinquency. Failure, omission, or violation of duty; misconduct. Often applied to falling behind on a debt.

Delinquent. 1. Overdue and unpaid. 2. Willfully and intentionally failing to carry out an obligation. 3. Short for "juvenile delinquent" or a minor who has done an illegal act or who has been proved in court to seriously misbehave.

Delivery. 1. The transfer of an object from one person to another (usually the transfer of goods that have been sold). 2. An act other than physically handing over an object that has the legal effect of a physical delivery.

Demand. 1. A forceful claim that presupposes that there is no doubt as to its winning. 2. The assertion of a legal right; a legal obligation asserted in the courts. 3. "On demand" is a phrase put on some **promissory notes** or other **negotiable instruments** to mean that the money owed must be paid immediately when requested by the **holder** of the note. These are called "*demand notes.*"

Demeanor. Physical appearance and behavior. The demeanor of a witness is not what the witness says, but how the witness says it, including, for example, tone of voice, hesitations, gestures, apparent sincerity, etc.

Demise. 1. A lease. 2. Any transfer of property (especially land). 3. Death.

Demonstrative evidence. All evidence other than **testimony**; evidence addressed directly to the senses; for example: a gun shown to the jury.

Demonstrative legacy. A gift in a **will** that is to be paid out of a particular part of the dead person's property.

Demur. To make a **demurrer** (see that word).

Demurrage. The money paid to a shipowner by a person who holds the ship beyond the contract time.

Demurrer. A legal pleading that says, in effect, "even if, for the sake of argument, the facts presented by the other side are correct, those facts do not give the other side a legal argument that can possibly stand up in court." The *demurrer* has been replaced in many courts by making a **motion to dismiss** (see that word).

Denial. 1. The part of a **pleading** that refutes the facts claimed in the other side's pleading. 2. A refusal or rejection; for example: a *denial* of welfare benefits to a family that makes too much money to qualify. 3. A deprivation or withholding; for example: a *denial* of a **constitutional** right.

Dep. 1. Short for "deputy." 2. Short for "department" ("dep't." is more common).

Dependent. 1. A person supported primarily by another person. 2. Conditional; for example: a *dependent contract* is one in which one side does not have to do something in the contract until the other side does something it is required to do.

Dependent relative revocation. The legal principle in some states that if a person **revokes** (takes back or cancels) a **will** with the intention of making a new one and that new one is either never made or is defective, there is a **rebuttable presumption** (an assumption) that he or she would have preferred the old will to no will at all.

Depletion allowance. The reduction of taxes on oil, minerals, and other natural resource products because they are being used up.

Deponent. Person who gives sworn **testimony** out of court (see **deposition**).

Depose. 1. Give sworn testimony out of court (see **deposition**). 2. Ask the questions of the person in no. 1; for example: a lawyer might say "I *deposed* Mr. Smith today."

Deposition. 1. The process of taking a witness' sworn **testimony** out of court. It is usually done by a lawyer with the lawyer from the other side given a chance to attend and participate. 2. The written record of no. 1.

Depreciation. 1. Fall in value or reduction in worth (usually due to deterioration or the passing of time). 2. The amount of the fall in value in no. 1 that is "written off" or charged to a particular time period for tax **deduction** purposes. If an equal amount of depreciation is taken in each year of a thing's useful life, it is called "*straight line*" depreciation. If most of the depreciation is taken early, it is called "*accelerated*" depreciation.

Derivative action. A lawsuit by a **stockholder** of a **corporation** against another person (usually an officer of the company) to enforce rights the shareholder thinks the corporation has against that person.

Derivative evidence. **Evidence** that is collected by following up on evidence gathered illegally is "*derivative*" and may not be used in a trial.

Derogation. Partial **repeal** or abolishing of a law by a later law that limits it or limits its effectiveness.

Descent. 1. **Inheritance** from parents or other ancestors. 2. Getting property by inheritance of any type, rather than by purchase or gift.

Descriptive word index. A large dictionary-like set of books that allows you to find which cases have discussed a topic by tracing down exact words or catchphrases; for example: if you are interested in cases involving tires that blowout during a skid, you might look up "tires," "blowouts" or "skidding."

Desertion. 1. Abandoning a military post and duty without permission and with no intention of returning. 2. Abandoning wife, husband or child with no intention of either returning or of reassuming the financial and other duties of marriage or parenthood.

Destroy. With regard to wills, contracts, or other legal documents, "destruction" does not necessarily mean total physical destruction. You can *destroy* a document's *legal effect* by less extreme methods, such as tearing it in half or writing over it.

Detainer. 1. The unlawful keeping of another person's property even if keeping that property was originally lawful. 2. Holding a person against his or her will.

Detention. Holding a person against his or her will. "*Detention for questioning*" is the holding of a person, by a policeman or similar public official, without making a formal **arrest**.

Determinable. Possibly ended; subject to being ended if a certain thing happens.

Determination. A final decision (usually of a court or other formal decision-maker such as a **hearing officer**).

Detinue. A legal action to get back property being unlawfully held by another person plus to get back **damages** for the wrongful withholding.

Detriment. 1. Any loss or harm. 2. Giving something up (a right, a benefit, some property, etc).

Devest. See **divest**.

Deviance. Noticeable differing from average or normal behavior. The word is usually applied to things society in general does not like, such as drug use.

Devise. 1. The gift of land or things on land by **will**. 2. Any gift by will.

Devisee. Person to whom land is given by will.

Devisor. Person who makes a **will** to give away land.

Devolution. The transfer or transition by process of law from one person to another of a right, **liability, title,** property, or office (often by death).

Devolve. To go by **devolution** (see that word).

Dewey decimal system. A library reference system that classifies all subjects by number; for example: the numbers in the 340's are for law, 343 is for criminal law, and 343.2 is for a special subject under criminal law. Each new number after the decimal point subdivides the previous number (and its subject) further.

Dicta. Opinions of a judge that are not a central part of the judge's decision even if the judge argues them strongly and even if they look like conclusions. One way to decide whether a particular part of a judge's opinion is *dicta* is to examine whether it was necessary to reach the result. If it could be removed without changing the legal result, it is probably dicta. If it is dicta, it is not binding **precedent** (see that word) on later court decisions, but it is probably still worth quoting if it helps your case.

Dictum. (Latin) 1. Singular of **dicta** (see that word). 2. Short for "*obiter dictum*" (a remark by the way, as in "by the way, did I tell you . . ."); a digression; a discussion of side points or unrelated points.

Digest. A collection of parts of many books, usually giving not only summaries, but also excerpts and condensations; for example: the **American Digest System** covers the decisions of the highest court of each state and of the Supreme Court. It is divided into volumes by time periods. It collects "**headnotes**" or summaries given at the top of each case and is arranged by subject categories.

Dilatory. Tending or intending to cause delay or gain time.

Diligence. Carefulness or prudence.

Diminution. Reduction.

Direct. Immediate or straight. This word, in different settings, may be the opposite of **indirect** (not direct), **collateral** (on the side), or **cross** (opposing) (see these words).

Direct evidence. Proof of a fact without the need for other facts leading up to it. In this sense, it is the opposite of **indirect** or **circumstantial** evidence (see these words). For example: if a person testifies that he or she saw John walking in the rain, it is *direct* evidence that John walked in the rain; but if the person testifies that he or she saw John wearing wet shoes, it is *circumstantial* evidence (see that word) that John walked in the rain. Another example of direct evidence: a live dodo offered to prove that dodos are not extinct.

Direct examination. The first questioning in a trial of a **witness** by the side that called that witness.

Direct tax. A tax that is paid directly to the government by the person taxed; for example: income tax is direct, but a manufacturing tax is not because it is passed on to the buyer in the form of higher prices.

Directed verdict. A situation in which the judge takes the decision out of the jury's hands by telling them what they must decide.

Director. 1. Head of an organization, group or project. 2. Person elected by the **shareholders** (owners) of a **corporation** to make all **corporate** decisions such as the hiring of the persons who actually run the day-to-day operations.

Directory. Advisory, instructing or **procedural**; for example: *directory* language in a **statute** that merely instructs an official may not invalidate (overturn) actions of an official who fails to follow instructions.

Disability. 1. Physical or mental: The absence of adequate physical or mental powers; the lowering of earning ability due to this absence. 2. Legal: The lack of legal capacity to do an act; for example: a married person is *disabled* from re-

103

marrying until the marriage ends in divorce or by death.

Disaffirm. Repudiate; take back consent once given; refuse to stick by former acts (usually used in situations where the person has a legal right to do so).

Disallow. Refuse, deny or reject.

Disbar. Take away a lawyer's right to practice law.

Discharge. 1. Release; remove; free; dismiss; for example: to *discharge* a **contract** is to end the obligation by agreement or by carrying it out; to *discharge* a prisoner is to release him or her; to *discharge* a court **order** is to cancel or revoke it; to *discharge* a person in **bankruptcy** is to release him or her from all or most debts; and to *discharge* a person from the army is to release him or her from service. 2. The documents showing that no. 1 has taken place; for example: *discharge papers* from the army. 3. Do or perform a duty.

Disciplinary rules. Specific things that a lawyer is prohibited from doing. They appear in the **Code of Professional Responsibility.**

Disclaimer. 1. The refusal, rejection, or renunciation of a claim, a power, or property. 2. The refusal to accept certain types of responsibility; for example: a *disclaimer clause* in a written sales contract might say "we give you, the purchaser, these promises . . . 1, 2, 3, etc., but *disclaim* all other promises or responsibilities."

Discontinuance. Another word for either **non-suit** or **dismissal** (see these words).

Discount. 1. A deduction or lowering of an amount of money, for example: a lower price. 2. Paying interest in advance.

Discovery. The formal and informal exchange of information between sides in a lawsuit. Two types of *discovery* are **interrogatories** and **deposition** (see these words).

Discretion. Power to act within general guidelines, but without either specific rules to follow or the need to completely explain or justify each decision or action.

Discretionary trust. A **trust** (see that word) that allows some leeway in carrying it out.

Discrimination. 1. The failure to treat equals equally; the setting up of illogical categories to justify treating persons unfairly. 2. Illegally unequal treatment based on race, religion, sex, or age.

Disfranchise. Take away the rights of a free citizen, such as the right to vote.

Dishonor. To refuse to accept or pay a **negotiable instrument** (see that word) when it comes due.

Disinterested. Impartial; not biased or prejudiced; not affected personally or financially by the outcome. (The word, however, does *not* mean "uninterested" and does *not* mean lacking an opinion).

Dismissal. A court order or judgment that puts a lawsuit out of court. It may be "with **prejudice**" (no further lawsuit may be brought by the same persons on the same subject) or "without prejudice."

Disorderly conduct. A vague term for actions that disturb the peace or shock public morality. The term may be more closely defined by state laws, but usually is not.

Disorderly house. A building with occupants who behave in a way that creates a neighborhood **nuisance.** These often include places for gambling or prostitution.

Disparagement. The discrediting, belittling, or "talking down" of something or someone. Under some circumstances, you can be sued for doing it; for example: *disparagement* of **title** and *disparagement* of **property.**

Disposable earnings. Gross or "total" pay, minus **deductions** required by law; this is not exactly the same as "take home pay."

Disposition. Final settlement or result; a court's *disposition* of a case may be to give a **judgment, dismiss** it, etc.

Dispositive facts. Facts that clearly settle a legal question in court.

Dispossession. Ouster; wrongfully putting a person off his or her property by force, trick or misuse of the law.

Dispute. A disagreement between persons about their rights and their legal obligations to one another.

Disqualify. Make ineligible; for example: a judge may be *disqualified* from deciding a case involving a company if the judge owns stock in that company.

Dissent. A judge's formal disagreement with the decision of the majority of the judges in a lawsuit. If the judge puts it in writing, it is called a *dissenting opinion.*

Dissolution. 1. Ending or breaking up; for example: *dissolution* of a **contract** is a **mutual** agreement to end it and *dissolution* of a **corporation** is ending its existence. 2. *Dissolution of marriage* is ending a marriage because there are "irreconcilable differences" between husband and wife. This is a **"no fault" divorce.** Sometimes, "dissolution" applies to any legal ending of a marriage, including a regular **divorce.**

Dissolve. End or cancel (see **dissolution**).

Distinguish. Point out basic differences; to distinguish a case is to show why it is irrelevant (or not very relevant) to the lawsuit being decided.

Distrain. To take another person's **personal property** either lawfully or unlawfully. For example: a landlord might distrain a tenant's property to make sure that back rent will be paid.

Distress. The process of **distraining** (see that word) property.

Distributee. **Heir**; person who inherits.

Distribution. Division by shares; for example: giving out what is left of a dead person's **estate** after taxes and debts are paid.

Distributor. Wholesaler.

District. A sub-division of many different types of areas (such as countries, states, or counties) for judicial, political or administrative purposes. "*Districting*" is the process of drawing a district's boundary lines for purposes of **apportionment.** (See that word).

District attorney. The top criminal prosecuting lawyer of each Federal district and of each state

district. On low-levels, this person may also be
called the "*county attorney*" or "*state's attorney.*"

District court. 1. Trial courts of the U.S., each one
in a Federal district that may be a whole state or
part of a state. 2. In some states, low-level state
courts.

Disturbing the peace. Vague term, defined in different ways in different places, for interrupting
the peace, quiet, or good order of a neighborhood.

Divers. 1. Many; several. 2. Different; many
different.

Diversion. A turning aside; for example: the unauthorized changing of the course of a river; the
unauthorized use of a company's funds or of **trust**
funds; or the turning aside of criminals or juvenile delinquents from jail into special **rehabilitation** programs.

Diversity of citizenship. A phrase used to explain
when Federal courts may take a case due to the
fact that the persons on one side of the case come
from a different state than the persons on the
other side. This basis for Federal court action is
called *diversity jurisdiction.*

Divest. Deprive, take away, withdraw, or cast
away; for example: you can divest yourself of a
car by selling it.

Dividend. A share of profits or property.

Divorce. The ending of a marriage by court order.
It is different from an **annulment** (which wipes
out the marriage from the beginning as if it never
existed in law) and from a **limited divorce** (also
called "**legal separation,**" "divorce a **mensa et
thoro,**" and "**from bed and board**") in that a

limited divorce separates the couples legally, but does not allow either one to remarry.

Dock. A name for the place in some courtrooms where the prisoner stays during a trial.

Docket. The list of cases set down for trial in a court.

Doctrine. A legal principle or rule.

Document. Anything with a message on it; for example: a contract, a map, a photograph of a message on wood, etc. An *ancient document* is an old document, produced from proper **custody** (safe-keeping), that is presumed to be genuine if it is over a certain age. And a *public document* is a document that is, or should be, open for public inspection.

Document of title. A piece of paper that is normally accepted in business as proof of a right to hold goods; for example: a **bill of lading** or a **warehouse receipt.**

Documentary evidence. Evidence supplied by writings and all other **documents** (see that word).

Doing business. A general, flexible term meaning carrying on enough business for profit within a state so that another person can sue the company in that state. "Doing business" also means that the state itself can tax the company or otherwise claim **jurisdiction** (see that word) over it.

Domain. Ownership and control (usually by the public); for example: national forests are in the *public domain* (owned and controlled by the U.S.). Some writings are also in the *public domain*, but the meaning is different (available for use and reprinting by anyone). Another use of the word is *"eminent domain"* (the right to take private property for public use).

Domestic. 1. Relating to the home. 2. Relating to the state; for example: a domestic corporation is a corporation created under the laws of the state in question. 3. Relating to the country.

Domicile. A person's permanent home, legal home, or main residence.

Domiciliary. Relating to a person's permanent home; for example: a *domiciliary administration* is the handling of a dead person's **estate** (property) in the state of the person's legal **domicile** and is the primary or central place where this is done.

Dominant. Something that has rights against another thing; for example: a *dominant estate* has rights (such as an **easement** . . . see that word) in another piece of land.

Dominant cause. See **proximate cause.**

Dominion. Ownership or power over something.

Donative. As a gift; for example: a *donative trust* is a **trust** set up as a gift for another person.

Donee. A person to whom a gift is made or a power is given.

Donor. A person making a gift to another or giving another person power to do something.

Doom. Old word for a law or for a judge's decision.

Dormant. "Sleeping," inactive, silent or concealed; for example: a *dormant partner* is a partner who has a financial interest, but takes no control over the business and is usually unknown to the public.

Double entry. A method of bookkeeping that shows every transaction as both a **debit** and a **credit** (see those words) by using both horizontal rows and vertical columns of numbers. If the total of the horizontal rows and the vertical columns is not the same, it is easier to find out where mistakes are than if the records were kept with only one "*entry*" for each item.

Double indemnity. Double insurance payoff if something happens in a certain way; for example: if a person dies, the payoff might be ten thousand dollars, but if the death is accidental, it might be twenty thousand dollars.

Double insurance. Insurance from more than one company on the same **interest** in the same thing. It is usually not possible to collect more than a thing is worth.

Double jeopardy. A second prosecution for the same crime once the first one is completed. This is prohibited by the U.S. Constitution.

Doubt. Uncertainty of mind about proof in a trial; for example: "*beyond a reasonable doubt*" is the standard for proof to convict a person as guilty of a crime. It is the highest standard of proof required in any type of trial, but does not mean "beyond *all* doubt."

Dower. A wife's right to all or part of her dead husband's property. This right is now regulated by statute and varies from state to state, but is the same within each state for either husband or wife (see **curtesy**).

Down payment. The cash that must be paid at the time that something is bought by **installments** (on time).

Draconian law. A law that is especially harsh or severe.

111

Draft. A **bill of exchange** or any other **negotiable instrument** (see these words) for the payment of money *drawn* by one person on another. A **check** is a type of *draft*.

Draftsman. A person who writes a legal document (especially the person who creates an original document) such as a **contract** or a **legislative bill.**

Draw. 1. Prepare a legal document. 2. To write out and sign a **bill of exchange** or make a **note** (see these words). 3. Take money out of a bank account.

Drawee. 1. A person to whom a **bill of exchange** (see that word) is addressed and who is requested to pay the amount of the bill. 2. A bank that has a deposit withdrawn from it.

Drawer. The person **drawing** a **bill of exchange** (see this word) or signing a check.

Droit. (French) Right, justice, a law, or the law.

Dry. Passive; inactive; for example: a *dry* trust is one in which the **trustee** is legal owner of property, but has no duties to perform other than the passive act of having the property in his or her name.

Duces tecum. (Latin) "Bring with you." The name for a type of **subpoena** (see that word) that commands a person to come to court and bring documents or other pieces of **evidence.**

Due. 1. Owing; payable. 2. Just, proper, regular, lawful, sufficient, or reasonable; for example: "due care" means proper or reasonable care for the situation.

Due date. Day a tax or debt must be paid.

Due notice. Reasonable notice (varies with the situation).

Due process of law. The *Due Process Clause* of the U.S. Constitution requires that no person shall be deprived of life, liberty, or property without due process of law. The requirements of due process are regularly changed by the Supreme Court. They vary in detail from situation to situation, but the central core of the idea is that a person should always have notice and a real chance to present his or her side in a legal dispute and that no law or government procedure should be **arbitrary** or unfair.

Dummy. Sham; make believe; set up as a "front"; for example: *dummy* **incorporators** are persons who initially set up a corporation to meet the formal requirements of a state's corporation laws and then drop out. It is perfectly proper in most cases.

Duress. Unlawful pressure on a person to do what he or she would not otherwise have done. It includes force, threats of violence, physical restraint, etc.

Duty. 1. An obligation to obey a law. 2. A legal obligation to another person. In this sense, when one person has a "**right**" to something, another person must have a "*duty*" to avoid interfering with that right. 3. Any obligation, whether legal, moral or ethical. 4. A tax on imports.

Duty of tonnage. Governmental port charges or port taxes on a boat.

Dyer Act. A 1919 law making it a Federal crime to take a stolen motor vehicle across a state line.

Dying declaration. Out of court words of a dying person about who killed him or her and how it happened. Normally, other persons' words are not good **evidence,** but here they are usually allowed.

E

E.B.T. *Examination before trial* of a **party** to a lawsuit. It is a part of the **discovery** process.

E.E.O.C. Equal Employment Opportunities Commission: a U.S. agency that attempts to end job discrimination by setting standards, bringing lawsuits, etc.

E.G. Abbreviation for the Latin "exempli gratia" (for the sake of example); used in most law books to take the place of "for example."

E.P.A. Environmental Protection Agency: an independent U.S. agency that enforces pollution control, does environmental research, etc.

E.R.D.A. Energy Research and Development Administration; a Federal agency.

Earned income. Money or other compensation received for work. It does not include the profits gained from owning property.

Earnest money. A deposit paid by a buyer to hold a seller to a deal and to show the buyer's good faith.

Easement. An *easement* on a piece of land is the right of a specific non-owner (such as a next-door neighbor) the government, or the general public to use part of the land in a particular way. This right usually stays with the land when it is sold. Typical *easements* include the right of the owner of a piece of land with no streetfront to use a specific strip of another person's land to reach the street, or the right of a city to run a sewer line across a specific strip of an owner's land. The word for the land that gives up an easement is "**servient**" and if there is one particular property that benefits from the easement, it is called "**dominant**."

Ecclesiastical courts. Religious courts that used to be powerful in England and that affected the development of the law. Religious law was called **canon law.**

Edict. A major law put out by a king or other head of state.

Effect. 1. To do, produce, accomplish or force. 2. A result.

Effective rate. See **tax rate.**

Effects. 1. Personal property. 2. Personal property of a person making a will or of a dead person.

Efficient cause. See **proximate cause.**

Ejectment. The name for an old type of lawsuit to get back land taken away wrongfully. It was used primarily to establish title to land and was brought against a fictitious defendant called the "*casual ejector.*"

Ejusdem generis. (Latin) Of the same kind or type.

Election. The act of choosing; for example: choosing among persons by voting. Also, a husband or wife may have to *elect* (choose) between what was left in a **will** by the other one and what state law reserves as a minimum share of a husband's or wife's **estate.** (A husband might leave a wife "the house and ten thousand dollars" and state law may allow the wife to take one-third of the husband's total estate. The wife can have one but not both of these.)

Elector. Voter.

Electoral college. A name for the persons chosen by voters to elect the president and vice-president. The *electoral college* is now almost a formality and the vote of the general public in each state directly controls the election.

Eleemosynary. Charitable.

Element. A basic part; for example: some of the *elements* of a **cause of action** for **battery** (see these words) are an intentional, unwanted physical contact. Each of these things ("intentional," "unwanted," etc.) is one "element."

Eligibility. Being legally qualified; for example: eligibility for social security benefits means meeting all the legal requirements to get them.

Emancipation. Setting free; for example: a child is *emancipated* when the child is old enough so that the parents have no further right to control or obligation to support him or her.

Embargo. 1. A government's refusal to allow the transportation of certain things in or out of the country. 2. A government's stopping the ships or planes of another country from coming in or going out.

Embezzlement. The **fraudulent** and secret taking of money or property by a person who has been trusted with it. This usually applies to an employee taking money and covering it up by faking business records or **account** books.

Emblements. Growing crops.

Embracery. Old word for an attempt to bribe a jury.

Eminent domain. The government's right and power to take private land for public use by paying for it.

Emolument. Any financial or other gain from employment.

Emphyteutic lease. A lease on land that is long term and can be passed on to another person as long as the rent is paid.

Empirical. Based on observation or experiment.

Employers' Liability Acts. See **workmen's compensation.**

En. (French) In; for example: *en ventre sa mere* means "in its mother's womb."

Enabling clause. The part of a **statute** that gives officials the power to put it into effect and enforce it.

Enabling statute. A law that grants new powers, usually to a public official.

Enact. Put a statute into effect; pass a statute through a **legislature;** establish by law.

Encroachment. Unlawfully extending property to take over another person's property; for example: putting a fence too far over a boundary line.

Encumber. Make property subject to a **charge** or **liability** (see **encumbrance**).

Encumbrance. A **claim, charge** or **liability** on property, such as a **lien** or **mortgage,** that lowers its value.

Endowment. Setting up a fund, usually for a public institution such as a school.

Enfeoffment. See **feoffment.**

Enfranchise. 1. Make free. 2. Give the right to vote.

Engage. Take part in or do; to "*engage*" in a particular activity is to do it more than once and probably regularly.

Engagement. Contract or obligation.

Engross. Make a final or "good" copy of a document.

Enhancement. Increasing or making larger; for example, a criminal penalty may be *enhanced* (made longer or worse) even though "enhancement" is usually thought of as being good.

Enjoin. Require or command; a court's issuing of an **injunction** (see that word) directing a person or persons to do, or, more likely, to refrain from doing certain acts.

Enjoyment. The exercise of a right; the ability to use a right.

Enlarge. 1. Make larger. 2. Extend a time limit. 3. Release a person from custody.

Enrolled bill. A **bill** that has gone through the steps necessary to make it a law.

Entail. An inheritance in land that can be passed on only to children, then children's children, etc.

Enter. 1. Go into. 2. Go onto land in order to take possession. 3. Become a part of. 4. Place formally on the **record**; write down formally in the proper place; for example: to "*enter an appearance*" is to submit a piece of paper to a court saying that you are now formally a part of a case, either as a **party** or as a lawyer.

Entering judgment. The formal act of recording a court's **judgment** in the court's permanent records after the judgment has been given or announced.

Enticement. An old form of lawsuit brought because of the seduction or taking away of a wife.

Entirety. As a whole; not divided into parts.

Entitlement. Absolute (complete) right to something (such as social security) once you show that you meet the legal requirements to get it.

Entity. A real being; a separate existence.

Entrapment. The act of government officials or agents (usually police) of **inducing** a person to commit a crime that the person would not have committed without the inducement. This is done for the purposes of prosecuting the person. It is not lawful in most cases and a criminal charge based on *entrapment* should fail.

Entry. 1. The act of making or entering a formal record by writing it down. 2. The thing written down in no. 1. 3. Going into a building unlawfully to commit a crime.

Enumerated. Mentioned specifically; listed.

Equal protection of laws. A constitutional requirement that the government shall in no way fail to treat equals equally, set up illegal categories to justify treating persons unfairly, or give unfair or unequal treatment to a person based on that person's race, religion, etc.

Equitable. 1. Just, fair and right for a particular situation. 2. An "*equitable action*" is a legal action based on a court's **equity** (see that word) powers.

119

Equity. 1. Fairness in a particular situation. 2. The name for a system of courts that originated in England to take care of legal problems when the existing laws did not cover some situations in which a person's rights were violated by another person. 3. A court's power to "do justice" where specific laws do not cover the situation. 4. The value of property after all charges against it are paid.

Equity of redemption. The right of a person whose property has been **foreclosed** on to get it back by paying off the whole mortgage plus costs of foreclosing.

Ergo. (Latin) Therefore.

Erratum. (Latin) Mistake.

Error. A mistake made by a judge in the procedures used at trial or in making legal rulings during the trial that allows one side in a lawsuit to ask a higher court to review the case. If the error is substantial, it is called "*reversible error*" by the higher court. If it is trivial, it is called "*harmless error.*"

Escalator clause. A contract term that allows a price to rise if costs rise. Or, in the case of a maximum payment regulated by the government (such as rent controls), for the price to rise if the maximum is raised or eliminated.

Escheat. The state's getting property because no owner can be found; for example: if a person dies and no person can be found who can legally inherit that person's property, the government gets it.

Escrow. Money, property, or documents belonging to person A and held by person B until person A takes care of an obligation to person C; for example: a mortgage company may require a homeowner with a **mortgage** to make monthly payments into an *escrow* account to take care of the yearly tax bill when it comes due.

Esq. Short for "Esquire"; a title given to lawyers.

Establish. **1.** Settle or prove a point. **2.** Set up, create, or found.

Establishment clause. That part of the U.S. Constitution that states "Congress shall make no law respecting an *establishment* of religion, etc."

Estate. **1.** The **interest** a person has in property; a person's right or **title** to property; for example: a *"future estate"* is a property interest that will come about only in the future if an uncertain event takes place. **2.** The property itself in which a person has an interest; for example: *real estate* (land) or a *decedent's estate* (things left by a dead person).

Estate tax. A tax paid on the property left by a dead person. It is paid on the property as a whole before it is divided up and handed out. This is the opposite of an **inheritance tax,** which is based on the money each individual inherits and is paid by each **heir** separately.

Estimated tax. Some persons with income other than salaries must "declare" and pay income tax every three months.

Estoppel. Being stopped from proving something (even if true) in court because of something said before that shows the opposite (even if false); for example: if a person signs a **deed,** that person

121

may be *estopped* from later going to court claiming that the deed is wrong.

Estoppel by judgment. The inability to raise an issue against a person in court because a judge has already decided that precise issue between the persons.

Estoppel certificate. A **mortgage** company's written statement of the amount due on a mortgage as of a particular date.

Et al. (Latin) Abbreviation for et alia ("and others"); for example: "*Smith et al.*" means Smith plus a list of other persons.

Et seq. (Latin) Abbreviation for et sequentes ("and the following"); for example: "*page 27 et seq.*" means "page twenty-seven and the following pages."

Et ux. Abbreviation for et uxor ("and wife") seen on old legal documents; for example: "This deed made by John Smith *et ux.*"

Et vir. (Latin) And husband.

Ethical considerations. General guidelines for proper behavior as a lawyer. These appear in the **Code of Professional Responsibility.**

Ethics. 1. Professional standards of conduct for lawyers and judges. **2.** Standards of fair and honest conduct in general.

Eviction. A landlord putting a tenant out of property either by taking direct action (a "*self-help*" *eviction*) or, more often, by going to court.

Evidence. 1. All types of information (observations, recollections, documents, concrete objects, etc.) presented at a trial or other hearing. **2.** Any information that might be used for a future trial.

Evidence law. The rules and principles about whether evidence can be **admitted** (accepted for proof)
in a trial and how to evaluate its importance.

Evidentiary fact. A fact that is learned directly
from **testimony** or other **evidence.** Conclusions
drawn from *evidentiary facts* are called "*ultimate
facts.*"

Ex. (Latin) A prefix meaning many things including: out of, no longer, from, because of, by, and
with.

Ex officio. 1. By the power of the office (official
position) alone. 2. Acting as a private citizen, not
as an official. (This is a popular, not legal, meaning.)

Ex parte. (Latin) With only one side present; for
example: an *ex parte order* is one made on the
request of one side in a lawsuit when (or because)
the other side does not show up in court (because
the other side failed to show up, because the other
side did not need to be present for the order to
issue, or because there *is* no other side.)

Ex post facto. (Latin) After the fact; an *ex post
facto law* is one that attempts to make an action a
crime that was not a crime at the time it was
done, or a law that attempts to reduce a person's
rights based on a past act that was not subject to
the law when it was done. Ex post facto laws are
prohibited by the Constitution.

Ex rel. "On relation"; when a case is titled "*State
ex rel. Doe v. Roe*" it means that the state is
bringing a lawsuit for Doe against Roe.

Examination. An investigation or questioning; for
example: the questioning of a witness under oath

or the questioning in a hearing of a **bankrupt** about his or her full financial situation.

Examiner. Name for a type of **hearing officer** or **administrative** judge.

Exception. 1. Leaving something or someone out intentionally; an exclusion. 2. A formal disagreement with a judge's refusal of a request or **overruling** of an **objection.** It is a statement that the lawyer does not agree with the judge's decision, but will save the objections until later (usually for an **appeal**). It is not necessary to take *exceptions* to accomplish this in most courts.

Excise. A tax on the manufacture, sale, or use of goods or on the carrying on of an occupation or activity.

Exclusionary clause. A part of a **contract** that tries to restrict the legal **remedies** available to one side if the contract is broken.

Exclusionary rule. 1. A reason why even **relevant** (see that word) **evidence** will be kept out of a trial. 2. *"The exclusionary rule"* often means the rule that illegally gathered evidence may not be used in a criminal trial.

Exclusive. Shutting out all others; sole; one only; for example: if a court has *exclusive jurisdiction* over a subject, no other court in the area can decide a lawsuit on that subject.

Exclusive agency. See **listing.**

Exclusive authorization. See **listing.**

Exculpate. Provide an **excuse** or **justification**; show that someone has not committed a crime or a wrongful act.

Exculpatory clause. A provision in a **trust** arrangement by which the **trustee** is relieved of all responsibility for things that go wrong or for losses if the trustee acts in good faith.

Excuse. A reason that will stand up in court for an unintentional action; for example: if you kill someone by accident and it was not your fault, it is *excusable homicide.*

Execute. Complete, make, perform, do or carry out; for example: to *execute a contract* is to sign it and make it valid, but to *execute an obligation* created by the contract is to carry it out or perform it.

Execution. 1. Carrying out or completion (see **execute**). 2. An official carrying out of a court's **order** or **judgment.** 3. Signing and finalizing (and handing over, if needed) a document such as a **deed.** 4. The government's putting a person to death.

Executive. 1. The branch of government that carries out the laws (as opposed to the **judicial** and **legislative** branches); the **administrative** branch. 2. A high official in a branch of government, a company, or other organization.

Executive order. A law put out by the president or a governor that does not need to be passed by the **legislature.**

Executor. Person selected by a person making a will to **administer** the will and to hand out the property once the person making the will dies.

Executory. Still to be carried out; incomplete; depending on a future act or event. Opposite of **executed.**

Exemplary damages. See **punitive damages.**

Exemplification. An official copy of a public document used as **evidence.**

Exemption. 1. Freedom from a general duty, service, burden, or tax. 2. **Deduction** from income of a certain amount for each family member. Each *exemption* lowers the income on which a person must pay taxes.

Exequatur. Having an American lawsuit *"clothed with an exequatur"* means having it **validated** by the local court in order to have it recognized and enforced overseas.

Exercise. Make use of; for example: to *"exercise a purchase option"* is to make use of a right to buy something by buying it.

Exhaustion of remedies. A person must take all reasonable steps to get satisfaction from an **administrative agency** before taking a problem with that agency to court (and to get satisfaction from a state government before going into Federal court).

Exhibit. 1. Any object or document offered as **evidence** (in a trial, **hearing, deposition, audit,** etc.). If accepted, it is marked to identify it. 2. Any document attached to a formal paper, such as a **pleading** or an **affidavit.**

Exoneration. 1. Clearing of a crime or other wrongdoing; **exculpation.** 2. Removal of a **burden** or a **duty.** 3. Right of a person who pays a debt for another person to be reimbursed by that person. 4. The right to be paid off on a **negotiable instrument.**

Expatriation. Voluntary act of giving up **citizenship** and leaving a country.

Expectancy. Something merely hoped for; for example: an **inheritance** under a **will** is an *expectancy* because the person making the will might change his or her mind.

Expert witness. A person possessing special knowledge or experience who is allowed to testify at a trial not only about facts (like an ordinary witness) but also about the professional conclusions he or she draws from these facts.

Expository statute. A law that is enacted to explain the meaning of a previously enacted law.

Express. Clear, definite, direct or actual (as opposed to **implied**); known by explicit words.

Expressio unius. (Latin) Short for "expressio unius est exclusio alterios" (the mention of one thing rules out others). This is a rule for **interpreting** documents. Most rules of this sort have their opposites, however, and are used by judges to justify decisions rather than to make them.

Expropriation. The taking of private property for public use.

Expunge. Blot out, obliterate or strike out; for example: to *expunge* and **arrest record** is to wipe it completely and physically "off the books."

Extension. 1. A lengthening of time; for example: in the **term** of a lease or in the time a person may pay a debt without extra payment. 2. "*Extending a case*" means a judge's applying the rule that the case stands for to another case that is only somewhat similar.

127

Extenuating circumstances. Surrounding facts that make a crime less evil or blameworthy. They do not lower the crime to a less serious one, but do tend to lower punishment.

Extinguishment. The ending of a right, power, contract, or property interest. It may end because of a **merging** with a bigger thing; for example: a right of **tenancy** *extinguishes* not only if the tenant moves out, but also if the tenant buys the house.

Extort. 1. To compel or coerce; for example: to get a confession by depriving a person of food and water. 2. To get something by illegal threats of harm to person, property, or reputation.

Extortion. Any illegal taking of money by using threats, force, or misuse of public office.

Extra. 1. Outside of. 2. In addition to.

Extradition. One country (or state) giving up a person to another one when the second country requests the person for a trial on a criminal charge.

Extrajudicial. Unconnected with court business.

Extraordinary remedy. A group of actions a court will take only if absolutely necessary. These include **habeas corpus** and **mandamus** (see these words).

Extraterritoriality. The operation of a country's laws outside of its physical boundaries; for example: the U.S.'s right to bring to trial and punish its soldiers in another country for crimes committed on a U.S. base there.

Extremis. (Latin) Last illness.

Extrinsic evidence. Facts drawn from things outside the contract or other document in question; for example: the fact that a person was forced to sign a contract is *extrinsic* to the "**face**" (words) of the contract itself.

Eyewitness. Person with first hand knowledge of an event; someone who can testify as to what he or she saw, or heard, or smelled, etc.

Eyre. A court of travelling judges in old England.

F

F. 1. Federal Reporter (see **National Reporter System**). 2. Following; for example: "26f." means "page 26 and the next page."

F.A.A. Federal Aviation Administration: the branch of the U.S. Department of Transportation that handles all air travel.

F.B.I. Federal Bureau of Investigation: the U.S. Justice Department branch that investigates all violations of Federal law that are not specifically handled by other agencies.

F.C.C. Federal Communications Commission: the U.S. agency that **regulates** television, telephone, radio, etc.

F.D.A. Food and Drug Administration: the branch of the U.S. Department of Health, Education and Welfare that **regulates** the safety of food, drugs, cosmetics, etc.

F.D.I.C. Federal Deposit Insurance Corporation: insures bank deposits for individual depositors.

F.E.A. Federal Energy Administration: **regulates** the use of energy sources such as oil and coal.

F.I.C.A. "Federal Insurance Contributions Act"; Social Security Tax.

F.N.M.A. Federal National **Mortgage** Association; a government sponsored, but privately owned purchaser of home mortgages. Also called "Fannie Mae."

F.O.B. "Free on board"; the selling price of goods includes transportation costs.

F.P.C. Federal Power Commission: **regulates** interstate transportation, production and use of electric power and natural gas.

F.Supp. Federal Supplement (See **National Reporter System**).

F.T.C. Federal Trade Commission: enforces prohibitions against **"unfair competition"** in business and "unfair or deceptive acts or trade practices"; enforces Federal laws such as Truth-in-Lending.

Face. The language of a document including everything in it (not just the front page), but excluding things about the document that do not appear in it; for example: a **contract** can be valid *"on its face"* even though a person was forced to sign it at gunpoint and no court would uphold it.

Face value. Just the amount of money written on a **note** or other financial document, not anything more for **interest** or other charges normally added on.

Facsimile. Exact copy

Fact. 1. An act; a thing that took place; an event. 2. Something that exists and is real as opposed to what should exist; for example: a *"question of fact"* is about what is or what happened, while a *"question of law"* is about how the law affects what happened and what should have happened according to law. **3.** Something that exists and is real as opposed to opinion or supposition.

Fact situation. A summary of the facts of a case without any comments or legal conclusions.

Factor. A person who is given goods to sell and who gets a commission for selling them.

Factum. (Latin) Act; fact; central fact or act upon which a question turns.

Failure of issue. Dying without children.

Fair comment. The **common law** (pre-**Constitutional**) right to comment, within limits, upon the conduct of public officials without being **liable** for **defamation** (see that word).

Fair hearing. Word many **administrative agencies** use for their trial-like decision-making process which is used when a person **appeals** an administrative decision. The hearing does not have to use full trial rules or procedures and is "fair" because it follows rules, not because persons always get what they need or deserve.

Fair market value. Price to which a willing seller and a willing buyer would agree for an item in the ordinary course of trade.

Fair trade. The fixing of a retail price for an item by the manufacturer.

Fair use. The limited use that may be made of something **copyrighted** without **infringing** the copyright.

False. **1.** Intentionally or knowingly untrue. **2.** Untrue.

False arrest. Any unlawful restraint or deprivation of a person's liberty. It is a **tort.**

False imprisonment. See **false arrest.**

False pretenses. A lie told to cheat another person out of his or her money or property.

Falsus in uno. (Latin) The rule that if a jury believes that any part of what a witness says is deliberately false, the jury may disregard it all as being false.

Family. A broad word that can mean, among other things: **1.** Any household or group of persons living together as a single group. **2.** Parents and children. **3.** Persons related by blood or marriage. "*Family*" is usually defined differently for different purposes; for example: it might mean different things under a state's zoning laws and its tax laws.

Family car doctrine (or Family purpose doctrine). The owner of a car will usually be **liable** for damage done by a family member driving the owner's car.

Fannie Mae. See **FNMA.**

Fatal. A mistake in legal procedure is "*fatal*" if it is serious enough to unfairly hurt the side that complains about it; for example: a fatal **error** (see that word) could cause a new trial.

Fault. **1.** Negligence; lack of care; failure to do a duty. **2.** Defect or imperfection. **3.** According to the **Uniform Commercial Code,** *fault* means "wrongful act, omission or breach."

Feasance. Doing an act; performing a duty.

Fed. **1.** Federal Reserve System: the central U.S. bank; sets money-supply policy. **2.** Short for Federal.

Federal. 1. A *Federal* union is a uniting of two or more states into one strong central government with many powers left to the states. 2. U.S.; the Federal government is the national as opposed to state government.

Federal question. Cases directly involving the U.S. Constitution, U.S. **statutes,** or treaties.

Federal Register. The first place that the rules and regulations of U.S. **administrative agencies** are published. Abbreviated "Fed. Reg."

Federalism. Several different levels of government (for example: city, state and national) existing side-by-side in the same area.

Federation. A formal group of persons, organizations, or governments loosely united for a common purpose.

Fee. 1. A charge for services. 2. An **inheritance** without any limitations placed on it; an **estate** with no restrictions on disposing of it and which will go, upon death, to a person's **heirs.**

Fee simple. Same as "**fee**" (see that word).

Fee tail. An **estate** that can be passed on only to children (or only to some other set line of **inheritance**).

Fellow servant rule. A rule (not much used now) that an employer is not responsible for the injuries one employee does to another employee if the employees were carefully chosen.

Felon. A person who commits a **felony** (major crime) and has not yet finished serving time for it.

Felonious. 1. Done with the intent to commit a major crime; for example: "*felonious assault*" is

133

an **assault** which, if successful, would have been a
felony. 2. Evil; malicious; unlawful.

Felony. 1. A serious crime. 2. A crime with a **sentence** of one year or more.

Felony-murder rule. An accidental killing committed while committing a **felony** may make that
killing a **murder.**

Feoffment. The old method of transferring full
ownership of land in England.

Feudal law. Law of property from the Middle Ages
in England.

Ff. An expression such as "p. 26ff" means "found
on page 26 and on the pages immediately following."

Fiat. (Latin) "Let it be done"; a command.

Fiction. A *legal fiction* is an assumption that something that is (or may be) false or non-existent is
true or real. Legal fictions are assumed or invented to help do justice; for example: bringing a
lawsuit to throw a non-existent "John Doe" off
your property used to be the only way to establish
a clear right to the property when legal **title** was
uncertain.

Fictitious. 1. Fake (and usually in bad faith). 2.
Non-existent; made up.

Fidelity bond. Insurance on a person against that
person's dishonesty. It is often required when a
person is in a position of trust, handles large sums
of money, and is seldom checked on by others.

Fiduciary. 1. A person who manages money or
property for another person and in whom that
other person has a right to place great trust. 2.
Situations like those in no. 1. 3. Any relationship

between persons in which one person acts for another in a position of trust; for example: lawyer and client or parent and child.

Fieri facias. (Latin) An old **writ** of **execution** commanding a **sheriff** to take goods to pay off a debt.

FIFO. "First in, first out," a method of calculating the worth of a merchant's **inventory.**

Fifth Amendment. 1. See **Bill of Rights.** 2. "*Taking the Fifth*" means refusing to answer a question because it might involve you in a crime.

File. 1. The complete court record of a case. 2. "To file" a paper is to give it to the court clerk for inclusion in the case record. 3. A folder in a law office (of a case, a client, business records, etc.).

Filiation proceeding. Same as **paternity suit** (see that word).

Final argument. Each side in a trial may give a last statement to the jury about what it thinks the facts are and how it thinks the law applies to these facts.

Final decision. This word has opposite uses: 1. The last action of a court; the one upon which an **appeal** can be based. 2. The last decision of a court or a series of courts from which there are no more appeals.

Financial statement. A summary of what a company owns and what it owes.

Finding. A decision (by a judge, jury, **hearing examiner,** etc.) about a question of fact; a decision about **evidence**; often called a "*finding of fact*" upon which a "*conclusion of law*" may be based.

Firm offer. A written offer (see that word), by a merchant, that will be held open for a certain length of time; a type of **option** that requires no **consideration** (see that word) to be valid.

First impression. New; a case or a question is "*of first impression*" if it presents an entirely new problem to the court and cannot be decided by **precedent.**

First instance. A *court of first instance* is a **trial** court as opposed to an **appeals** court.

Fiscal. Financial; the *fiscal* year is a period of time, equal to a calendar year, but starting on the day that the state or company uses as "day one" for its business records. This is often January, April, July, or October first.

Fishing trip. **1.** Using the courts to find out information beyond the fair scope of the lawsuit. **2.** The loose, unfocused questioning of a **witness** or the overly broad use of the **discovery** process.

Fixed asset. A thing (such as a machine) that is essential to the operation of a business.

Fixed charges. Business costs that continue whether or not business comes in; for example: rent.

Fixture. Anything attached to land or a building. The word is sometimes used to mean those attached things that once attached may *not* be removed by a tenant. It usually means those things attached that *may* be removed.

Flagrante delicto. (Latin) In the act of committing the crime.

Floating capital. Money used to meet current expenses.

Floating lien. An arrangement in which later property purchased by someone with a **secured** debt or

lien (see these words) on property becomes subject to that debt or lien.

Flotsam. The wreckage of a ship found floating in the water.

Followed. A case is followed by a later case if it is used to decide the later case.

Forbearance. 1. Refraining from action (especially action to enforce a right). 2. Holding off demanding payment on a debt that is due.

Force. 1. Unlawful or wrongful violence; for example: *forceable entry* is taking possession or entering another person's property against that person's will or by using "force" in its ordinary meaning. 2. "In force" means in effect and valid.

Force majeure. (French) Irresistible, natural, or unavoidable force; for example: an earthquake.

Forceable detainer. The act of a person who originally had a right to possession of land or a building and then refuses to give up the property when that right is ended.

Forced sale. A sale made to pay off a court's **judgment,** ordered by that court, and done according to rules set by that court.

Foreclosure. Action by a person who holds a **mortgage** to: 1. take the property away from the mortgagor (such as the homeowner); 2. end that homeowner's rights in the property; and 3. sell the property to pay off the mortgage debt. Both the process (which is usually but not always done by lawsuit) and the result are called "*foreclosure.*"

Foreign. Belonging to, coming from, or having to do with another country or another state; for example: a Maine court would call a **corporation**

incorporated in and based in Ohio a *foreign* corporation.

Foreman. The leader of a **jury** who speaks for it.

Foreseeability. What a reasonably careful and thoughtful person would expect and plan for at the time of an occurrence and under the same circumstances; not hindsight.

Forensic. Having to do with courts and law; for example: *forensic medicine* is medical knowledge or medical practice involved with court **testimony** or other legal matters.

Forfeit. To lose the right to something due to neglect of a duty, due to an offense, or due to a **breach** of **contract**; for example: if a **defendant** fails to show up for trial, he or she may *forfeit* the bail bond.

Forgery. 1. Making a fake document (or altering a real one) with intent to commit a **fraud.** 2. The document itself in no. 1.

Form. 1. A model to work from (or a paper with blanks to be filled in) of a legal document such as a **contract** or a **pleading.** 2. The language, arrangement, conduct, procedure, or legal technicalities of a legal document or a legal **proceeding** as opposed to the "**substance**" or subject of the document or proceeding.

Formal party. A person who is involved in a lawsuit in name only and has no real interest in the proceedings.

Formed design. A deliberate and set intention to commit a crime (particularly a killing).

Forms of action. The special, individual, technical ways each different type of lawsuit used to have to be brought in court. If a legal problem did not fit into one of these pigeonholes (such as "**trover**," "assumpsit" or "**replevin**"), it could not be brought in many courts.

Fornication. Unlawful sexual intercourse between unmarried persons.

Forswear. Swear to something you know is untrue. This is broader than "**perjury**" (see that word), but not as serious.

Forthwith. An unnecessarily formal word meaning immediately; as soon as possible.

Fortuitous. Happening by chance or accident; unexpected; unforeseen; unavoidable; does *not* mean "lucky."

Forum. (Latin) A court.

Forum non conveniens. (Latin) "Inconvenient court." If two or more courts both have proper **venue** (see that word) for a case, a judge may rule that a lawsuit must be brought in the other court for either the convenience of or fairness to the parties.

Forwarding fee. Money paid to a lawyer who **refers** a client to another lawyer. The money is paid by the lawyer who receives the client.

Foundation. Basis; for example: the *foundation* of a trial is the group of issues in dispute between the sides (as set out in the **pleadings**).

Four corners. Same as **face** (see that word) of a document, that is, the document itself without outside information about it.

Franchise. 1. A business arrangement in which a person buys the right to sell, rent, etc., the products or services of a company and use the compa-

139

ny's name to do business. **2.** A special right given by the government, such as the right to vote or to form a corporation.

Fraud. Any kind of trickery used by one person to cheat another.

Fraudulent. Cheating; for example: a "fraudulent conveyance" is a debtor's transfer of property to someone else in order to cheat a **creditor** who might have a right to it.

Freedom of speech. The Constitutional right to say what you want as long as you do not interfere with others' rights. These other rights are protected by the laws of **defamation,** public safety, etc.

Freehold. Ownership of land, either unrestricted or restricted by a time limit only.

Friend of the court. See **amicus curiae.**

Friendly fire. A fire that remains contained where intended, but may do damage anyway.

Friendly suit. A lawsuit brought by agreement to settle a point of law that affects opposing persons.

Frisk. Superficial running of hands over a person's body in order to do a quick search.

Frivolous. Legally worthless; for example: a pleading that clearly has no legal leg to stand on, even if every fact it claims is true, is *frivolous.* An **appeal** that presents no legal question or is so lacking in substance that it could not possibly succeed is *frivolous.*

Frolic. An employee's act that has nothing to do with what he or she is employed to do.

Fruit. Product of; material result; for example: rental income is the fruit of renting land out and stolen money is the "fruit of crime."

Frustration. "Frustration of contract" occurs when carrying out a bargain has become impossible because of some change or occurrence that is not the fault of the persons making the deal.

Fugitive from justice. A person who commits a crime and either leaves the area or hides to avoid prosecution.

Full faith and credit. The Constitutional requirement that each state must treat as valid, and enforce where appropriate, the laws and court decisions of other states.

Fund. 1. A sum of money set aside for a particular purpose. 2. Money and all other assets (such as stocks or bonds) on hand.

Fundamental law. A country's constitution or basic governing principles.

Fungible. Things that are easily replaced one for another. For example: pounds of rice are fungible because one may be substituted for another, but paintings are not fungible.

Future acquired property. Property that is made part of a mortgage on presently owned property.

Future earnings. Estimated money that would have been made in the future if an injury had not occurred.

Future interests. Present rights in property that give the right to future possession or use; for example: the right to own property and use it after ten years go by.

Futures. Contracts promising to buy or sell standard commodities (rice, soybeans, etc.) at a future date and at a set price; these are "paper" deals and involve profit and loss on promises to deliver, not possession of the actual commodities.

G

G.A.O. General Accounting Office: assists the U.S. Congress in financial matters; **audits** and investigates Federal programs; settles claims against the U.S., etc.

G.N.M.A. General National Mortgage Association: a government organization that operates special programs in which housing mortgages are bought and sold to encourage private lending in certain types of housing. Also called "Ginnie Mae."

G.S.A. General Services Administration: manages all U.S. property.

Gaol. Jail.

Garnishee. A person who holds money or property belonging to a **debtor** and who is subject to a **garnishment** (see that word) proceeding by a **creditor.**

Garnishment. A legal proceeding taken by a **creditor** after a **judgment** is received against a **debtor.** If the creditor knows that the debtor has money or property with someone else (such as a bank account or wages paid by an employer), the creditor first has the money tied up by legal process and then takes as much of it as state laws allow to pay off the debt.

Gen. General.

General. A whole group as opposed to an individual in it or only a part of it; applying to all as opposed to some or to one; the opposite of general is often "**special**" or "**limited.**"

General Assembly. **1.** The entire **legislature** of many states. **2.** The lower house of many state legislatures. **3.** The large policy making meeting of the United Nations.

General assignment for creditors. A transfer of all rights to a **debtor's** property to a **trustee** who settles the debtor's affairs and distributes money to the **creditors.**

General assistance (or General relief). A local form of aid to the poor that sometimes has state backing, but involves no Federal funds. It is usually temporary.

General average loss. A loss at sea that will be shared by the shipowner and all owners of cargo shipped. This happens if the lost or damaged items (often thrown overboard) were intentionally lost to save the ship and the rest of the cargo.

General building scheme. The division of a piece of land into separate building lots that are sold with identical restrictions on each as to how the land may be used.

General creditor. A person who is owed money, but who has no **security** (for example, a **mortgage**) for the debt.

General digest. See **American Digest System.**

General execution. A court **order** to a sheriff or another court official to take any **personal property** of a defendant in order to pay off a **judgment** against that person.

General jurisdiction. The power of a court to hear and decide any type of case that comes up within its geographical area.

General lien. A right (arising from a **contract**) to hold **personal property** of another person until payment of a debt is made.

General verdict. See **verdict.**

General warranty deed. A transfer of land that includes the formal, written promise to protect the buyer against all claims of ownership of the property.

Gerrymander. Changing political boundaries or districts in a state or country in order to accomplish an improper purpose, such as to give a voting advantage to one political party.

Gift. Any willing transfer of money or property without payment close to the value of the thing transferred.

Ginnie Mae. See **GNMA.**

Gloss. An explanation of a passage in a book or document that is usually put on the same page.

Glossary. **1.** Dictionary. **2.** Small dictionary; specialized dictionary.

Going public. Selling **shares** in a **corporation** to the general public.

Good. Valid; legally sufficient.

Good behavior. A vague term, applied differently to the conduct required for public officials to keep their jobs, for criminals to get out of jail early, etc.

Good cause. Legally sufficient; not arbitrary.

Good faith. **1.** Honest; honesty in fact. **2.** For a merchant, *good faith* also means "the observance of reasonable commercial standards of fair dealing in the trade" according to the **Uniform Commercial Code.**

Goods. A general word that can have a meaning as broad as all property (excluding land) or as narrow as items for sale by a merchant.

Goodwill. The reputation and built-up business of a company. It can be generally valued as what a company would sell for over and above the value of its physical property and money owed to it.

Government instrumentality doctrine. A legal rule that any organization run by a branch of government may not be taxed.

Grab law. Aggressive collection (see that word).

Grace. 1. A favor. 2. A holding off on demanding payment of a debt or enforcing some other right. Often called *"grace days."*

Grace period. A short period of time an **insurance policy** stays in effect after the **premium** payment is due.

Graduated tax. See **tax rate.**

Grand jury. See **jury.**

Grand larceny. A **theft** of money or property worth above a certain amount which is set by law.

Grandfather clause. An exception to a restriction that allows all those already doing something to continue doing it even if they would be stopped by the new restriction.

Grant. 1. Give or confer. 2. Transfer of land, usually by **deed.** 3. A gift or subsidy.

Grantee. Person to whom a **grant** is made or land is **deeded.**

145

Grantor. Person making a **grant** or **deeding over** land.

Gratuitous. Without payment or other real **consideration.**

Gratuitous licensee. A non-business visitor; a social guest.

Gravamen. The basis, gist, or material part of a **charge, complaint,** etc.

Grievance procedure. An orderly, regular way of handling problems between workers and employers.

Gross. 1. Great or large. 2. Flagrant or shameful. 3. Whole or total.

Gross income. 1. Money taken in (as opposed to "**net**" income, which is money taken in minus money paid out). 2. Under the Federal tax laws, *gross income* is money taken in minus "**exclusions**" (such as gifts or interest on tax-free **bonds**); it is formally defined as "all income from whatever source derived" in the Internal Revenue Code.

Ground rent. Rent paid for land when the tenant has put up the building.

Grounds. Basis, foundation, or points relied on; for example: "grounds" for a **divorce** may include **adultery, cruelty,** etc.

Group legal services. Legal help given to members of an organization or employees of a company. It is paid for in advance on a group basis, often similar to health insurance.

Guarantee. Same as **guaranty** (see that word).

Guaranty. 1. The same as a merchant's **warranty** (promise) that goods are of a certain quality, will be fixed if broken, will last a certain time, etc. 2.

A promise to fulfill an obligation (or pay a debt) if the person who has the obligation fails to fulfill it; for example: John contracts with Ron that if Ron lends Don five dollars and Don fails to pay it back in a week, John will pay it.

Guardian. A person who has the legal right and duty to take care of another person or that person's property because that other person (for example, a child) cannot legally take care of himself or herself. The arrangement is called "*guardianship.*"

Guardian ad litem. A **guardian** (see that word), usually a lawyer, who is appointed by a court to take care of another person's interests during a lawsuit involving that person.

Guest statute. Laws in some states that do not permit a person who rides in another person's car as a *guest* (without payment or other business purpose) to sue that person if there is an accident unless the accident involves more than **ordinary negligence.**

Guilty. 1. Responsible for a crime. **2.** Convicted of a crime. **3.** Responsible for a **civil wrong,** such as **negligence.**

H

H.B. "House Bill"; a **bill** in the process of going through the House of Representatives on its way to becoming a law.

H.D.C. Holder in due course.

H.E.W. Department of Health, Education and Welfare: the U.S. Cabinet department that, in addition to what its name states, runs Social Security, the Food and Drug Administration, and many special "human services" programs.

H.R. House of Representatives.

H.U.D. Department of Housing and Urban Development: the U.S. Cabinet department that coordinates Federal housing and land use policy and funds housing construction through a variety of programs.

Habeas corpus. (Latin) "You have the body"; a judicial **order** to someone holding a person to bring that person to court. It is most often used to get a person out of unlawful imprisonment by forcing the captor and the person being held to come to court for a decision on the legality of the imprisonment or other holding (such as keeping a child when someone else claims **custody**).

Habendum. The part of a **deed** that describes the ownership rights being transferred.

Habitability. The requirement that a rented house or apartment be fit to live in.

Habitual. Regular, common and customary; more than just frequent. Some states have "*habitual criminal*" laws that may apply to a person who has been convicted of as few as two crimes.

Habitual intemperance. Regular drunkenness that is serious enough to interfere with a normal home or job. This is grounds for a **divorce** in many states. Also, some states include drug addiction under the label.

Harbor. 1. Shelter, house, keep, or feed. 2. Shelter or conceal a person for an illegal purpose, such as to protect a criminal from the police.

Hard cases. Cases where fairness requires being loose with legal principles.

Hatch Act. A Federal law to prevent certain types of political activity (such as holding public office) by Federal employees.

Have and hold. A common formal phrase in a **deed** that is no longer necessary to make the deed effective.

Head of family. A person who actually supports a group of related persons living together.

Head of household. A special category of Federal taxpayer. To be allowed to pay at "head of household" rates, you must meet several tests; for example: unmarried or legally separated, pay over half the support of your *dependants*, etc.

Headnote. A summary of a case placed at the beginning of the case when it is collected and published.

Hearing. 1. A court proceeding. 2. A trial-like proceeding that takes place in an **administrative agency** or other non-court setting. 3. A meeting of a **legislative committee** to gather information. 4. A *"public hearing"* may involve an agency showing a new plan or proposed action to the public and allowing public comment and criticism.

Hearing examiner (or Hearing officer). A judge-like official in an **administrative agency.**

Hearsay. Second-hand **evidence**; facts not in the personal knowledge of the witness, but a repetition of what others said that is used to prove the truth of what those others said; oral or written evidence that depends on the believability of something or someone not available to the court.

Hearsay exception. **Evidence** that will be admitted as evidence in a trial because it fits under a special rule even though it is **hearsay** (see that word) and would normally be kept out because of this. For example, **dying declarations** are a *hearsay exception* in some situations.

Heart-balm Act. State laws either eliminating or restricting lawsuits based on **breach of promise to marry.**

Heat of passion. A state of violent and uncontrollable provoked anger that may reduce the legal definition of a killing from **murder** to **manslaughter.**

Heir. A person who inherits property.

Held. Decided; as in "the court held that"; (see definition no. 2 of **hold**).

Henceforth. An unnecessarily formal word meaning "now and in the future."

Hereafter. An unnecessarily formal word meaning "in the future."

Hereditaments. Anything that can be **inherited.** Objects that can be inherited are called "*corporeal hereditaments*" and rights that can be inherited are called "*incorporeal hereditaments*".

Herein. A vague word meaning "in this document." ("*Hereinabove*" and "*hereinafter*" are just as vague, adding only "before this" and "after this" to the definition.)

Hereto. An unnecessarily formal word meaning "to this."

Heretofore. A vague and unnecessary word meaning "before" or "in times past."

Herewith. An unnecessarily formal word meaning "in this" or "with this."

Hermeneutics. Legal hermeneutics is the art of **construing** and **interpreting** legal documents.

Hierarchy. An ordering of persons, things, or ideas by rank or level with more at the bottom than at the top. A typical hierarchy is the army (many privates, some majors, very few generals, etc.). Most **bureaucracies** are arranged this way.

High crimes and misdemeanors. The basis for **impeachment** in the U.S. **Constitution.** Opinions differ as to the exact meaning of the phrase. It may include **felonies**; it may include offenses against the U.S. that have serious governmental or political consequences; or it may be whatever the U.S. **Congress** decides it is.

Hitherto. An unnecessarily formal word that means "in the past."

Hoc. This.

Hold. 1. To possess or own something lawfully and by good **title.** 2. To decide; a judge who decides how law applies to a case or "declares **conclusions of law**" is said to "*hold that* . . . ." 3. Conduct or have take place; for example: to "*hold court.*"

Hold harmless. Agree to pay claims that might come up against another person.

Hold over. 1. Keep possession as a **tenant** after the **lease** period ends. 2. Stay in office after the **term** of office is up.

Holder. A person who has legally received possession of a **negotiable instrument** (see that word), such as a **check,** and who is entitled to get payment on it.

Holder in due course. A **holder** (see that word) who buys a **negotiable instrument** thinking that it is **valid** and having no knowledge that any business involving it is shady. The Uniform Commercial Code defines it as "a holder who takes the instrument for value, in good faith and without notice that it is overdue or has been dishonored or of any defense against or claim to it."

Holding. The core of a judge's **decision** in a case. It is that part of the judge's written **opinion** that applies the law to the facts of the case and about which can be said "the case means no more and no less than this." When later cases rely on a case as **precedent,** it is only the *holding* that should be used to establish the precedent. A holding may be less than the judge said it was. If the judge made broad, general statements, the holding is limited to only that part of the generalizations that directly apply to the facts of that particular case. "Holding" is the opposite of **"dicta."**

Holding company. A company that exists primarily to control other companies by owning their **stock.** A *personal holding company* is formed by a few persons to avoid high personal **income taxes.** This type of company is subject to a special Federal income tax.

Holograph. A **will, deed,** or other legal document that is entirely in the handwriting of the signer.

Home relief. See **general assistance.**

Home rule. Local self-government.

Homestead exemption. Laws allowing a head of a family to keep a home and some property safe from **creditors.**

Homicide. Killing another person (not necessarily a crime).

Hon. Short for "honorable," often placed before a judge's name.

Honor. To **accept** (or pay) a **negotiable instrument,** such as a **check,** when it is properly **presented** for acceptance (or payment).

Honorary trust. A **trust** that gets no special tax advantages, but is not quite a private, ordinary trust; for example, to "feed the pigeons in Clark Park." Some states allow these trusts, but most do not.

Hornbook. A book summarizing the basic principles of one legal subject.

Hostile fire. A fire that either escapes from where it was contained or a fire that was never intended to exist at all.

Hostile witness. A **witness** called by one side who shows so much **prejudice** or hostility to that side that he or she can be treated as if called by the other side. This allows **cross-examination** of your own witness.

Hotchpot. Mixing of property belonging to several persons in order to divide it equally; taking into account money or property already given to children when dividing up the property of a dead person in order to equalize shares.

House. **1.** One of the branches of a legislature; either the "*upper house*" or the "*lower house.*" **2.**

The lower branch of a two part **legislature** such as Congress is called "the House."

Housebreaking. Breaking into and entering a house to commit a crime. Some states call it **burglary** if done at night.

Household. A **family** (see that word) living together (plus, sometimes, servants or others living with the family).

Hung jury. A jury that cannot reach a **verdict** (decision) because of strong disagreement among jurors.

Hypothecate. 1. To **pledge** or **mortgage** a thing without turning it over to the person making the loan. 2. **Securing** repayment of a loan by holding the **stock, bonds,** etc. of the **debtor** until the debt is paid, with the power to sell them if it is not paid.

Hypothesis. A theory or working assumption.

Hypothetical question. A process of setting up a series of facts, assuming that they are true, and asking for an answer to a question based on those facts. In a trial, *hypothetical questions* may be asked of **expert witnesses** only. For example, a gun expert might be asked "If this gun had a silencer, could a shot be heard from a hundred feet away?"

I

I.C.C. 1. Interstate Commerce Commission: regulates interstate railroads, trucking companies, etc. 2. Indian Claims Commission: handles claims of Indians against the U.S.

I.e. (Latin) That is.

I.R.S. Internal Revenue Service: the U.S. tax collection agency.

Ibid. (Latin) The same; in, from, or found in the same place (same book, page, case, etc.).

Idem. (Latin) The same; exactly the same thing.

Illegal. Contrary to the criminal law; breaking a law (not just improper or **civilly** wrong).

Illegitimate. 1. Contrary to law; lacking legal authorization. 2. A child born to unmarried parents.

Illicit. Prohibited; unlawful.

Illusory promise. A statement that looks like a promise that could make a **contract,** but, upon close examination of the words, promises nothing real or legally binding.

Immaterial. Not necessary; not important; without weight; trivial.

Immediate cause. 1. The last event in a series of events, which, without any further events, produced the result in question (this may be different from "**proximate cause**"). 2. **Proximate cause** (see that word).

Immediate issue. Children.

Imminent. Just about to happen; threatening.

Immunity. 1. Any exemption from a duty that the law usually requires. 2. Freedom from a duty or a penalty. 3. Freedom from prosecution involving subjects on which you have given **testimony** to a **grand jury, legislature,** etc.

Immunity bath. Automatic **immunity** (see that word) from **prosecution** when you testify, whether or not you request it.

Impair. Weaken, make worse, lessen, or otherwise hurt.

Impanel. Making up a list of **jurors** for a trial or selecting those who will actually serve.

Impeach. 1. See **impeachment.** 2. Show that a **witness** is untruthful, either by **evidence** of past conduct or by showing directly that the witness is not telling the truth.

Impeachment. 1. See **impeach.** 2. The first step in the removal from public office of a high public official such as a governor, judge or president. In the case of the U.S. President, the House of Representatives makes an accusation by drawing up "*articles of impeachment*," voting on them, and presenting them to the Senate. This is impeachment. But impeachment has popularly come to include the trial of the president in the Senate and conviction by two-thirds of the Senators.

Impediment. Legal inability to make a contract; for example: an *impediment to marriage* might be a prior marriage that is still **valid.**

Impertinence. **Irrelevance** in the sense that the proof offered may be relevant to an issue, but the issue itself is irrelevant to the trial.

Implead. Bring into a lawsuit; for example: If A sues B and B sues C in the same lawsuit, B **impleads** C.

Implied. Known indirectly; known by analyzing surrounding circumstances or the actions of the persons involved; the opposite of **express.**

Implied remedies. A private lawsuit to protect a **Constitutional right** may be permitted by a court even if no particular lawsuit is specifically provided for by law. This lawsuit (a remedy) is implied in the right itself.

Implied warranty. The legal conclusion that a **merchant** promises that what is sold is fit for normal use, or, if the merchant knows what the buyer wants the thing for, that it is fit for that particular purpose. Unless these *implied warranties* are **expressly** excluded (for example, by clearly labeling the thing sold "**as is**") a merchant will be held to them.

Impossibility. That which cannot be done. A contract is not binding and cannot be enforced if it is physically impossible (for example, to be in two places at once), legally impossible (for example, to make the contract at age four), or logically impossible (for example, to sell a car for one thousand dollars when the buyer pays two thousand for it). These are all examples of "*objective impossibility*." However, "*subjective impossibility*" (such as not having enough money to pay for something you have contracted to buy) will not get you out of a contract.

Imposts. Taxes; import taxes.

Impound. Take a thing into the **custody** of the law until a legal question about it is decided.

Imprimatur. (Latin) "Let it be printed"; official government permission to publish a book. This is not needed in the U.S.

Imprisonment. 1. Putting a person in prison. 2. Depriving a person of personal liberty in any physical way.

Improvement. An addition or change to land or buildings that increases the value; more than a repair or replacement.

Imputed. Something is "*imputed*" to a person if, even though that person does not know a fact, he or she *should* have known it (both legally and actually) or if, even though that person is not physically responsible for something, he or she is legally responsible; for example: if a person does certain kinds of activities, **income** will be imputed to him or her for tax purposes whether or not the money was actually made.

Imputed knowledge. If the facts are available to a person and if it is that person's duty to know those facts, knowledge may be imputed to that person and he or she is treated legally as if the facts are known.

Imputed negligence. If David is **negligent** and Paul is responsible for David's actions, David's negligence is *imputed* (carried over or attributed) to Paul.

Imputed notice. If Linda is given notice of something (a fact, a lawsuit, etc.) and Linda is Ruth's **agent** (lawyer, manager, etc.) then notice to Linda can be *imputed* as notice to Ruth.

In blank. Without restriction; signing a **negotiable instrument,** such as a **check,** without making it **payable** to anyone in particular (leaving the "pay to" space empty).

In camera. (Latin) **1.** "In chambers"; in a judge's private office. **2.** A hearing in court with all spectators excluded.

In common. More than one person sharing something whole; for example: if two people own a house "*in common*," they both own all of it.

In evidence. 1. Facts or things that are already before the court as **evidence.** 2. "*Facts in evidence*" may be those facts already fully proved.

In extremis. (Latin) In the last illness before dying.

In forma pauperis. (Latin) "As a pauper"; permission to sue in court without paying any court costs.

In kind. The same type of thing; for example: a loan is returned "*in kind*" when a closely similar, but not identical, object is returned.

In lieu of. Instead of; in place of.

In loco parentis. (Latin) In the place of a parent; acting as a parent with respect to the care and supervision of a child; the power to discipline a child as a parent can.

In medias res. (Latin) Into the heart or middle of a subject without introduction or preface.

In pais. (French) 1. An act done informally as opposed to being done by taking legal action. 2. An act done informally as opposed to being done by making a formal document. 3. See **pais.**

In pari delicto. (Latin) In equal fault; equally guilty.

In pari materia. See **pari materia.**

In perpetuity. Forever.

In personam. (Latin) A lawsuit brought to enforce rights against another person as opposed to one brought to enforce rights in a thing against the whole world (**in rem**). For example: a suit for automobile accident injuries is in *personam* because it is against the driver or owner only. A suit to establish **title** to land is *in rem* because, even if there is a person fighting the claim on the other side, a victory is binding against the whole world and a "thing" is primarily involved.

In re. (Latin) "In the matter of." This is a prefix to the name of a case concerned with a thing, rather than with a lawsuit directly between two persons; for example: *"in re Brown's Estate"* might be the title of a proceeding in **probate** court to dispose of the property of a dead person. The words are also used when a child is involved; for example: *"in re Mary Smith"* might be the title of a child **neglect** proceeding even though it is really against the parents. *"In re"* should *not* be used in an ordinary sentence as a substitute for "concerning."

In rem. (Latin) A lawsuit brought to enforce rights in a thing against the whole world as opposed to one brought to enforce rights against another person. For an example of each type of suit, see **in personam**. Also, there is a type of lawsuit in between *in rem* and *in personam* called *"quasi in rem"* or "sort of concerning a thing." These are **actions** that are really directed against a person, but are formally only directed against property; for example: a **mortgage foreclosure.**

In specie. (Latin) **1.** In the same or similar form or way. **2.** Exactly the same; **specific performance** (see that word).

In terrorum. (Latin) "In threat": name given to a gift in a **will** that is given on the condition that the person taking the money or property will refrain from **contesting** the will to get a bigger share.

In toto. (Latin) In whole; completely.

Inadmissible. Facts or things that cannot be **admitted** into **evidence** in a trial.

Inadvertence. 1. Lack of attention or carelessness. 2. Excusable mistake or oversight.

Inalienable. Cannot be given away, taken away, or sold; for example: "*inalienable rights*" are those basic Constitutional rights that cannot be taken away.

Inc. **Incorporated**; for example: "Pink Ink, Inc." is the Pink Ink Corporation.

Incapacity. 1. Lack of legal ability or power to do something; for example: a child has a legal *incapacity* to vote or make **contracts.** 2. An injury bad enough to prevent working.

Incarceration. Confinement in a jail or prison.

Incest. Sexual intercourse between a man and woman who, according to state law, are too closely related by blood.

Inchoate. Partial, unfinished, unripened; for example: an "*inchoate instrument*" is a document, such as a **deed,** that is **valid** between the **parties,** but is not "complete" and valid against anyone else until it is registered or **recorded** with the proper officials.

Incidental. Depending upon something else more important; for example: "*incidental damages*" are the "side costs" of a broken contract, such as storing the goods you thought were sold.

Incite. Urge, provoke, strongly encourage or stir up.

Income. 1. Money gains from business, work, or investments. 2. All financial gain.

Income averaging. Reducing your taxes by showing that your income in prior years was far lower and by paying tax on your average income for those years.

Income splitting. Reducing total family taxes by giving income-producing property (such as **stocks**) to a family member who pays taxes at a lower rate.

Income tax. A tax on profits from business, work, or **investments,** but not on the growth in value of investments or property.

Incompatibility. 1. Two or more things incapable logically, physically, or legally of existing together. 2. The inability of a husband and wife to live together in marriage; *"incompatibility"* is "**grounds**" for a **divorce** in some states. In these states, a divorce may be granted without either person being at fault.

Incompetency. Lack of ability or legal right to do something. This word often refers to the condition of persons who lack the mental ability to manage their own affairs and who have someone appointed by the state to manage their finances.

Incompetent evidence. Evidence that may not be **admitted** into **evidence** in a legal proceeding.

Inconsistent. Contradictory, so that if one thing is **valid,** another thing cannot be valid. Or, if one thing is allowed to happen, another thing cannot be.

Inconvenience. A broad word meaning anywhere from trivial to serious hardship or injustice.

Incorporate. Formally create a **corporation**; the persons who do this initially are called "incorporators."

Incorporate by reference. Make a part of something by mere mention; for example: in document A, say that document B is a part of document A, just as if document B were actually written out in document A. This is a space-saving technique.

Incorporeal. Without body; the opposite of **corporeal** (see that word).

Increment. 1. One piece or part of a piece-by-piece increase. 2. Anything gained or added. 3. The process of gaining or adding to something.

Incriminate. Expose yourself or another person to the danger of **prosecution** for a crime.

Incriminatory. Tending to show guilt.

Inculpate. 1. Accuse of guilt or crime. 2. Involve in guilt or crime.

Incumbent. A person who presently holds an office (usually an elected public office).

Incumber. See **encumber.**

Incumbrance. See **encumbrance.**

Incur. Get; get something bad, such as a debt or **liability** because the law places it on you; for example: you *incur a liability* when a court gives a money **judgment** against you.

Indecent. Offensive to public morality.

Indefeasible. A right that cannot be defeated, **revoked,** or taken away in any way is called "*indefeasible.*"

Indefinite term. A jail or prison sentence for a length of time up to a certain maximum.

Indemnify. Compensate or reimburse a person who has suffered a loss.

Indemnity. A contract to compensate or reimburse a person for possible losses of a particular type; a type of **insurance.**

Indenture. Old word for a formal paper, such as a **deed,** with identical copies for each person signing it.

Independent contractor. A person who contracts with an employer to do a particular piece of work by his or her own methods and under his or her own control.

Indeterminate. With the exact time period not set; for example: an *indeterminate sentence* is a criminal sentence with a maximum or minimum set, but not the exact amount of time. Some states have judges set only indeterminate sentences and have special boards decide the exact sentence later.

Indicia. Indications; pointers; signs; circumstances that make a certain fact probable, but not certain; for example: *indicia of partnership* are those facts that would make you believe that a person was a partner in a business even if it doesn't seem so on the surface.

Indictment. A formal accusation of a crime, made against a person by a **grand jury** upon the request of a **prosecutor.**

Indirect cost. Same as **fixed cost** (see that word).

Indirect evidence. Same as **circumstantial evidence** (see that word).

Indispensable party. A person who has such a stake in the outcome of a lawsuit that the judge will not make a final decision unless that person is formally **joined** as a **party** to the lawsuit.

Indorse. To sign a paper or document.

Indorsement. 1. Signing a **negotiable instrument,** such as a check, in a way that allows the piece of paper, and the rights it stands for, to transfer to another person. 2. Signing any **document** "on the back."

Inducement. 1. That thing, statement, or promise by a person that convinces another person to make a deal. 2. The thing that convinces someone to do something.

Industrial union. Labor union whose members may have different skills, but who work for the same type of industry (printing, clothing manufacture, etc.).

Infamy. Loss of good reputation because of **conviction** of a major crime.

Infancy. A general word for being a very young child. In some states, this means the same as **minority** (see that word).

Infant. 1. A person under the age of adulthood. 2. A very young child.

Inference. A fact or proposition that is shown to be probably true because it is the logical result of another fact or proposition that has already been proved or admitted to be true; for example: if the first four books in a set of five have green covers, it is a logical *inference* that the fifth book has a green cover.

Inferior court. 1. Any court but the highest one in a court system. 2. A court with special, limited responsibilities, such as a **probate** court.

Infirmity. A defect; for example: if the papers that transfer a **title** are **defective,** the title transfered has an *infirmity.*

Information. 1. A formal accusation of a crime made by a proper public official such as a **prosecuting** attorney. 2. A sworn, written accusation of a crime that leads to an **indictment**. 3. Personal knowledge of something. (But *"information and belief"* may mean no more than a person's opinion.)

Informed consent. A person's agreement to allow something to happen (such as surgery) that is based on a full disclosure of facts needed to make the decision intelligently.

Infra. (Latin) 1. Below or under. 2. Within. 3. Later in this book; for example: *"infra p. 236"* means "look at page 236, which is further on."

Infraction. 1. A violation of a minor law. 2. A violation or **breach** of a contract or a duty.

Infringement. 1. A **breach** or violation of a right. 2. The unauthorized making, using, selling, or distributing of something protected by a **patent, copyright,** or **trademark.**

Ingrossing. Making a perfect copy of the final rough draft of a document in order to have the document in its final, official form.

Inherent. Derived from and inseparable from the thing itself; for example: *"inherent danger"* is the danger some objects have by merely existing.

A bomb is probably inherently dangerous, while a hammer is probably not.

Inherent vice. Basic defect.

Inherit. To receive property from a dead person either by the effect of **intestacy** laws or from a **will.**

Inheritance. Property received from a dead person, either by the effect of **intestacy** laws or from a **will.** An *inheritance tax* is the tax that the person who inherits pays. This is not an **estate tax** (see that word).

Initiative. The power of the people to enact laws by voting without the need for passage by the **legislature.**

Injunction. A judge's order to a person to do or to refrain from doing a particular thing; for example: a court might *issue an injunction* (or "**enjoin**") a company from dumping wastes into a river. An injunction may be *preliminary* or *temporary* until the issue can be fully tried in court or it may be *permanent* or *final* after the case has been decided.

Injure. 1. Hurt or harm. 2. Violate the legal rights of another person.

Injurious falsehood. A false statement that causes intentional injury is an *injurious falsehood* even if it is not **defamation** (see that word).

Injury. Any wrong, hurt, or damage done to another person's rights, body, reputation or property.

Innocent. 1. Not guilty. 2. Not responsible for an action or event. 3. In good faith or without knowledge of legal problems involved.

Inoperative. Not now in effect.

Inns of Court. Associations that prepare English law students to practice in court.

Inquest. A **coroner's hearing** into the cause of a person's death when that death was either violent or suspicious.

Inquisitorial system. A system in which the judge acts to dig out facts and also to represent the state's interest in a trial. It is the opposite of the **adversary system** (see that word) we have in U.S. trials.

Insane. See **insanity.**

Insanity. Insanity is a legal, not a medical word. It has different meanings in different situations; for example: the use of the word is different in a criminal **prosecution,** a **probate** hearing on the **validity** of a **will,** a **defense** to a **contract** lawsuit, a **proceeding** to put a person away in a mental hospital, or an appointment of a **guardian.** Even within each situation, both the word and the concepts behind it are vague and difficult to apply to any specific set of facts. It is no more precise or useful than "crazy" or "nuts." For example: one state allows locking up "insane persons" in a mental hospital and defines "insane persons" as "persons who need restraint or treatment in a mental hospital."

Insecurity clause. A section of a **contract** that allows a **creditor** to make an entire debt come due if there is a good reason to think that the **debtor** cannot or will not pay.

Insolvency. The condition of being **insolvent** (see that word).

Insolvent. The condition of some persons (or organizations) who either cannot pay debts as they come due or whose **assets** are less than **liabilities.**

Inspection. The right to see and copy documents, enter land, or do other things in order to gather evidence through the **discovery** process.

Installment. A regular, partial payment on a debt.

Instance. 1. Forceful request. 2. Situation or occurrence.

Instant. Present or current.

Instigate. Push into action (especially a bad action or a crime); **abet.**

Institute. An old word for some books about the law.

Institution. 1. A public organization such as a college or a prison. 2. The start of anything; for example: the commencement of a lawsuit. 3. A basic system of laws.

Instructions. Directions given by the judge to the jury explaining how they should go about deciding the case. This may include a summary of the questions to be decided, the laws that apply, and the **burden of proof** (see that word).

Instrument. 1. A written document; a formal or legal document such as a contract or a will. 2. Short for "**negotiable instrument**" (see that word).

Instrumentality. A **corporation** that is totally controlled by another corporation.

Insurable interest. A person's real financial interest in another person or in an object. The "interest" is the fact that a person will suffer financially if the insured person dies or the insured object is lost. An **insurance contract** must involve an *insurable interest* or it may be a form of gambling and unenforceable.

Insurance. A **contract** in which one person pays money and the other person promises to reimburse the first person for specified types of losses if they occur. The person agreeing to compensate for losses is usually called the *"insurer"* or *"underwriter"*; the person who pays for this protection is the *"insured"*; the payment to the insurer is a *"premium"*; the written contract is a *"policy"*; the thing or person being protected is the *"insurable interest"*; and the types of harm protected against are *"risks"* or *"perils."* A few of the more common types of insurance (and the situations they cover) are as follows: *automobile liability* (injury to other persons or their property from an accident involving a car you own or drive); *casualty* (accidents and injuries); *credit life* (to pay off a car or other major purchase in case of death while installments are still owed); *group* (insurance provided at lower rates through an employer or other defined group of people); *homeowners* (a set of different types of insurance that usually includes fire, theft, and liability); *self* (putting aside money into an account that will be used to pay claims if they come up); *straight life* (life insurance with continuing payments); *term* (insurance that ends at the end of a certain time period); *title* (protection against claims made on the title of land you own); *unemployment* (a government program through your job) and *workmen's compensation* (see that word).

Insured. 1. A person who buys insurance on property or life. 2. A person whose life is insured.

Insurer. The person or company that provides insurance.

Intangibles. Property that is really a right, rather than a physical object; for example: bank accounts, **patents,** etc.

Integrated. Made whole or complete.

Integrated agreement. An agreement is integrated when the persons making it agree on a document or documents as the final and complete expression and explanation of the agreement. This complete and written document is called an "**integration.**"

Integrated bar. A system in which all lawyers who practice before the courts of a geographical area must belong to one organization which is supervised by the highest court of that area.

Integration. The process of making whole or complete; see "**integrated**" and words following.

Intemperance. See **habitual intemperance.**

Intent. The resolve or purpose to use a particular means to reach a particular result. "*Intent*" usually explains *how* a person wants to do something and *what* that person wants done, while "**motive**" explains *why*. These words often get confused.

Intention. Determination to do a certain thing (see **intent**).

Inter. (Latin) Among or between; for example: "*inter se*" means "among themselves."

Inter alia. (Latin) "Among other things"; usually used when what is being mentioned is only part of what there is; for example: "We found in the box, *inter alia*, a book."

Inter vivos. (Latin) "Between the living"; describes an ordinary gift, as opposed to a gift made shortly before dying to avoid **estate** taxes. It also describes an ordinary **trust** as opposed to one set up under a **will.**

Interest. 1. A broad term for any right in property; for example: both an owner who **mortgages** land and the person who lends the owner money on the mortgage have an *interest* in the land. 2. The extra money a person receives back for lending money to another person; money paid for the use of money.

Interference. The state of affairs when two different persons claim a **patent** on what may be the same discovery or invention.

Interim. Temporary; meanwhile.

Interior. Department of the Interior: the U.S. Cabinet department that manages public lands, Indian affairs, natural resources, etc.

Interlineation. Writing between the lines.

Interlocutory. Provisional; temporary; while a lawsuit is still going on.

Internal Revenue Code. The United States **tax** laws.

International Court of Justice. A branch of the United Nations that settles voluntarily submitted disputes between countries and also gives **advisory opinions** to the branches of the U.N.

International law. 1. *Public international law* is the customary law that applies to the relationships and interactions between countries. 2. *Private international law* is the set of principles that determines which country's courts should hear a dispute and which country's laws should apply to each situation. It is sometimes called *"conflict of laws."*

Interpleader. A procedure in which persons having claims against another person may be forced to enter into a lawsuit or risk losing their claim; for example: if A is sued by B for a debt and A thinks that C might have a legitimate claim against A for the same debt, A may *interplead* C (join C as a **party**) to the suit.

Interpol. International Criminal Police Organization: a coordinating group for law enforcement.

Interpolate. Insert words into a completed document.

Interpretation. The process of discovering or deciding the meaning of a written document by studying only the document itself and not the circumstances surrounding it; deciding what a document means as opposed to what it should mean.

Interrogatories. 1. Written questions sent from one side in a lawsuit to another attempting to get written answers to factual questions. These are a part of the formal **discovery** process in a lawsuit and usually take place before the trial. 2. Written questions addressed to any **witness.**

Interstate compact. An agreement between or among states that has been passed as law by the states and has been approved by Congress.

Intervening cause. A cause of an accident or other injury that will remove the blame from the wrongdoer who originally set events in motion. It is also called an *"intervening act,"* *"intervening agency,"* or *"intervening force."*

Intervenor. A person who voluntarily **enters** (becomes a **party** in) a lawsuit between other persons (see **intervention**).

Intervention. A proceeding by which a person is allowed to become a **party** to a lawsuit by joining the **plaintiff,** joining the **defendant,** or making separate claims.

Intestacy. See **intestate.**

Intestate. 1. Dying without making a **will**; dying without making a valid will; dying and leaving some property that is not covered by a will. 2. A person who dies without making a valid will.

Intestate succession. **Inheritances** distributed to **heirs** according to a state's laws about who should collect. This is done when there is no valid **will.**

Intolerable cruelty. Same as **cruelty** (see that word).

Intra. "Within"; for example: *intrastate commerce* is business carried out entirely within one state as opposed to **interstate commerce** (see that word).

Intrinsic evidence. Facts learned from a **document** itself, not from outside information about it.

Introduction of evidence. The submission of **evidence** for possible acceptance in a trial.

Inure. Take effect; result; for example: if "benefits inure to Mr. Smith," they will come to him and take effect for him.

Invalid. 1. Inadequate; useless. 2. Not binding; lacking legal force.

Inventory. A detailed list of articles of property.

Investment. Using money to make money (buying **stocks,** putting cash in a savings account, etc.).

Investment credit. A tax break on some property bought for business purposes.

Investment securities. Stocks, bonds, etc.

Invitation. 1. Asking someone to come onto your property. 2. Keeping land or a building in such a way as to make persons think that you want them to come in; for example: a store owner "*invites*" the public to come in. In the law of **negligence,** a person must be more careful for the safety of any person "invited" in than for the safety of a person who is merely *allowed* onto property.

Invitee. A person who is at a place by **invitation** (see that word). Note: a social caller may not be an "*invitee*," but a "**licensee**" (see that word).

Invoice. A list sent by a merchant that details goods sent to another person (often a purchaser) and usually gives prices item by item.

Involuntary manslaughter. The unintentional, but still illegal, killing of another human being. This is defined differently in different states.

Ipse dixit. (Latin) "He himself said it"; a statement that depends for its persuasiveness on the authority of the person who said it.

Ipso facto. (Latin) "By the fact itself"; "by the mere fact that."

Irregularity. Failure to proceed properly; failure to take the proper formal steps in the proper way while involved in a lawsuit or doing some official act. An irregularity is not an illegal act, but it may be serious enough to **invalidate** or otherwise harm what a person is trying to accomplish.

Irrelevant. Not related to the matter at hand; for example: *irrelevant evidence* is **evidence** that will

175

not help to either prove or disprove any point that matters in a lawsuit.

Irreparable injury. Probable harm that cannot be properly fixed by money alone and that is serious enough to justify an **injunction** (see that word).

Irresistable impulse. Loss of control due to **insanity** that is so great that a person cannot stop from committing a crime. This is one of many vague "*tests*" to decide whether a person will be treated as a criminal and put away in jail or treated as a mental patient and put away in a mental hospital.

Irrevocable. Incapable of being called back, **revoked** (see that word), stopped or changed.

Issue. **1.** To send forth, put out, or **promulgate** officially; for example: when a court *issues* a **writ** or other legal paper, it gives it to a **court officer** to be **served on** (delivered to) a person. **2.** One single point in dispute between two sides in a lawsuit. An issue may be "*of law*" (a dispute about how the law applies to the case) or "*of fact*" (about the truth of a fact). **3.** Descendants (children, grandchildren, etc.). **4.** A group of **stocks** or **bonds** that are offered or sold at the same time. **5.** The first transfer of a **negotiable instrument** such as a check.

Itemize. List by separate articles or items; break down something by listing its separate parts.

J

J. **1.** Judge; for example: "*Johnson, J.*" means Judge Johnson. **2.** Journal.

J.D. Short for "Juris Doctor" or "Doctor of Jurisprudence." This is now the basic law degree, replacing the "LL.B." in the late 1960's. There are many other law degrees offered in other countries and many advanced law degrees offered here and elsewhere. These include the LL.M., LL.D., B.L., J.C.D., D.C.L., etc. Their exact names are not important; you need to know who gives the degree to know exactly what it means.

J.P. Justice of the Peace; a low-level local judge.

Jactitation. False boasting or false claims.

Jail. A place of confinement that is more than a police station lockup and less than a prison. It is usually used to hold persons either convicted of **misdemeanors** (minor crimes) or persons who cannot get out on bail while awaiting trial.

Jailhouse lawyer. A popular name for a prisoner who helps other prisoners with legal problems, such as getting **sentences** reduced.

Jeopardy. 1. Danger; hazard; peril. 2. The risk of **conviction** and punishment faced by a **defendant** in a criminal trial.

Jetsam. Goods thrown off a ship to lighten it in an emergency.

Jobber. 1. A person who buys and sells for other persons. 2. A wholesaler.

John Doe. A made-up name used in some types of lawsuits where there is no real **defendant,** in a legal proceeding against a person whose name is not yet known, or as a name for a person in an example used to teach law.

Joinder. Joining or uniting together; for example: *joinder of parties* is the bringing in of a new person who joins together with the **plaintiff** as a plaintiff or the **defendant** as a defendant; *joinder of issue* is when a lawsuit gets by the preliminary stages and issues are clearly laid out with one side asserting the truth of each point and the other side asserting its falsity; *non-joinder* is the failure to bring in a person who is necessary as a party to a lawsuit.

Joint. Together; as a group; united; undivided; for example: a *"joint return"* is a combined reporting of income taxes by a husband and wife.

Joint adventure (or Joint venture). A "one-shot" grouping together of two or more persons in a business. If they have a continuing relationship, it may be a **partnership** (see that word).

Joint and several. Both together and individually; for example: a **liability** or debt is *joint and several* if the **creditor** may sue the **debtors** either as a group (with the result that the debtors would have to split the loss) or individually (with the result that one debtor might have to pay the whole thing).

Joint estate. Ownership of property by more than one person where, when anyone dies, the others get that person's share.

Joint stock company. A company that is more than a **partnership,** but less than a **corporation** (see these words). It is similar to a corporation in most ways, but all owners are **liable** for company debts.

Jones Act. A Federal law that permits ship employees (such as merchant seamen) to sue for **damages** if injured.

Journal. 1. A book that is written in regularly, such as an **account** book, in which all expenses and all money taken in are written down as it happens. 2. A periodical magazine such as a *law journal.*

Judge. 1. The person who runs a courtroom, decides all legal questions, and sometimes decides entire cases. 2. To decide.

Judge advocate. A military legal officer who may act as a judge or a lawyer.

Judgment. The official decision of a court about the rights and claims of each side in a lawsuit. *"Judgment"* usually refers to a final decision that is based on the facts of the case and made at the end of a trial. There are, however, other types of judgments; for example: a *consent judgment* is the putting of court's approval on an agreement between the sides about what the judgment in the case should be; a *default judgment* is one given to one side because the other side does not show in court or fails to take proper **procedural** steps; and an *interlocutory judgment* is one given on either a preliminary or a side issue during the course of a lawsuit.

Judgment creditor. A person who has proven a debt in court and is entitled to use court processes to collect it. The person owing the money is a *judgment debtor.*

Judgment note. The paper a debtor gives to a creditor to allow *confession of judgment* (see that word).

Judgment-proof. Persons against whom a money **judgment** will have no effect (persons without money, persons protected by wage-protection laws, etc.).

Judicare. Publically financed legal services (often allowing a person the choice of a lawyer).

Judicature. Relating to the **judicial** branch of government; the judicial branch of government; for example: in England, the *Judicature Acts* set up their modern system of courts.

Judicial. 1. Having to do with a court. 2. Having to do with a judge. 3. The branch of government that interprets the law and that judges legal questions.

Judicial notice. The act of a judge in recognizing the existence or truth of certain facts without bothering to make one side in a lawsuit put them in **evidence.** This is done when the facts are either common knowldge and undisputed (such as the fact that Argentina is in South America) or are easily found and cannot be disputed (such as the text of the Constitution).

Judicial question. An issue that the courts may decide, as opposed to one that only the **executive** branch may decide (a political question) or that only the **legislature** can decide (a legislative question).

Judicial review. The court's power to declare a **statute unconstitutional** and to interpret laws.

Judiciary. The branch of government that interprets the law; the branch that judges; for exam-

ple: the Judiciary Act of 1789 set up the system of
Federal courts.

Junior. An interest or a right that collects after or
is subordinate to another interest or right.

Jural. 1. Having to do with the basic or fundamental law of rights and obligations. 2. Legal rather
than moral rights and obligations.

Jurat. Name for the statement on an **affidavit**
about where, when, and before whom it was
sworn to.

Juridical. 1. Having to do with the court system or
with a judge. 2. Regular; conforming to law and
court practice.

Juris doctor. Doctor of laws; the basic law degree,
replacing the Bachelor of Law degree or LL.B. It
is abbreviated "**J.D.**"

Jurisdiction. 1. The geographical area within
which a court (or a public official) has the right
and power to operate. 2. The persons about
whom and the subject matters about which a
court has the right and power to make decisions
that are legally binding.

Jurisdictional. 1. Having to do with **jurisdiction**
(see that word). 2. Essential for gaining jurisdiction; for example: the "*jurisdictional amount*" is
the value of a claim being made in a case. Some
courts take only those cases that have jurisdictional amounts above or below a certain money limit;
and *jurisdictional facts* are those things a court
must know before taking and keeping a case (such
as whether the **defendant** has been properly
served, etc.).

Jurisdictional dispute. A conflict between unions, either as to which union should represent certain workers or as to which union's members should do a certain type of work.

Jurisprudence. The study of law and legal philosophy.

Jurist. Judge.

Juristic act. An act intended to and capable of having a legal effect.

Juristic person. A person for legal purposes; this includes both **natural persons** (individuals) and **artificial persons** (**corporations**).

Juror. A person who is a member of a **jury**.

Jury. A group of persons selected by law and sworn in to look at certain facts and determine the truth. The two most common types of juries are the *grand jury* (persons who receive complaints and accusations of crime, hear preliminary evidence on the complaining side, and make formal accusations or **indictments**) and a *petit jury* or *trial jury* (usually twelve, but sometimes six persons who decide **questions of fact** in many trials). There are also **coroner's juries** (see that word) and others.

Jury box. The enclosed place where the jury sits in a trial.

Jury commission. A committee of private citizens that picks **jurors**. In some places, this job is done by a jury **clerk**.

Jury list. 1. List of those **jurors** selected to try a case. 2. List of all jurors commanded to be in court to be selected for various cases. **3.** List of all possible jurors.

Jus. 1. (Latin) Right or justice. **2.** Law or the whole body of law; for example: "*jus gentium*" (law of nations) is **international law. 3.** A particular right.

Jus tertii. (Latin) The right of someone not involved in a lawsuit to property that is involved in the suit.

Just. 1. Legal or lawful. **2.** Morally right; fair; words like "*just cause*" and "*just compensation*" include both meanings (no. 1 and no. 2) of "just."

Justice. 1. Fairness and equality in treatment by the law. **2.** Department of Justice: the U.S. Cabinet department that manages the country's legal business. It represents the U.S. in both civil and criminal matters, runs the Federal prison system, and has specialized departments that handle **antitrust,** civil rights, the Federal Bureau of Investigation, Immigration and Naturalization, the Law Enforcement Assistance Association, etc. **3.** A judge of many types of high courts, such as the U.S. Supreme Court.

Justice of the peace. One type of low-level local judge.

Justiciable. Proper to be decided by a court; for example: a "*justiciable controversy*" is a real dispute that a court may handle.

Justification. A reason that will stand up in court for an intentional action that would otherwise be unlawful; a just cause; for example: self-defense may be *justification* for a killing.

Juvenile court. A court set up to handle cases of either **delinquent** or **neglected** children (see these words).

K

Kangaroo court. A popular expression for an unofficial court with no legal powers.

Keep. To carry on or manage (a hotel); to tend or shelter (a dog); to maintain continuously (a record book); to store (a box); to continue without change (a ship's course); or to protect (a child).

Keogh Plan. See **retirement income credit.**

Key numbers. A reference system that classifies legal subjects by specific topics and subtopics, with a "Key number" (☜) attached to each topic. It allows you to find cases by subject in the **American Digest System** and the **National Reporter System** (see these words).

Kidnapping. Taking away and holding a person illegally.

Kin (or Kindred). 1. Blood relationship. **2.** Any relationship.

Kind. See **In kind.**

King's Bench (or Queen's Bench). An English court that developed most of the "**common law**" (see that word) that has become the basis for American law.

Kiting. Writing checks on an account before money is put in to cover them.

Knowingly. With full knowledge and intentionally; willfully.

L

L.E.A.A. Law Enforcement Assistance Administration: a U.S. agency under the **Justice** Department that gives funds to state and local governments to fight crime.

L.Ed. *Lawyer's Edition* of the U.S. Supreme Court Reports.

L.J. **Law Journal** (see that word).

LL.B. "Bachelor of Laws"; the basic law degree up until the late 1960's. Replaced by "J.D."

LL.M and LL.D. Advanced law degrees (masters and doctorate). Other initials are also used for some advanced law degrees (see **J.D.** for a list of examples).

L.R. 1. **Law Reports** (see that word). 2. **Law Review** (see that word).

L.S. Short for "locus sigilli" or "the place of the seal." These letters once were placed next to a signature to make a **contract** formally binding.

L.S.A.T. Law School Aptitude Test; "the law boards."

Labor. Department of Labor: the U.S. Cabinet department that **regulates** working conditions, labor-management relations, manpower development, etc. However, the National Labor Relations Board (**N.L.R.B.**) is an independent agency.

Labor dispute. A controversy between an employer and employees or an employer and a union involving wages, hours, working conditions, or the question of who has the right to speak for the employees.

Labor union. A formal organization of employees formed to improve compensation and working conditions of every type.

Laches. A delay (in pursuing or enforcing a claim or right) that is so long that the person against whom you are proceeding is unfairly hurt or **prejudiced** by the delay itself. This will keep you from winning.

Land grant (or Land patent). A gift (usually with conditions attached) of land from the government to a private person, organization, or business.

Landlord. The owner of land or a building that is rented or leased to a **tenant.**

Landrum-Griffin Act. A Federal law, passed in 1959, that gave several new rights to individual union members (such as the requirement that unions must have a fair **constitution**). It also changed the **Taft-Hartley Act** in several ways; some pro-union, some pro-employer.

Lapse. **1.** The end or failure of a right because of neglect to enforce or use it within a time limit. **2.** The failure of a gift by **will.**

Larceny. Stealing of any kind.

Lascivious. Tending to excite lust; impure; obscene; immoral.

Last clear chance. A legal principle that a person injured in (or having property harmed by) an accident may win **damages** even when **negligent** if the person causing the damage could have avoided the accident after discovering the danger.

Last resort. A *court of last resort* is one from which there is no **appeal.**

Latent. **1.** Hidden; for example: a *latent defect* is something wrong (with an article sold or with the **validity** of a legal document) that cannot be discovered by ordinary observation or care. **2.** Dormant, **passive,** or "put away."

Lateral support. The right to have land supported by adjoining land; for example: digging that causes a cave-in on the property next door violates this right.

Law. **1.** That which must be obeyed. **2.** A statute; an act of the legislature. **3.** The whole body of principles, standards, and rules put out by a government. **4.** The principles, standards and rules that apply to a particular type of situation; for example: "*juvenile law.*"

Law day (Law date). A court-set day after which a **mortgagee** can no longer pay off a debt on real estate and get the land back from **foreclosure.**

Law journal (or Law review). A publication put out by a law school with articles on legal subjects such as court decisions and legislation.

Law merchant. The generally accepted customs of merchants. These customs have standardized over the years and become a part of the formal law.

Law of Nations. See **public international law.**

Law of the case. Any decision or ruling on a case by an **appeals** court becomes the "*law of the case*" in any subsequent case on the subject between the same persons.

Law of the land. **1.** A law or rule that is in force throughout the country or, sometimes, throughout a geographical area. **2.** A country's custom, which gradually becomes as important legally as

187

written law.   3. Basic ground rules of **due process** and **equal protection** (see these words) that give rights to every person.

Law reform.   Using the courts to make basic changes in the laws, often by bringing **test cases.**

Law Reports.   Published books in a series that contain cases decided by a court.

Law Week.   *U.S. Law Week* is a **loose-leaf service** with "hot off the press" news from the Supreme Court, other courts, and some legislatures.

Lawful.   Legal; authorized by law; not forbidden by law.

Lawsuit.   A **civil action**; a court proceeding to enforce a right (rather than to convict a criminal).

Lawyer.   A person licensed to practice law; other words for "lawyer" include: *attorney, counsel, solicitor* and *barrister.*

Lay.   Non-professional; for example: a lawyer would call a non-lawyer a lay person and a doctor would call a non-doctor a lay person.

Lay advocate.   A **paralegal** who specializes in representing persons in **administrative hearings.**

Layaway.   Putting down a deposit to hold a purchase for later pickup (this is *not* necessarily an "**installment sale**" involving **credit**).

Leading case.   A case that either established a legal principle or is otherwise very important in an area of law.

Leading question.   A question that shows a **witness** how to answer it or suggests the preferred answer.

Lease.   1. A **contract** for the use of land or buildings, but not for their ownership.   The **lessor** is called the **landlord** and the **lessee** is the **tenant**. **2.** A contract for the use of something, but not for its ownership. **3.** A long-term loan of something in exchange for money. Also, a *sublease* is a lease made to another person by a person to whom something is leased.

Leaseback. A sale of land with a **lease** of the same land from the buyer back to the seller.

Leasehold. Land or buildings held by **lease.**

Least fault divorce. Comparative rectitude (see that word).

Leave. 1. To give by **will. 2.** Permission; for example: *"leave of court"* is permission from a judge to take an action in a lawsuit that requires permission (to file an **amended pleading,** for example).

Ledger. A business **account** book, usually set up by categories.

Legacy. 1. A gift of money by **will. 2.** Any gift by will.

Legal. 1. Required or permitted by law. **2.** Not forbidden by law. **3.** Concerning or about the law. **4.** Having to do with an old *court of law* as opposed to a court of **equity** (see that word).

Legal age. The age at which a person becomes old enough to make contracts. This is generally eighteen to twenty-one in most states, but it may be lower for specific purposes.

Legal aid. A place that provides free legal help to poor persons.

Legal assistant. See **paralegal.**

Legal cap. Long legal stationery with a wide left-hand margin and a narrow righthand margin.

Legal cause. See **proximate cause.**

Legal cruelty. See **cruelty.**

Legal detriment. A person acquires a *"legal detriment"* when making a contract by taking on **liabilities** or duties that are enforceable in court or by changing financial position in some way.

Legal ethics. 1. The moral and professional duties owed by lawyers to their clients, to other lawyers, to the courts, and to the public. 2. The study of no. 1.

Legal executive. A highly trained English **paralegal.**

Legal fiction. See **fiction.**

Legal proceedings. Any actions taken in court or connected with a lawsuit.

Legal realism. A philosophy of law that takes psychology, sociology, economics, politics, etc. into account in order to explain how legal decisions are made.

Legal representative. A person who takes care of another person's business involving courts, especially **executors** or **administrators** of **wills.**

Legal residence. Actually living in a place and intending to stay there.

Legal right. A right that should win if tested in court.

Legal Services Corporation. The organization that runs the Federally funded program of legal aid.

Legal tender. Official money (dollar bills, coins, etc.).

Legal worker. See paralegal.

Legalese. Unnecessary legal jargon.

Legatee. A person who **inherits** something in a
will.

Legislate. To enact or pass laws. A *legislator* (person who makes laws) works in the *legislature*
(lawmaking branch of government) on *legislation*
(laws, **statutes, ordinances,** etc.). This work of
legislation (passing laws) is a *legislative* function
(lawmaking, as opposed to "**executive**," which is
carrying out laws, or "**judicial**," which is interpreting laws).

Legislation. 1. The process of thinking about and
passing or refusing to **pass** laws (**statutes, ordinances,** etc.). 2. Statutes, ordinances, etc.

Legislative. Lawmaking, as opposed to "**executive**"
(carrying out or enforcing laws), or "**judicial**"
(interpreting or applying laws).

Legislative courts. Courts that have been set up by
legislatures (Congress, state legislatures, etc.),
rather than those set up originally by the U.S.
Constitution.

Legislative facts. General facts that help an **administrative agency** to decide general questions of
law and policy and to make rules. They are the
opposite of **adjudicative facts** (see that word).

Legislative history. The background documents
and records of hearings held on a **bill** as it became
a law.

Legislative intent rule. Decide what the lawmakers
meant or wanted when they passed a law by
looking at the legislative record (**hearing** reports,
etc.). This is one of several possible ways of
interpreting statutes. It is different from the
legislative purpose rule (see that word).

Legislative purpose rule. Look at what the law was before the present law was passed and decide by looking at the law itself what the law was trying to change. This is one of several possible ways of interpreting statutes. It is different from the **legislative intent rule** (see that word).

Legislator. A lawmaker, such as a U.S. Senator, a member of a city council, etc.

Legitimate. 1. Lawful or legal (also, a child born to a married couple is called *legitimate*). 2. To make lawful.

Lessee. A person who **leases** or rents something from someone. A lessee of land is a **tenant.**

Lesser included offense (Lesser offense). A crime that is a part of a more serious crime; for example: **manslaughter** is a lesser crime included in the description of **murder.**

Lessor. Person who leases or rents land or a building to another person.

Let. 1. To **award** a contract (such as a building job) to one of several bidders. 2. To **lease.**

Letter. 1. The strict, precise, literal meaning of a document; the exact language (of a law, for example) rather than the spirit or broad purpose. 2. A formal document; for example: a *"letter of attorney"* is a document giving a person **power of attorney** (see that word).

Letter of credit. A statement by a bank or other financer that it will back up or pay the financial obligations of a merchant involved in a particular sale.

Letters of administration (or Letters testamentary). Court papers allowing a person to take charge of the property of a dead person in order to **distribute** it.

Letters of marque and reprisal. See **marque and reprisal.**

Levy. 1. To **assess,** raise, or collect; for example: to *levy a tax* is to either **pass** one in a **legislature** or to collect one. 2. To seize or collect; for example: to *levy on a debtor's property* is to put it aside by court **order** in order to pay **creditors.** 3. The **assessment** or seizure itself in no. 1 and no. 2.

Lewd. Morally impure in a sexual sense; **lascivious.**

Lex. (Latin) Law; a collection or body of laws.

Lex fori. (Latin) The law of the **forum** or court; the law of the state or country where the case is decided.

Lex loci. (Latin) The law of the place; the law of the state or country where the event being sued on took place; for example: "*Lex loci delictus*" is the law of the place where the crime took place.

Leze majesty. (French) **Treason** (see that word).

Liability. A broad word for legal obligation, responsibility, or debt.

Liable. Responsible for something (such as harm done to another person); bound by law; having a duty or obligation enforceable in court against you by another person.

Libel. 1. Written **defamation** (see that word); published false and **malicious** written statements that injure a person's reputation. 2. The first pleading in an admiralty (maritime or ocean-ship) court, corresponding to the **complaint** of an ordinary **civil** lawsuit. Also, the name for some specialized

complaints in some places, such as a *"divorce libel."*

Libelant. Plaintiff (see that word).

Libelous. Defamatory; tending to injure reputation.

Liberty. 1. Freedom from illegal personal restraint. **2.** Personal rights under law.

Library of Congress system. A method of finding books, first by subject area (law is "K") and then by a number assigned in time order by the Library of Congress.

License. 1. Formal permission to do something specific (usually given by the government). **2.** The document that gives the permission in no. 1. **3.** Acting without any legal restraint; disregarding the law entirely.

Licensee. 1. A person who holds a **license**. **2.** A person who is on property with permission, but without any enticement by the owner and with no financial advantage to the owner; often called a *"mere licensee"* as opposed to an **"invitee"** in negligence law. Note: in some situations, an invited personal guest is a *licensee, not* an *invitee.*

Licentiousness. 1. Doing what you want with total disregard for ethics, law, or others' rights. **2.** Lewdness or lasciviousness; moral impurity in a sexual context.

Lien. A claim, charge, or liability against property that is allowed by law, rather than one that is part of a contract or agreement; for example: a *mechanic's lien* is the right of a workman to hold property worked on until paid for the services, and a *tax lien* is the government's placing of a financial obligation on a piece of property that must be paid if taxes are not paid. Other types of *liens* are **judgment, landlord's,** and **mortgage.**

Lieu. (French) "Place"; "*in lieu of*" means "instead of."

Life estate. A property right that is good until someone dies, but that cannot be passed on to an **heir.**

Life in being. The remaining length of time a specific person already born has to live.

LIFO. "Last in, first out," a method of calculating the worth of a merchant's **inventory.**

Lift. Raise up; remove.

Limitation. 1. A restriction. 2. A time limit; for example: a "*statute of limitations*" is a law that sets a maximum amount of time after something happens for it to be taken to court, such as a "*three year statute*" for lawsuits based on a contract, or a "*six year statute*" for a criminal prosecution. 3. *Limitation* of a case is a judge's refusing to apply the rule that decided it to deciding another case.

Limited. 1. Partial or restricted; for example: *limited liability* is the legal rule that the owners (**shareholders**) of a **corporation** cannot usually be sued for **corporate** actions (unless the owners are involved in **fraud** or a crime) and, thus, the most they can lose is the value of their investment. 2. "Limited" is also the English and Canadian word for "Corporation." It is abbreviated "Ltd."

Lindberg Act. A Federal law prohibiting the transportation of a **kidnapped** person across a state line.

Line of credit. The maximum amount of credit a merchant or bank will give to a customer.

Lineal. In a line; for example: *lineal relationships* are those of father and son, grandson and grandmother, etc.

Liquidate. 1. Pay off or settle a debt. 2. **Adjust** or settle the amount of a debt. 3. Settle up affairs and distribute money, such as the money left by a dead person or by a company that goes out of business.

Liquidated. 1. Paid or settled up. 2. Determined, settled or fixed; for example: a *"liquidated claim"* is a claim or debt with a definite amount fixed either by agreement or by a court's action.

Liquidation. 1. See **liquidate.** 2. Winding up business and ending a company.

Lis pendens. 1. A pending lawsuit. 2. A warning notice that **title** to property is in **litigation** and that anyone who buys the property gets it with legal strings attached.

Listing. A **real estate agent's** right to sell land. An *open* or *general listing* is the right to sell that may be given to more than one agent at a time. An *exclusive agency listing* is the right of one agent to be the only one other than the owner who may sell the property during a period of time. An *exclusive authorization to sell listing* is a written **contract** that gives one agent the sole right to sell the property during a time period. This means that even if the owner finds the buyer, the agent will get a **commission.** *Multiple listing* occurs when an agent with an exclusive listing shares information about the property sale with many members of a real estate association and shares the sale commission with an agent who finds the buyer. And, a *net listing* is an arrangement in which the seller sets a minimum price he or she will take for the property and the agent's commission is the amount the property sells for over that minimum selling price.

Litigant. A **party** to (participant in) a lawsuit.

Litigate. **1.** Actively carry on a lawsuit. **2.** Carry on the **trial** part of a lawsuit.

Litigation. A lawsuit.

Litigious. **1.** Fond of bringing lawsuits; bringing too many lawsuits. **2.** Disputable; subject to disagreement.

Littoral. Having to do with a shore, bank, or side of a body of water.

Livery. Old word for formal transfer and delivery of something (especially land).

Living trust. A **trust** that will take effect while the person setting it up is still alive, as opposed to one set up under a **will.** It is also called an **"inter vivos trust."**

Loan shark. A person who lends money at an **interest** rate higher than the legal maximum.

Lobbying. Attempting to persuade a **legislator** (Congressman, etc.) to vote a certain way on a bill or to introduce a bill.

Local action. A lawsuit that may be brought in only one place.

Loco parentis. See **in loco parentis.**

Lockout. An employer's refusal to allow employees to work. This is not an individual matter between an employer and a single employee, but a tactic in employer-union disputes.

Locus. (Latin) Place; for example: "*locus delicti*" means the place where a crime was committed.

Lodger. A person who lives in a part of a building run by another and does not have total control over the rooms lived in. Two examples of lodgers are a person in a boardinghouse or a traveller in a motel.

Logging in. An initial record (a "log") of the name of persons brought to a police station. The *logging in* process may be combined with **booking** (see that word).

Long-arm statute. A state law that allows the courts of that state to claim **jurisdiction** over (decide cases directly involving) persons or property outside the state.

Loose-leaf service. A set of books in loose-leaf binders that gives up-to-the-minute reports on one area of law, such as Federal taxes. As the law changes, new pages replace old ones. Three big publishers of these are Prentice-Hall, Commerce Clearing House, and Bureau of National Affairs.

Loss. A broad word that can mean anything from *total loss* (dropping a coin accidently in the ocean) through *partial loss* (a drop in the value of a **stock**) to *technical loss* ("loss" of an eye might mean the loss of use of the eye for practical purposes. In general, the legal use of the word is close to its ordinary use.

Lot. 1. An individual piece of land. 2. A thing or group of things that is part of one separate sale or delivery.

Lump-sum settlement. **1.** Payment of an entire amount of money owed at one time rather than in payments. **2.** Payment of a fixed amount of money to take care of an obligation that might otherwise have gone on forever; for example: *"lump-sum alimony"* might be a payment of one large sum to avoid the possibility of having to pay a changeable amount of money on a regular basis for a long time.

Lunacy. See **insanity.**

M

Magistrate. **1.** A low-level judge, usually with limited functions and powers; for example: the U.S. Magistrates perform this job for the Federal courts.

Magna Charta. A document signed by the English king in 1215 that defined and gave many basic rights for the first time in England.

Maintenance. **1.** Meddling with a lawsuit that doesn't concern you. **2.** See **separate maintenance.**

Majority. **1.** Full legal age to manage your own affairs. **2.** More than half; fifty-one is *a majority* of votes when one hundred persons vote.

Maker. Person who initially signs a **negotiable instrument,** such as a check, and by doing so promises to pay on it.

Mala fides. (Latin) Bad faith.

Mala in se. (Latin) **1.** Wrong in and of itself. **2.** Morally wrong.

Malfeasance. Wrongdoing; doing an illegal act (especially by a public official).

Malice. Ill will; intentionally harming someone; having no moral or legal justification for harming someone.

Malice aforethought. An intention to seriously harm someone or to commit a serious crime.

Malicious. Done intentionally, from bad motives and without excuse; for example: "*malicious prosecution*" is bringing charges against someone in order to harm that person and with no legal justification for doing it. If the person prosecuted wins, that person can sue the person who brought the charges for *malicious prosecution*.

Malicious mischief. The criminal offense of intentionally destroying another person's property.

Malpractice. Professional misconduct or unreasonable lack of skill. This word usually applies to bad or unfaithful work done by a doctor or lawyer.

Manager. 1. Person chosen to run a business or a part of one. 2. A member of the House of Representatives who is chosen to prosecute an **impeachment** trial in the Senate.

Mandamus. (Latin) "We command." A court **order** that tells a public official or government department to do something. It may be sent to the **executive** branch, the **legislative** branch, or a lower court.

Mandate. 1. Judicial command to act; see **mandamus.** 2. Authorization to act.

Mandatory. Required; must be followed or obeyed.

Mandatory authority. **Binding authority** (see that word).

Man-in-the-house rule. Some states used to deny **welfare benefits** (see these words) to poor families solely because a man lived with them. This is now **unconstitutional** (see that word).

Mann Act. A Federal law against transporting women across state lines for immoral purposes (especially prostitution).

Manslaughter. An unlawful killing of a person without **malice** (see that word).

Margin. 1. The percentage of the cost of a **stock** that must be paid in advance when purchasing it. 2. A boundary or boundary line.

Marginal rate. See **tax rate.**

Marital. Having to do with marriage; for example: the "*marital deduction*" is the amount of money a wife or husband can inherit from the other without paying **estate** taxes.

Maritime law. The law of ships, ocean commerce, and sailors.

Market price (or Market value). See **fair market value.**

Marketable title. Formal right to land that is legally valid and clear from doubt; having the land's "papers in order."

Marque and reprisal. The request made to the ruler of one country to seize the citizens or goods of another country until some wrong done by that other country is straightened out. It is prohibited by the U.S. Constitution.

Marshal. A person employed by Federal courts to keep the peace, deliver legal orders, and perform duties similar to those of a state **sheriff.**

Marshaling. Arranging, ranking, or disposing of things in order; for example: *marshaling assets and claims* is collecting them up and arranging the debts into the proper order of priority and then dividing up the assets to pay them off.

Martial law. Government by the military.

Martindale-Hubbell. A set of books that lists many lawyers by location and type of practice. It also has one volume that gives summaries of each major area of the law in each state.

Massachusetts trust. A **business trust** (see that word).

Master. 1. An employer who has the right to control the actions of an employee. 2. A *"special master"* is a person appointed by a court to carry out the court's orders in certain types of lawsuits. A special master might, for example, supervise the sale of property under a **decree** (**order**) that it be sold. Federal courts have masters to perform a wide variety of information gathering jobs for a trial.

Material. Important; probably necessary; having effect; going to the heart of the matter; for example: a *"material allegation"* in a legal **pleading** is a statement that is essential to the **claim** or **defense** being used and without which the pleading would have little or no legal effect.

Material fact. 1. The basic reason for a contract, without which it would not have been started. 2. A fact that is central to winning or deciding a case. 3. A fact which, if told to an **insurer,** would have influenced the insurer to refuse insurance, cancel insurance, or raise its cost.

Material issue. A question that is formally in dispute between persons and is properly brought before the court.

Material witness. A person who can give testimony no one else can give. In an important criminal case, a *material witness* may sometimes be held by the government against his or her will.

Matter. 1. Central, necessary, or important fact. 2. Event, occurrence, or transaction. 3. Subject of a lawsuit. 4. Name for certain special types of legal proceedings; for example: "*In the matter of John Jones*" might be the name for a child **neglect** case.

Matter of fact. A question that can be answered by using the senses or the **testimony** of **witnesses.**

Matter of law. A question that can be answered by applying the law to the facts of a case.

Matter of record. Anything that can be proved by merely checking in a court record. The word is sometimes broadened to include anything that can be proved by checking any official record.

Maturity. The time when a debt or other obligation becomes due or a right becomes enforceable.

Maxim. A general statement about the law that works when applied to most cases.

Mayhem. The crime of violently giving someone a serious permanent wound.

Mechanic's lien. A workman's legal claim to hold property worked on (or at least to file formal papers **securing** a right to property) until charges are paid.

Mediation. Outside help in settling a dispute. The person who does this is called a **mediator.**

Meeting of minds. Agreement by each person entering into a deal on the basic meaning and legal effect of the **contract.**

Membership corporation. A non-profit, non-**stock** corporation created for social, charitable, political, etc., purposes.

Memorandum. 1. An informal note or summary of a meeting, a proposed agreement, etc. 2. A note from one member of an organization to another. 3. A written document that proves a **contract** exists. 4. A **brief** (see that word) of law submitted to a judge in a case.

Memorandum decision. A court's *decision* that gives the **ruling** (what it decides and orders done), but no **opinion** (reasons for the decision).

Mens rea. (Latin) Guilty mind; wrongful purpose; criminal intent.

Mensa et thoro. (Latin) Bed and board; a type of **limited divorce** (see that word).

Mental anguish (or Mental suffering). In deciding payment for harm done, "mental anguish" may be as limited as the immediate mental feelings during an injury or as broad as grief, shame, humiliation, dispair, etc.

Mental cruelty. See **cruelty.**

Mercantile. Commercial; having to do with buying and selling, etc.

Merchantable. Fit to be sold; of the general type described and fit for the general purpose for which it was bought.

Merger. 1. The union of two or more things (usually, when one is smaller or of less importance than the other and ceases to exist once the joining together is complete); for example: when two companies *merge*, the smaller becomes a part of the larger. Also, two rights can merge. If a tenant buys the house he or she lives in, the right of **tenancy** merges and is ended with the right of ownership. **2.** If a written contract is intended as the final expression of an agreement between persons, it can not be contradicted by prior agreements; these *merge* into the contract.

Merits. **1.** The central part of a case; the "meat" of one side's legal position. **2.** The substance or real issues of a lawsuit, as opposed to the form or the legal technicalities it involves. *"Judgment on the merits"* is a final resolution of a lawsuit after hearing all **evidence.**

Mesne. Middle, intermediate; for example: *"mesne process"* includes the legal papers and court **orders** in between the start and finish of a lawsuit.

Metes and bounds. Measuring land by boundary lines and fixed points and angles.

Military law. The law that regulates the armed forces and its members.

Mineral right. A right to either take minerals out of the ground or to receive payment for minerals taken out.

Ministerial. **1.** Done by carrying out orders, rather than by making many choices of how to act. In this use of the word, a police chief's actions would be **"discretionary"** (see that word) and a police officer's actions *"ministerial."* **2.** Done by carrying out a general policy (whether or not there is much choice of action) rather than by setting or making **policy**. In this sense of the word, a police chief's actions would be *ministerial* and the police board's would be **discretionary**.

Minor. 1. A person who is under the age of full legal rights and duties. 2. Less or lower.

Minority. 1. Being a **minor** (see that word). 2. Less than half. 3. Groups with only a small percentage of the total population.

Minute book. The record book kept by the **clerk** of some courts that lists a summary of all **orders** in each case by case number.

Minutes. Written notes of a meeting.

Miranda warning. The warning that must be given to a person **arrested** or taken into **custody** by a policeman or other official. It includes the fact that what you say may be held against you and the right to remain silent and to contact a lawyer.

Miscarriage of justice. A legal proceeding or other official action that does unfair harm to a person.

Misdemeanor. A criminal offense less than a **felony** that is usually punishable by a **fine** or less than a year in jail.

Misfeasance. 1. The improper doing of an otherwise proper act; doing something wrong. 2. Doing an illegal or improper act.

Misprision. Failure to carry out a public duty, such as the duty to properly carry out a high public office or the failure to report a crime.

Misrepresentation. 1. A false statement that is not known to be false is an *innocent misrepresentation*. 2. A false statement made when you should have known better is a *negligent misrepresentation*. 3. A false statement known to be false and meant to be misleading is a *fraudulent misrepresentation*.

Mistake. An unintentional error or act. A *"mistake of fact"* is a mistake about facts that is not caused by a **negligent** failure to find out the truth. A *"mistake of law"* is knowledge of the true facts combined with a wrong conclusion about the legal effect of the facts.

Mistrial. A trial that the judge ends and wipes out completely because of a major defect in procedure.

Mitigating circumstances. Facts that do not **justify** or **excuse** an action, but that can lower the amount of moral blame, and thus lower the criminal **penalty** or **civil damages** for the action.

Mitigation of damages. Facts showing that the size of a claim for **damages** is unjustified.

Mittimus. The name for a court **order** sending a convicted person to prison or transferring records from one court to another.

M'Naghten's rule. One of many rules, proposed over the years in different cases, to determine whether a person will be held criminally responsible for an act. According to the *"Rule in M'Naghten's Case,"* a person is "not guilty because of **insanity**" if, at the time of the offense, "a defect of reason produced by a disease of the mind" caused the person to "not know the nature of the act" or to "not know right from wrong."

Model Acts. Proposed laws put out by the National Conference of Commissioners on Uniform State Laws (but not those proposed as **"Uniform Laws"**); for example: the *Model Public Defender Act.*

Modification. A change or alteration (usually a minor one).

Modus. (Latin) Method, means, manner or way; for example: "*modus operandi*" is a method of operation (usually refers to criminal behavior).

Moiety. Half.

Monopoly. The ability of one or a few companies to control the manufacture, sale, distribution, or price of something.

Moore. *Moore's Federal Practice*; a treatise on practice before the Federal courts.

Moot. 1. A subject for argument; undecided; unsettled. 2. Abstract; not a real case involving a real dispute. 3. For the sake of argument; practice; for example: "*moot court*" is a mock court in which law students practice arguing cases.

Moral turpitude. Immoral conduct; a criminal act involving more than a technical breaking of the law.

Moratorium. An enforced delay; for example: a city may impose a suspension or temporary delay in giving out building permits if it is necessary to protect the environment.

Mortgage. One person putting up land or buildings (or, in the case of a **"chattel mortgage," personal property**) in exchange for a loan. A mortgage usually takes one of three forms: 1. The ownership of the property actually transfers in whole or in part to the lender. 2. The ownership does not change at all and the mortgage has the same effect as a **lien** (see that word). 3. The property is put into **trust** with an independent person until the debt is paid off.

Most favored nation. An agreement between two countries that says that each will treat the other as well as it treats the country it treats best. The main effect of "most favored nation" status is lowered import taxes.

Motion. 1. A request that a judge make a ruling or take some other action; for example: a "*motion to dismiss*" is a request that the court throw the case out. 2. The formal way something is proposed in a meeting.

Mouthpiece. Slang for "lawyer."

Movant. Person who makes a **motion** (see that word).

Move. To make a **motion** (see that word).

Moving cause. See **proximate cause.**

Multi-level distributorship. See **pyramid sales scheme.**

Multiplicity of actions. Improperly bringing more than one lawsuit on the same subject when one would do.

Mun. Municipal (see that word).

Municipal. Having to do with local government; for example: *municipal bonds* are **bonds** issued by a local government to raise money and a *municipal ordinance* is a local law or regulation.

Municipal corporation. City; also called a "*municipality.*"

Muniments. Documents that are evidence of **title,** such as **deeds.**

Murder. The unlawful killing of another human being that is **premeditated** (planned in advance) or has **malice aforethought** (see that word).

Mutatis mutandis. (Latin) With necessary changes in detail.

Mutilation. Cutting, tearing, erasing, or otherwise changing a document in a way that changes or destroys its legal effect.

Mutual. Done together; **reciprocal**; for example: *mutual wills* are separate wills that were made out as part of a deal, each one done because of the other one.

Mutual company. A company in which the customers are the owners who get the profits.

Mutual fund. An investment company that pools investors' money and buys shares of stock in many companies. It does this by selling its own shares to the public.

Mutuality of contract. The principle that each side must do something or promise to do something to make a contract binding and valid.

N

N.A.L.S. National Association of Legal Secretaries; a group that provides information and professional **certification** for legal secretaries.

N.B. (Latin) Abbreviation for "nota bene"; mark well; note well; or observe; used to single out one thing for special emphasis.

N.E. North Eastern Reporter (see **National Reporter System**).

N.L.A.D.A. National Legal Aid and Defender Association.

N.L.R.B. National Labor Relations Board: regulates labor-management activities such as **collec-**

tive bargaining, union elections, unfair labor practices, etc.

N.O.V. See **non obstante veredicto.**

Naked. Incomplete; without force.

National Reporter System. A system of sets of books that collects all cases from state supreme courts by region. (For example, the North Eastern Reporter has Illinois, Indiana, Massachusetts, New York and Ohio. It is abbreviated "N.E." and its more recent books are N.E.2d or "second.") The Reporter System also has sets for all Federal cases, some lower court cases state-by-state, and a **digest** for each region. It has become the official place for some states to publish their decisions.

Nationality. Country of which a person is a **citizen.**

Natural law. 1. Rules of conduct that are thought to be the same everywhere because they are basic to human behavior. 2. Basic moral law.

Naturalization. Becoming a **citizen** of a country.

Ne exeat. (Latin) A court paper forbidding a person from leaving the area.

Neglect. 1. Failure to do a thing that should be done. 2. Absence of care in doing something. 3. Failure to properly care for a child.

Negligence. The failure to exercise a reasonable or ordinary amount of **care** in a situation that causes harm to someone or something. It can involve doing something carelessly or failing to do something that should have been done. Negligence can vary in seriousness from **gross** (recklessness or willfulness), through *ordinary* (failing to act as a reasonably careful person would) *to slight* (not much).

Negligent. Careless (see **negligence**).

Negotiable instrument. A signed document that contains an uncondititional promise to pay an exact sum of money either when demanded or at an exact future time. Further, it must be marked payable "to the **order** of" a specific person or payable "to **bearer**" (the person who happens to have it). *Negotiable instruments* include **checks, notes,** and **bills of exchange.** There is a whole branch of law concerning them and a special vocabulary of ordinary sounding words (such as "**holder**") that have specialized meanings in this area.

Negotiate. 1. Discuss, arrange or bargain about a business deal. 2. Discuss a compromise to a situation. 3. Transfer a "**negotiable instrument**" (see that word) from one person to another.

Nemo. (Latin) No one; no person.

Net. The amount remaining after subtractions; for example: *net assets* are what is left after subtracting what you owe from what you have.

Next cause. See **proximate cause.**

Next friend. A person who acts formally in court for a child without being that child's legal **guardian.**

Next of kin. 1. Persons most closely related to a dead person. 2. All persons entitled to **inherit** from a person who has not left a **will.**

Nihil. (Latin) Nothing.

Nil. (Latin) Nothing.

Nisi. (Latin) "Unless"; a judge's **rule, order,** or **decree** (see these words) that will take effect *unless* the person against whom it is issued comes to court to "**show cause**" why it should not take effect.

Nisi Prius. (Latin) "Unless before"; in American law, a trial court.

No contest. See **nolo contendere.**

No fault. **1.** A type of automobile insurance, required by some states, in which each persons's own insurance company pays for injury or damage up to a certain limit no matter whose fault it is. **2.** Popular name for a type of **divorce** in which a marriage can be ended because it has simply broken down.

Nolle prosequi. (Latin) The ending of a criminal case because the **prosecutor** decides or agrees to stop prosecuting. When this happens, the case is "*nolled*" or "*nol. prossed.*"

Nolo contendere. (Latin) "I will not contest it"; a **defendant's** plea of "*no contest*" in a criminal case. It means that he or she does not directly admit guilt, but submits to **sentencing** or other punishment.

Nominal. **1.** In name only. **2.** Not real or substantial; slight; token.

Non. (Latin) Not; for example: "*non compos mentis*" means "not of sound mind" (this includes idiocy, **insanity,** severe drunkenness, etc.).

Non obstante veredicto. (Latin) "Notwithstanding the verdict"; a judge's giving **judgment** (victory) to one side in a lawsuit even though the jury gave a **verdict** (victory) to the other side.

Non prosequitur. (Latin) "He does not follow up"; a **judgment** given to a **defendant** because the

plaintiff has stopped carrying on the case. This is now usually a "**motion to dismiss.**"

Non vult contendere. Nolo contendere (see that word).

Non-age. Not yet of legal age; still a **minor** (see that word).

Non-conforming use. Use of a piece of land that is permitted even though that type of use is not usually permitted in that area by the **zoning** laws.

Non-feasance. Failure to perform a required duty (especially by a public official).

Non-recognition. See **recognition.**

Non-suit. The ending of a lawsuit because the **plaintiff** has failed to take a necessary step or accomplish a necessary action.

Non-support. Failure to provide financially for a wife (or, sometimes, for a husband). It is **grounds** for a **divorce** in some states.

Norris-LaGuardia Act. A Federal law, passed in 1932, to prevent many types of **injunctions** against strikers and to prohibit "**yellow dog**" **contracts.**

Notary public. A semi-public official who can administer **oaths,** certify the validity of documents, and perform other witnessing type duties needed by the business and legal worlds.

Notation voting. Voting (by a board, legislature, etc.) without any meeting. It is not permitted in most situations.

Note. A document that says the person who signs it promises to pay a certain sum of money at a certain time.

Notes of decisions. References to cases that discuss the laws printed in an **Annotated Statutes** book.

Notice. 1. Knowledge of certain facts. Also, "*constructive notice*" means a person should have known certain facts and will be treated as if he or she knows them. 2. Formal receipt of the knowledge of certain facts; for example: "*notice*" of a lawsuit usually means that formal papers have been delivered to a person (*personal notice*) or to the person's **agent** (*imputed notice*).

Notice to quit. Written notice from a **landlord** to a **tenant** that the tenant will have to move.

Novation. The substitution by agreement of a new **contract** for an old one with all the rights under the old one ended. Usually, the substitution of a new person who is responsible for the contract and the removal of an old one.

Nudum pactum. (Latin) "Nude pact" or bare agreement; a promise or action without any **consideration** (payment or promise of something of value) other than good will or affection.

Nuisance. 1. Anything that annoys or disturbs unreasonably, hurts a person's use of his or her property, or violates the public health, safety, or decency. A *nuisance* may be subject to a private lawsuit or a public prosecution. 2. Use of your own land that does anything in no. 1.

Null. No longer having any legal effect or **validity.**

Nullity. "Nothing"; of no legal force or effect.

Nunc pro tunc. (Latin) "Now for then"; retroactive effect; for example: a judge may sometimes issue an **order** to have a legal effect that starts at an earlier date, in effect *backdating* the order.

Nuncupative will. An oral **will.** It is valid in a few states.

O

O.M.B. Office of Management and Budget: helps the U.S. President in financial matters; oversees the budget; investigates and assists government efficiency; etc.

O.R. Short for "own recognizance" or release without **bail** (see **recognizance**).

Oath. Formal swearing that you are bound by conscience either to tell the truth or to faithfully do something.

Obiter dictum. (Latin) See **dictum.**

Object. 1. Purpose. 2. State that an action by the other side in a lawsuit (such as the use of a particular piece of **evidence**) is improper, unfair, or illegal and ask the judge for a ruling on the point; state that an action by the judge is wrong.

Objection. 1. The process of objecting (see **object**). 2. Disapproval.

Obligation. A broad word that can mean any **duty**, any legal duty, a duty imposed by a contract, a formal written promise to pay money, a duty to the government, etc.

Obligee. Person to whom a **duty** is owed.

Obligor. Person who owes another person a **duty**.

Obliteration. Erasing or blotting out written words. (Sometimes lining out or writing over is *obliteration* even if the words still show.)

Obscene. A general word, best defined as what the United States Supreme Court allows a **prosecutor** to successfully prosecute as immoral, indecent, or lewd at the present time.

Obscenity. See **obscene.**

Obstructing justice. Interfering by words or actions with the proper working of courts or court officials; for example: trying to keep a **witness** from appearing in court.

Occupancy. Physical possession of land or buildings either with or without legal right or **title.**

Occupation. 1. Physical possession. 2. Business or profession.

Of counsel. 1. Person employed as a lawyer in a case. 2. Person who helps the primary lawyer in a case.

Of course. As a matter of right; actions that a person may take in a lawsuit either without asking the judge's permission or by asking and getting automatic approval.

Of record. Entered on the proper formal records; for example: "*counsel of record*" is the lawyer whose name appears on the court's records as lawyer in a case.

Off. Postponed indefinitely.

Offense. **Crime** or **misdemeanor**; any breaking of the criminal laws.

Offer. 1. To make a proposal; to present for acceptance or rejection. 2. To attempt to have something admitted into **evidence** in a trial; to **introduce** evidence. 3. An "*offer*" in contract law is a proposal to make a deal. It must be communicated successfully from the person making it to the person to whom it is made and it must be definite and reasonably certain in its terms.

Officer of the court. Includes court employees such as judges, **clerks, sheriffs, marshals, bailiffs,** and

constables (see these words).   Lawyers are also
officers of the court and must obey court rules.

Officers.   The persons who actually run an organization at the top (president, secretary, etc.).

Official notice.   The same as **judicial notice** (see
that word), but for an **administrative agency.**

Offset.   Set-off (see that word).

Olograph.   See **holograph.**

Ombudsman.   (Swedish) A person who acts as the
government's "complaint bureau" with the power
to investigate official misconduct, help fix wrongs
done by the government, and sometimes, prosecute the wrongdoers.

Omnibus.   (Latin) Containing two or more separate
and independent things; for example: an "*omnibus bill*" is a piece of **legislation** concerning two or
more entirely different subjects.

On all fours.   See "**all fours.**"

On demand.   Payable immediately.

On or about.   Approximately; a phrase used to
avoid being bound to a more precise statement
than the law requires; for example: "*On or about
July 15th.*"

One.   A useless word when put in front of a word
that needs no number; for example: "one Susan
Grant testified that . . .."

Onus probandi.   (Latin) **Burden of proof** (see that
word).

Open.   1. Begin. **2.** Make visible or available. **3.**
Remove restrictions, reopen, or open up; for example: to *open a judgment* is to keep it from
going into effect and to look at the case again. **4.**

Visible or apparent. **5.** With no limit as to time or as to amount.

Open-end contract. A **requirements contract** (see that word).

Open-end credit. Credit cards and "revolving charges" where you can pay a part of what you owe each month on several different purchases.

Open-end mortgage. A **mortgage** agreement in which amounts of money may be borrowed from time to time on the same agreement.

Open shop. A business where non-union persons may work.

Opening statement. In an opening statement to a jury at the start of a trial lawyers for each side explain what they think about: the law that applies to the case, what the facts are, and how the facts will be proved.

Operation of law. The way in which rights or **liabilities** sometimes come to or fall upon a person automatically, without his or her cooperation.

Opinion. **1.** A judge's statement of the decision he or she has reached in a case. **2.** A document prepared by a lawyer for a client that gives the lawyer's conclusions about how the law applies to a set of facts in which the client is interested.

Opinion evidence. Evidence of what a witness thinks, believes, or concludes about facts, rather that what the witness saw, heard, etc. *Opinion evidence* is usually accepted only from an **expert witness** (see that word).

Oppression. **Unconscionability** (see that word).

Opprobrium. Shame.

Option. A **contract** in which one person pays money for the right to buy something from or sell something to another person at a certain price and within a certain time period.

Oral contract. A **contract** that is not entirely in writing or not in writing at all. (Similarly, an oral **will** is either partly in writing or not in writing at all.)

Order. 1. A written command or direction given by a judge; for example: a *restraining order* is a judicial command to a person to temporarily stop a certain action or course of conduct. 2. A command given by a public official. 3. "*To the order of*" is a direction to pay something. These words (or "pay to the **bearer**") are necessary to make a document a **negotiable instrument** (see that word). A document with these words on it is called "*order paper.*"

Ordinance. A local or city law, rule or **regulation.**

Organic. Basic; for example: an *organic act* is a law giving self-government to a geographical area, and *organic law* is the basic, fundamental law of a government (its basic unwritten assumptions and its constitution).

Organization. Almost any group of persons with legal or formal ties may be an organization. So may almost any business.

Original jurisdiction. The power of a court to take a case, try it, and decide it (as opposed to the power of a court to hear and decide an **appeal**).

Origination fee. Charge for finding, placing or starting financing; for example: for a **mortgage** on a house.

Ostensible. Apparent or visible; for example: *ostensible authority* is the power a person seems to have (especially the power a **principal** seems to give to an **agent**).

Over. Continued (on the next page or in the next session of a court).

Overdraft (or Overdraw). Taking out more money by check from a bank account than you have in the account.

Overhead. **Fixed costs** (see that word).

Overrule. **1.** To reject or supercede; for example: a case is *overruled* when the same court or a higher court in the same system rejects the legal principles on which the case was based. This ends the case's value as **precedent.** **2.** To reject an **objection** made during a trial.

Overt. Open; clear; for example: an *overt act* in criminal law is more than mere preparation to do something criminal; it is at least the first step of actually attempting the crime.

Oyer and terminer. (French) "Hear and decide"; some higher state criminal courts are called by this name.

Oyez. "Hear ye"; the word cried out in some courtrooms to get attention at the start of a court session.

P

P. Pacific Reporter (see **National Reporter System**).

P.C. Professional Corporation; a special **corporation** set up by doctors, lawyers, or other professionals who work together.

P.-H. Prentice-Hall (see **loose-leaf service**).

P.J. Presiding judge.

P.L.I. *Practicing Law Institute*; a non-profit organization that publishes books and holds seminars to educate lawyers.

P.U.C. Public Utilities Commission; state agencies that regulate power companies, railroads, etc.

Packing. Trying to get a favorable decision from a jury (or a court, an agency, etc.) by improperly placing specific persons on the jury (court, etc.).

Pact. A bargain or agreement.

Pactum. (Latin) A bargain or agreement.

Pairing. Two persons (one for and one against a **bill** in a **legislature**) agreeing to refrain from voting. This allows them both to be absent for the vote.

Pais. (French) Outside the court; the countryside; for example: a matter "**in pais**" (see that word) has to do with facts (that happened outside the courtroom), not with law (that is decided inside the courtroom) and is tried "*per pais*" (by the jury).

Palpable. Plain, clear, easily seen, or notorious. (The word usually refers to an **error,** an **abuse** of authority, or something else wrong.)

Pander. To pimp or solicit for prostitution.

Panel. 1. Jury list. 2. Group of judges (smaller than the entire court) who decide a case. 3. "*Open panel*" legal services is a plan in which legal help is paid in advance (usually by a type of insurance) and a person can choose his or her own lawyer. *"Closed panel"* is paid in advance legal services given by a specific group of lawyers.

Paper. 1. "The papers" are all the documents connected with a lawsuit. 2. "Paper" may be short for "**commercial paper**" or a **negotiable instrument** (see that word). 3. "Paper" may mean "only paper"; for example: a *"paper title"* is a document of **title** to something that may or may not be valid. 4. When a prosecutor *"papers"* a case, it means, in some places, that it *will* be formally **prosecuted,** and, in other places, that it will *not* be formally prosecuted any more.

Par. At face value; for example: if a hundred dollar **bond** sells in the bond market for one hundred dollars, it sells *"at par."*

Paralegal. A paralegal is a non-lawyer who needs legal skills to do a job. Most persons who work for lawyers (such as legal secretaries or "legal assistants") are *paralegals*, and many persons who work for **agencies** and do legally related work are paralegals. It is a general word that takes into account the types of work done, the amount of legal knowledge needed, the work setting, and the type of supervision.

Parallel citation. A case (or other legal document) that is published in more than one place.

Paramount title. A **holder in due course** (see that word) has the best right to a document (and to all the money or property it stands for) in all but a few circumstances; for example: if the property were originally stolen, the real owner has *"paramount title."*

Parcener. An old word for a **joint heir**; a person who inherits property along with another person's inheriting it (each person inherits the whole thing). "*Co-parcener*" means the same thing as "parcener."

Pardon. A president's or governor's power to release a person from punishment for a crime.

Parens patriae. (Latin) The right of the government to take care of minors and others who cannot legally take care of themselves. The use of this power to deprive a person of freedom has been limited by recent laws and decisions.

Parent corporation. A company that fully controls another company.

Pari delicto. (Latin) Equal fault.

Pari materia. (Latin) "On the same subject"; interdependent; for example: laws *pari materia* must be read together to know what effect each should have.

Pari passu. (Latin) Equally; without preference.

Parity. Equality.

Parliamentary law. Rules and customs by which **legislatures** (and many other types of meetings) are run.

Parol. Oral; not in writing; for example: *parol evidence* is oral **evidence** or the evidence a **witness** gives. It usually refers to evidence about an agreement's meaning that does not appear in the written **contract.**

Parol evidence rule. A legal doctrine that says when persons put their agreement in writing, the meaning of the written agreement cannot be changed by using prior oral agreements (unless

224

there was a **mistake** or **fraud** in preparing the written contract).

Parole. A release from prison before a **sentence** is up that depends on the person's "keeping clean" and doing what he or she is supposed to do while out. If the person fails to meet the "*conditions of parole*" the rest of the sentence must be served.

Particular average loss. A loss of property at sea that is the result of negligence or accident and that must be borne by the owner of the property.

Particulars. The details of a legal **claim** or of separate items on an **account**.

Parties. See **party**.

Partition. Dividing land owned by several persons into smaller pieces owned by each one individually.

Partner. A member of a **partnership** (see that word). A "*dormant,*" "*silent,*" or "*sleeping*" partner is a person who is in a partnership, but is not known as a partner by the public, does not take an active hand in the business, and, if also a "*special*" or "*limited*" partner, puts in a fixed amount of money, gets a fixed amount of profit, and is usually not **liable** for anything beyond the investment itself.

Partnership. A contract between two or more persons to carry on a business together and to share money and labor put in and profits or losses taken out. It is not a **corporation** (see that word).

Party. 1. A person concerned with or taking part in any matter, affair, or proceeding. 2. A person who is either a **plaintiff** or a **defendant** in a lawsuit. A *real party* is a person who actually stands to gain or lose something from being a part of the case, while a *formal* or *nominal party* is one who has only a technical or "name only" interest. **3.** A *"third party"* is a person who is not directly involved in a contract, but who is or might be affected by it. **4.** Of two or more parts; for example: a *"party wall"* is put up between two properties.

Party of the first part. A wordy and unnecessary phrase used instead of repeating the name of a **party** to a document; for example: if a **contract** is between Freeway Motors and John Driver, the contract should use "Freeway Motors," "Freeway," "seller," etc., rather than "party of the first part."

Pass. **1.** Say or pronounce; for example: a judge *"passes sentence"* on a **convicted** defendant. **2.** Enacted successfully; for example: a **bill** "passes" when a legislature votes "yes" on it. **3.** Examine and determine; for example: a jury *"passes upon"* the issues in a lawsuit. **4.** Transfer or become transferred; for example: when a **deed** is properly made out, property *passes* from one person to another.

Passim. (Latin) "Here and there"; found in various places.

Passive. Inactive.

Patent. **1.** Open, evident, plainly visible. **2.** A right (given by the Federal government to a person) to control the manufacture and sale of something that person has discovered or invented. **3.** A grant of land by the government to an individual.

Patentable. A discovery or invention that includes a new idea is "*patentable*" or suitable to be given a patent.

Paternity suit. A court action to prove a person is the father of an illegitimate child and to enforce support obligations.

Pauper. A poor person who cannot support him or herself and requires financial help from the government.

Pawn. To give **personal property** (such as a camera) to another person (usually called a *pawnbroker*) as **security** for a debt. A pawned item is held until the money loaned is paid back. If the money is not paid back within a certain time, the item is sold.

Payable. 1. Owing and to be paid in the future. 2. Owing and due for payment now.

Payee. The person to whom a **negotiable instrument** (such as a check) is made out; for example: "pay to the **order** of John Doe."

Peace bond. A **bond** to guarantee good behavior for a period of time.

Peculation. **Embezzlement** (see that word).

Pecuniary. Monetary; related to money.

Pederasty. Anal intercourse between men; a crime in many states.

Peers. Equals; however, a "trial by a jury of peers" does not mean by persons exactly equal to the defendant, but merely by citizens chosen fairly.

Penal. 1. Punishable; concerning a penalty. 2. Criminal; for example: a *penal code* is the set of criminal laws for a country, state, etc.

Penal damages. See **punitive damages.**

Penalty. 1. A punishment imposed by law. 2. A sum of money promised by one person to another to be paid if the first person fails to do something called for in a **contract** between them.

Pendency. While **pending** (see that word).

Pendent jurisdiction. The right of a **Federal** court to decide all questions in a case even if only some of them involve Federal law.

Pendente lite. (Latin) "Pending the suit"; while a lawsuit is in progress.

Pending. As yet undecided; begun but not finished.

Penology. The study of prisons and criminal punishment.

People. 1. A nation or state. 2. All persons in a nation or state as one whole group.

Peppercorn. A dried pepper berry; something of **nominal** (extremely small), but real value.

Per. (Latin) By; through; by means of; during; for example: "*per annum*" means by the year or yearly and "*per autre vie*" means during the life of another person.

Per capita. (Latin) "By heads"; by the number of individual persons, each to share equally. Sometimes, the opposite of "**per stirpes**" (see that word).

Per curiam. (Latin) "By the court": an **opinion** backed by all the judges in a particular court, and usually with no one judge's name on it.

Per se. (Latin) In and of itself; taken alone; inherently.

Per stirpes. (Latin) "By roots"; a method of dividing a dead person's **estate** by giving out shares equally "by representation" or by family groups; for example: if John leaves three thousand dollars to Mary and Sue, and Mary dies, leaving two children (Steve and Jeff), a *per stirpes* division would give one thousand and five hundred dollars to Sue and seven hundred and fifty dollars each to Steve and Jeff. A **"per capita"** (see that word) division would give one thousand dollars to each of the three living descendants.

Percentage lease. A **lease** of a building with the rent based on the dollar value of sales by the tenant in the building.

Peremptory. 1. Absolute; conclusive; final or arbitrary. 2. Not requiring any explanation or cause to be shown; for example: a *"peremptory challenge"* to a **juror** means that one side in a trial has been given the right to throw out a certain number of possible jurors before the trial without giving any reasons.

Peremptory ruling. A judge's ruling that takes the final decision away from the jury; for example: a **directed verdict** or **judgment notwithstanding the verdict** (see these words).

Perfect. 1. Complete; enforceable; without defect. 2. To tie down or "make perfect"; for example: to *"perfect a title* is to **register** it in the proper place so that your ownership is protected against all persons, not just against the person who sold to you.

Performance. Carrying out a **contract,** promise, or other **obligation** according to its terms, so that the obligation ends. *Specific performance* is being required to do exactly (or as close to exactly as is fair) what was required. A court may require specific performance if one person fails to perform one side of a deal and money **damages** will not properly pay back the other side for harm done.

Perjury. Lying while under **oath.**

Permissive. Allowed or endured.

Perpetuating testimony. A procedure for taking and preserving **testimony** (usually by **deposition**) of persons who are in very bad health, very old, or about to leave the state.

Perpetuation of evidence. Making sure that **evidence** is available for a possible trial later.

Perpetuity. Any attempt to control the **disposition** of your property by **will** that is meant to last longer than the life of a person alive when you die (or at least conceived by then) plus twenty-one years. The attempt will fail in most states. This is called the *"Rule against perpetuities."*

Perquisites. Benefits of a job in addition to the salary; for example: a company car for personal use.

Person. 1. A human being (a "natural" person). 2. A **corporation** (an "artificial" person). Corporations are treated as persons in many legal situations. Also, the word *"person"* includes corporations in most definitions in this dictionary.

Personal. 1. Having to do with a human being. 2. Having to do with movable property as opposed to land and buildings.

Personal injury. 1. Any harm done to a person's rights, except for property rights. 2. **Negligence actions** such as for automobile accidents.

Personalty. Personal property; movable property.

Persuasive authority. All sources of law that a judge might use (but is not required to use) in making up his or her mind about a case; for example: legal encyclopedias or related cases from other states. A case may be strongly persuasive if it comes from a famous judge or a nearby powerful court.

Petit jury (or Petty jury). "Small jury" or trial jury.

Petition. 1. A written request to a court that it take a particular action. In some states, the word is limited to written requests made when there is no other side in a case (**ex parte** . . . see that word), and in some states, "*petition*" is used in place of "**complaint**" (see that word) as the first **pleading** in a lawsuit. 2. A request made to a public official.

Petition in bankruptcy. A paper filed in a **bankruptcy** (see that word) court by a **debtor** requesting **relief** from debts. It can also be filed by **creditors** asking that a person be put into bankruptcy involuntarily.

Petitioner. Same as "**plaintiff**" (see that word) in many states.

Petitory action. A lawsuit to establish **title** to land as opposed to a lawsuit to gain physical possession of the land.

Philadelphia lawyer. Originally praise of a lawyer's skill, this word has come to mean sly or tricky.

231

Physical fact. An indisputable law of nature or a scientific fact.

Picketing. Persons gathering outside a place to disturb its activities or to inform persons outside of grievances, opinions, etc. about the place.

Plagarism. Taking all or part of the writing of another person and passing it off as your own.

Plain error rule. The principle that an **appeals** court can **reverse** a **judgment** because of an **error** in the proceedings even if the error was not **objected** to at the time.

Plain meaning rule. If a law seems clear, take the simplest meaning of the words and do not read anything into it. This is one of several possible ways of interpreting statutes.

Plaintiff. Person who brings (starts) a lawsuit against another person.

Plat. A map showing how a piece of land will be subdivided (divided up) and built upon.

Plea. 1. The **defendant's** formal answer to a criminal **charge**. The defendant says: "**guilty**," "not guilty" or "**no contest**" (see these words). **2.For the use of the word in most modern civil** lawsuits, see **pleading.** 3. Older word for several types of civil motions; for example: a "*plea in abatement*" has been replaced in most places by a "**motion to dismiss**" (see that word) for a technical reason, such as the suit's being brought in the wrong court.

Plea bargaining. Attempts at making a deal between a **prosecutor** and a criminal **defendant's** lawyer about the charges to which the defendant will **plead** guilty and about other arrangements, such as the prosecutor's recommendation of a **sentence** to the judge.

Plead. 1. Make or file a **pleading** (see that word). 2. Argue a case in court.

Pleading. 1. The process of making formal, written statements of each side of a case. First the **plaintiff** submits a paper with facts and claims; then the **defendant's** paper submits facts and counter-charges; then the plaintiff responds; etc., until all issues and questions are clearly posed for a trial. 2. "*A pleading*" is one of the papers mentioned in no. 1. The first one is a "**complaint**," the response an "**answer**," etc. "*The pleadings*" is the sum of all these papers. Sometimes, **motions** and other court papers are called pleadings, but this is not strictly correct.

Pledge. Handing over physical possession of a piece of **personal property** (such as a radio) to another person who holds it until you pay off a debt to that person.

Plenary. Full; complete; of every person or every thing.

Plurality. The greatest number; for example: if Jane gets ten votes and Don and Mary each get seven, Jane has a *plurality* (the most votes), but not a **majority** (more than half of the votes).

Pocket part. An addition to many lawbooks that updates them until a new edition comes out. It is found inside the back cover and should always be looked for when doing legal research.

Point. 1. An individual legal proposition, argument, or question raised in a lawsuit. "*Points and authorities*" is the name for a document prepared to back up a legal position taken in a lawsuit (for example, to support or oppose a **motion**). **2.** One percent; a term used by **mortgage** companies to describe an initial charge made for lending money.

Police power. The government's right and power to set up and enforce laws to provide for the safety, health, and general welfare of the people; for example: the power to **license** occupations such as barbering.

Policy. **1.** The general operating procedures of an organization. **2.** The general purpose of a **statute** or other law. **3.** A type of lottery by betting on numbers; the "numbers game" **4.** "*Public policy*" is the general good of the state and its people. A contract is "against public policy" if carrying it out will be harmful to the public. **5.** For "*insurance policy*," see **insurance.**

Political question. A question that the courts will not decide because it concerns a decision properly made by only the **executive** branch of government; for example: only the executive branch has the right to decide whether or not a foreign country has become an independent nation.

Political rights. Rights concerning a citizen's participation in government; for example: the right to vote.

Poll tax. A tax, now illegal, on the right to vote.

Polling the jury. Individually asking each member of a jury what his or her decision is.

Polls. A *challenge to the polls* is an objection to the selection of a particular **juror,** made before the jury (often a **grand jury**) convenes.

Polygamy. Having more than one wife or husband. It is a crime in the U.S.

Popular name tables. Reference charts that help find **statutes** if their popular names are known; for example, you could find the official name and **citation** of the "Sherman Act" from a *popular name table.*

Positive evidence. See **direct evidence.**

Positive law. Law that has been **enacted** by a **legislature.**

Posse commitatus. (Latin) "The power of the state"; the group of citizens who may be gathered by the **sheriff** or other law officer to help enforce the law, usually on an emergency basis.

Possession. 1. Ownership and control of **personal property.** 2. Rightful control of land or buildings; for example: a **tenant** may have *possession.* 3. Simply holding something; for example: having an illegal drug in your pocket is called "*possession.*"

Possessory action. A lawsuit to gain actual control of property as opposed to one that attempts to get legal ownership to property; for example: an **eviction** is a *possessory action.*

Post-date. To put a date on a document that is later than the date the document is signed.

Post-mortem. (Latin) "After death"; an autopsy or examination of a body to determine the cause of death.

Posting. Writing down an **entry** (such as money spent for a lamp) into an **account** book.

Pourover. A **will** that leaves some money or property into an existing **trust** is called a "*pourover* *will"* and a trust that does the same thing is a *"pourover trust."*

Power. 1. The right to do something. 2. The ability to do something. 3. A combination of no. 1 and no. 2.

Power of appointment. A part of your **will, deed,** or separate document that gives someone the power to decide who gets your money or property or how it will be used.

Power of attorney. A document authorizing a person to act as attorney for the person signing the document.

Power of sale. The right of a **mortgage** holder or mortgage **trustee** to sell the property if payments are not made.

Pp. Pages.

Practicable. Stuffy word meaning "feasible"; can be done.

Practice. 1. Custom, habit, or regular repetition. 2. Formal court procedure; the way a lawsuit is taken to and through court as opposed to what it is about; for example: a *practice manual* is a book of forms and procedures to use in **pleading** and court practice. 3. Engaging in a profession, such as law. 4. Doing things that are only permitted to be done by a member of a profession; for example: giving legal advice or arguing a case in court is the *"practice of law."*

Praecipe. A formal request that the court **clerk** take some action; a **motion** that does not need a judge's approval, and, if done correctly, will be carried out by the court clerk; for example: in most places a lawyer can **enter an appearance** in a case by *praecipe.*

Prayer. Request; that part of a legal **pleading,** such as a **complaint,** that asks for **relief** (help, specific court action, something from the other side, etc.).

Preamble. Introduction (usually saying why a document, such as a **statute,** was written).

Precatory. Expressing a wish; advisory only; not legally binding in most situations.

Precedent. **1.** A court decision on a *question of law* that gives **authority** or direction on how to decide a similar question of law in a later case with similar facts. **2.** Something that must happen before something else may happen; see **condition precedent.**

Precept. Command by a person in authority.

Precinct. A police or election district within a city.

Precipe. See **praecipe.**

Precognition. Examination of a **witness** before trial.

Pre-emption. **1.** First right to buy something; for example: *"pre-emptive rights"* are the rights of some **stockholders** to first chance at buying any new stock the company issues. **2.** The first right to do anything; for example: when the Federal government *"pre-empts the field"* by passing laws in a subject area, the states may not pass conflicting laws and sometimes may not pass any laws on the subject at all.

Preference. **1.** A **creditor's** right to be paid before other creditors. **2.** The act of an **insolvent** (broke) **debtor** in paying off a creditor more than a fair share of what is left; for example: if John owes Mary ten dollars and Don ten dollars, but has only ten dollars left and pays it all to Mary, this is a *preference*. If a debtor gives a creditor preference shortly before going into **bankruptcy,** the bankruptcy court may be able to get that money back in to be divided fairly.

Preferred stock. See **stock.**

Prejudice. **1.** Bias; a preconceived opinion; leaning towards one side in a dispute for reasons other than an evaluation of the justice of that side's position. **2.** A judge's prejudice refers not to an opinion about the subject of the case, but to the judge's bias towards one of the *persons* in the dispute. **3.** All rights are lost; for example: if a case is "*dismissed with prejudice*" it cannot be brought back into court again. **4.** Substantially harmful to rights; for example: *prejudicial error* is serious enough to be **appealed.**

Premeditation. A prior determination to do something; thinking in advance about how to do something (usually a crime).

Premium. The money paid for **insurance coverage.**

Preponderance of evidence. Greater weight of evidence, not as to quantity (number of witnesses), but as to quality (believability and greater weight of important facts proved).

Prerogative. **1.** A special privilege. **2.** Special official power.

Prerogative writs. Actions a court will take only under special circumstances. These include, for example, **mandamus** and **habeas corpus** (see these words).

Prescription. A method of getting legal ownership of **personal property** (everything but land) by keeping it in your possession openly, continuously, and with a claim that it belongs to you. This must be done for a length of time set by state law.

Present. 1. Immediate. 2. See **presentment.**

Presentence investigation. An investigation by court-appointed social workers, **probation officers,** etc. into a criminal's background and prospects for rehabilitation.

Presentment (or Presentation). 1. A **grand jury's** charging a person with a crime that it has investigated itself without an **indictment** given to it by a prosecutor. In some states, it is an informal document; a statement, not a charge. 2. Showing a **negotiable instrument,** such as a check, and asking for payment on it.

Presents. "These presents" is an obsolete phrase for "this legal document."

Presumption. A conclusion or inference drawn. A *presumption of fact* is a conclusion that because one fact exists (or one thing is true) another fact exists (or another thing is true). If no new facts turn up to prove the presumption wrong, it is evidence as good as any direct proof of the fact. A *presumption of law* is a rule of law that whenever a certain set of facts shows up, a court must automatically draw certain legal conclusions; for example: the *presumption of innocence* is that whenever a person is charged with a crime, he or she is innocent until proved guilty, so the government must make the case. Presumptions can be *rebuttable* (good until destroyed by more facts) or *conclusive, absolute* or *irrebuttable* (an inference that must be drawn from a set of facts no matter what).

Presumptive. May be inferred.

Pretermitted heir. A child (or sometimes any descendant) either unintentionally left out of a **will** or born after the will is made.

Prevailing party. The person who wins a lawsuit (even if not by as much as asked for or desired).

Preventive detention. Holding persons against their will because they are likely to commit a crime. This practice is **unconstitutional** in most but not all situations.

Preventive law. Legal help and information designed to help persons to avoid legal problems before they occur.

Prima facie. (Latin) At first sight; on the face of it; presumably; a fact that will be considered to be true unless disproved by contrary **evidence**; for example: a *prima facie case* is a case that will win unless the other side comes forward with evidence to dispute it.

Primary authority. Binding authority (see that word).

Primary evidence. The best evidence to prove a point; for example: the document itself is the best evidence of what it says, so it is "*primary.*"

Prime 1. Original. **2.** Most important.

Primogeniture. 1. First child born to a husband and wife. **2.** An outdated rule that the first son **inherited** everything.

Principal. 1. Chief; most important; primary. **2.** A sum of money as opposed to the profits made (**interest**) on that money. **3.** An employer or anyone else who has another person (an **agent**) do things for him or her. **4.** A person directly involved with committing a crime as opposed to an **accessory** (see that word).

Principle. A basic legal truth, doctrine, or generalization.

Prior hearing. A hearing by an **administrative agency** that in some situations must be given to a person before taking any action that harms the person.

Prison. A place for the long-term holding of persons **incarcerated** for a crime.

Prisoner. Anyone deprived of liberty by the government either because of an accusation of a crime or **conviction** of a crime.

Privacy. The right to be left alone; this right is generally "balanced" against other rights such as "*freedom of the press*."

Private. Concerning individuals, not the general public and not the government; for example: *private law* is the law of relationships between person and person, not person and government; one subject in private law is "**contracts**."

Private attorney general. A private individual who goes to court to enforce a public right for all citizens.

Private international law. See **conflict of laws**.

Private law. 1. A **statute** passed to affect one person or group, as opposed to a **public law** (see that word). **2.** The law of relationships among persons and groups (such as the law of **contracts,** divorce, etc.) as opposed to **public law** (see that word).

Privies. See **privity** and **privy.**

Privilege. 1. An advantage; a right to preferential treatment. 2. An exemption from a duty others like you must perform. 3. The right to speak or write **defamatory** (personally damaging) words because the law allows them in certain circumstances; for example: words are privileged if spoken completely "in the line of public duty." 4. A basic right; for example: the "*privileges and immunities*" guaranteed to all by Article IV and the Fourteenth Amendment of the U.S. Constitution. 5. A special advantage as opposed to a right; an advantage that can be taken away again.

Privileged communication. See **confidentiality.**

Privileges and immunities. The constitutional requirement that no state may treat a person from another state unfairly.

Privity. 1. Private or "inside" knowledge. 2. A close, direct financial relationship; for example: both the **executor** (person who **administers** a **will** and hands out property) and an **heir** (person who gets the property) are in **privity** with the **testator** (person who wrote the will and gave away the property). Also, *privity of contract* exists among those persons who actually took part in making the deal and have rights and duties because of it; for example, a manufacturer and a seller may be "in privity," but not the manufacturer and the buyer.

Privy. 1. A person who is in **privity** (see that word) with another person. The plural is *privies.* 2. Private.

Prize. A ship taken by one country from another with which it is at war.

Pro. (Latin) For.

Pro bono publico. (Latin) For the public good. When abbreviated to "*pro bono*," it stands for free legal work done for some charitable or public purpose.

Pro forma. (Latin) As a matter of form; a mere formality.

Pro hac vice. (Latin) For this one particular occasion only.

Pro rata. Proportionately; by percentage; by a fixed rate; by share; for example: if Tom, Dick, and Harry are owed two, four, and six dollars respectively by John, but John has only six dollars to give out, a *pro rata* sharing would be one, two, and three dollars respectively.

Pro se. (Latin) For himself or herself; in his or her own behalf; for example: "*pro se representation*" means that a person will handle his or her own case in court without a lawyer.

Pro tanto. (Latin) For that much; to the extent of.

Pro Tem. (Latin) Short for "Pro tempore"; for the time being.

Probable cause. A reasonable suspicion, provable by facts, that a crime has been committed. It does not depend on what the official finds out after an **arrest** or **search** is made, but on what the official knew before taking action.

Probate. 1. The process of proving that a **will** is genuine and giving out the property in it. 2. The name in some states for a court that handles the

distribution (giving out) of **decedents' estates** (dead persons' property) and other matters such as **insanity commitments**.

Probation. Allowing a person convicted of a criminal offense to stay out of jail under supervised conditions (by a "*probation officer*").

Probationer. A person free on **probation** (see that word).

Probative. Tending to prove or actually proving something.

Probative facts. Facts that actually prove other facts necessary to a valid issue in a lawsuit; **evidentiary facts**.

Procedural law. The rules of carrying on a lawsuit (how to enforce rights in court) as opposed to "**substantive law**" (the law of the **rights** and **duties** themselves).

Procedure. The rules and methods of carrying on a lawsuit (**pleading,** making **motions,** presenting **evidence,** etc.).

Proceeding. 1. A **case** in court. 2. The orderly progression of a case in court. 3. The recorded history of a case.

Proceeds. Money or property gained from a sale.

Process. 1. A court's ordering a defendant to show up in court or risk losing a lawsuit without being represented; a **summons**. 2. Any court **order** that "takes **jurisdiction** over" (brings formally under the court's power) a person or property. 3. Regular, legal method of operating.

Prochein ami. (French) **Next friend** (see that word).

Proctor. 1. Someone appointed to manage another person's affairs. 2. A lawyer or representative.

Procure. 1. Make something happen; get something for someone. 2. Solicit customers for a prostitute.

Produce. Bring forward; show; yield up; for example: a "*motion to produce*" or a "*motion for production*" is a request that the judge order the other side to show you specific documents.

Producing cause. See **proximate cause.**

Professio juris. A made-up Latin word for an agreement in a **contract** to have the law of one particular state or country decide all questions involving the contract.

Proffer. 1. Offer or present. 2. **Avowal** (see that word).

Profit. All gains including both money and increases in the value of property.

Profits a prendre. (French) The right to take the growing crops of another person's land.

Progressive tax. A tax that charges the rich a larger proportion of their wealth than it charges the poor; for example: Federal *income tax* is progressive, at least in theory. The opposite of a progressive tax is a **regressive** tax. This hits the poor harder. An example is a sales tax. Even though everyone pays the same tax, it takes a larger part of a poor person's money to pay it.

Prohibition. 1. An order to stop certain actions or warning not to engage in them; for example: *a writ of prohibition* is an order from a higher court telling a lower one to stop proceeding with a lawsuit. 2. Popular name for the period in American history when the manufacture or sale of alcoholic beverages was illegal.

Promise. 1. A statement that morally, legally, or some other way binds the person who makes it to do something. 2. In legal language, *a promise* is an oral or written statement from one person to another, given for something of value in return. It binds the person making the promise to do something and gives the other person the legal right to demand that it is done.

Promissory estoppel. The principle that if Person A makes a promise and expects Person B to do something in reliance upon that promise, then Person B does act in reliance upon that promise, the law will usually help Person B enforce the promise.

Promissory note. 1. A written promise with no strings attached to pay a certain sum of money by a certain time. 2. A **negotiable** *promissory note* is a signed written promise, with no strings attached, to pay an exact sum of money immediately, when asked for, or by a certain date to either "the **order** of" a specific person or to "**bearer**" (the person who physically has it).

Promoter. Person who forms a **corporation.**

Promulgate. Publish; announce officially; put out formally.

Proof. The result of convincing **evidence**; the conclusion drawn that evidence is enough to show that something is true or that an argument about facts is correct.

Proper. Fit, suitable, or appropriate; for example: *a proper party* to a lawsuit is a person who has a real, substantial interest in the suit's outcome, who can conveniently be added to the suit as a **party**, but without whom the suit can still be decided.

Property. 1. Ownership of a thing; the legal right to own a thing. 2. Anything that is owned or can be owned, such as land, automobiles, money, **stocks, patents,** etc.

Proponent. The person who offers something, puts something forward, or proposes something.

Propound. To offer, propose, or put forward something; for example: to *propound a will* is to put it forward and request that it be accepted as valid by the **probate** court.

Proprietary. Having to do with ownership.

Prorate. To divide or share proportionately or by shares; see **pro rata.**

Prorogation. 1. Agreement in a **contract** to allow the courts of one particular state or country to decide all disputes involving the contract. 2. A delay, putting off, or **continuance.**

Prosecute. 1. Begin and follow up on a **civil** lawsuit. 2. Charge a person with a crime and bring that person to trial. The process is called **prosecution,** the procedure is called a *prosecution*, the person who was harmed by the crime or who made the complaint is a *prosecuting witness*, and the public official who presents the government's case is called the **prosecutor.**

Prosecutor. 1. Public official who presents the government's case against a person accused of a crime and who asks the court to convict that person. 2. The private individual who accuses a person of a crime is sometimes called the *private prosecutor.*

Prosecutorial discretion. The power of the **prosecutor** (see that word) to decide whether or not to prosecute a person, to decide how serious a charge to press, how large a penalty to request, what kind of a **plea bargaining** deal to accept, etc.

Prospective. Looking forward; concerning the future; for example: *a prospective law* is one that applies to situations that arise after it is enacted. Most laws are prospective only.

Prospectus. **1.** A document put out to describe a **corporation** and to interest persons in buying its **stock.** **2.** A document put out to interest persons in any financial deal (such as the offer to sell a building).

Prostitution. A person offering her (in some states, his or her) body for sexual purposes in exchange for money. A crime in most states.

Protective order (or Protection order). A court's **order** that temporarily allows one side to hold back from showing the other side documents or other things that were properly requested.

Protest. **1.** A written statement that you do not agree to the legality, justice, or correctness of a payment, but you are paying it while reserving your right to get it back later. **2.** A formal certificate of the **dishonor** of a **negotiable instrument** (see these words) you have **presented** for payment. It is signed by a **notary** and gives notice to all persons **liable** on the negotiable instrument that they may have to pay up on it.

Prothonotary. Head **clerk** of some courts.

Protocol. **1.** The first draft of an agreement between countries or the preliminary document opening an international meeting. **2.** Formalities.

Province. Duty or area of responsibility.

Provisional Temporary or preliminary; for example: a *provisional remedy* is a court **order** or an action permitted by a court that helps to enforce the law on a temporary basis. These include **temporary injunctions** and **attachments** (see these words).

Proviso. A condition, qualification, or limitation in a document.

Provocation. An act by one person that triggers a reaction of rage in a second person. *Provocation* may reduce the severity of a crime such as a killing of the second person by the first. It may also be a **defense** to a **divorce** based on **cruelty.**

Proximate cause. The real cause of an accident or other injury. It is not necessarily the closest thing in time or space to the injury and not necessarily the event that set things in motion. It is a general word for a general idea. Some other names for the same idea are "causa causans," "causa proxima," and "dominant," "efficient," "immediate," "legal," "moving," "next," or "producing" cause.

Proxy. **1.** A person who acts for another person (usually to vote in place of the other person in a meeting the other can not attend). **2.** A piece of paper giving the right mentioned in no. 1.

Prudent person rule. A **trustee** (see that word) may invest **trust** funds only in traditionally safe investments or risk being personally responsible for losses.

Public. 1. Having to do with a state, nation, or the community as a whole. 2. Open to all persons.

Public defender. A free lawyer, employed by the government to represent poor persons accused of a crime.

Public domain. 1. Land owned by the government. 2. Free for anyone to use; no longer protected by **patent** or **copyright.**

Public interest. A broad term for anything that can affect the general public's finances, health, rights, etc. *"Public interest law"* is non-profit legal practice for a public cause, such as protection of the environment.

Public law. 1. The study of law that has to do with either the operation of government or the relationship between the government and persons (examples are **constitutional law, administrative law, criminal law,** etc.). 2. The name for the original form that United States and some state laws come out in; for example: "Public Law No. 223."

Public policy. A vague word that can be as broad as "what is good for (or will not harm) the general public" or "the law."

Public service commission (or Public utilities commission). A state agency that regulates the business of railways, power companies, etc.

Publication. Making public; for example: in copyright law, *publication* is offering a book or other thing to the public by sale or distribution; in the law of **defamation,** *publication* usually means communicating the information to another person; in the law of **wills,** *publication* is telling a **witness** that you intend a document to be your will; and in the law of court procedure, *publication* of a legal notice is publishing it in a newspaper.

Publish. See **Publication.**

Puffing. Salesmanship by a seller that is mere general bragging about what is sold, rather than definite promises about it or intentionally misleading information.

Punitive damages. Money awarded by a court to a person who has been harmed in a particularly malicious or willful way by another person. This money is not related to the actual cost of the injury or harm suffered. Its purpose is to keep that sort of act from happening again by serving as a warning. It is also called "**exemplary damages.**"

Purchase. 1. Buy. 2. According to the **Uniform Commercial Code,** "*purchase*" includes "any voluntary transaction creating an interest in property, including a gift."

Purchase money mortgage. A buyer financing part of a purchase by giving a **mortgage** on the property to the seller as **security** for the loan.

Purchase order. A document that authorizes a person or a company to deliver goods or perform services. It promises to pay for them.

Purge. 1. Cleanse, clear or **exonerate** from a charge, from guilt, or from a **contract.** 2. In **wills**: to knock out a person named in a will (because that person is prohibited from getting anything) without destroying the rest of the will.

Purport. **1.** To imply, profess outwardly, or give the impression (sometimes, a false impression). **2.** The meaning, intent, or purpose of something.

Pursuant. In accordance with; in carrying out; for example: "Pursuant to my authority as governor" means "I have the authority to do what I am about to do because I am governor, and that thing is . . . ."

Purview. The purpose, scope, and design of a **statute** or other **enacted** law.

Putative. **Alleged,** supposed, or commonly known as; for example: a *putative father* is the alleged father of an **illegitimate** child.

Pyramid sales scheme. A type of sales pitch that promises that once you buy an item, you get paid for each additional buyer you find for the company. It is also known as a "referral sales plan," a "chain referral plan" and a "multi-level distributorship." It is illegal in many forms.

Q

Q. **1.** Quarterly. **2.** Question.

Q.V. (Latin) Quod vide; "which see" or "look at." This is a direction to the reader to look in another place in the book (or in another book) for more information. This dictionary uses the phrase "*see that word*" where most lawbooks would say "*Q.V.*"

Qua. (Latin) As; considered as; in and of itself; for example: the *trustee qua trustee* is not **liable**" means that the **trustee** is not liable as a trustee (but might be liable as an individual).

Quaere. A question, query or doubt; when used before a phrase it means that which follows is an open question.

Qualification. **1.** Possessing the personal qualities, property, or other necessary things to be eligible to fill a public office or take on a particular duty. **2.** Limitation or restriction.

Qualify (or Qualified). See **qualification.**

Qualified acceptance. A "*qualified acceptance*" is not an **acceptance** at all, but a **counteroffer** (see that word) because an acceptance (see that word) of a deal must be unqualified and unrestricted.

Quantum meruit. (Latin) "As much as he deserved"; an old form of **pleading** a lawsuit for compensation for work done.

Quantum valebat. (Latin) "As much as they were worth"; an old form of **pleading** a lawsuit for payment for goods sold and delivered.

Quare. (Latin) "Wherefore"; for example: "*quare clausum fregit*" (wherefore he broke the close) is an old form of **pleading** a lawsuit for **damages** against someone who **trespasses** on your land.

Quash. Overthrow; **annul**; completely do away with (usually refers to a court stopping an **order** or an **indictment**).

Quasi. (Latin) "Sort of"; analogous to; for example: a "*quasi-contract*" is an obligation "sort of like" a contract that comes, not from an agreement, but from a relationship between persons or from their actions.

Quasi-judicial. The case-deciding function of an **administrative agency.**

Quasi-legislative. The rulemaking function of an **administrative agency.**

Query. Question (see **quaere**).

Qui. (Latin) He (or she); he (or she) who.

Quia timet. (Latin) "Because of fears"; a request to a court, similar to a request for an **injunction** (see that word).

Quick assets. Property that can be turned into cash for immediate use.

Quid pro quo. Something for something; the giving of one valuable thing for another; "**consideration** (see that word) that makes a **contract valid.**

Quiet. Free from interference or disturbance; for example: an "*action to quiet title*" is a way of establishing clear ownership of land.

Quit. Leave or give up possession of a place.

Quitclaim deed. A **deed** that passes on to the buyer all those rights or as much of a **title** as a seller actually has. A *quitclaim deed* does not **warrant** (promise) that the seller actually has full title to the land to pass on.

Quo animo. (Latin) "With what intention or motive" (see **animus**).

Quo warranto. (Latin) "With what authority"; a proceeding in which a court questions the right of a person (usually a public official) to take a certain action or to hold a certain office.

Quod. (Latin) That which; that.

Quorum. The number of persons who must be present to make the actions of a group (such as a **board**) valid. This number is often a majority (over half) of the whole group, but is sometimes much less or much more.

R

R.O.R. Release on own **recognizance** (see that word).

Race statute. In a state with a *"race statute,"* a person who first **records** (files) a claim (such as a **deed**) has the legal right to that claim. This means that in these states, if Joan sells a house to Tom, then sells it again to Ellen, then Ellen files the deed, Ellen's deed will probably be good against Tom.

Rape. The crime of a man imposing sexual intercourse by force upon an unwilling woman. Also, *"statutory rape"* is the crime of a man having sexual intercourse with a girl under a certain state-set age.

Ratable. Proportional; adjusted by some formula or percentage.

Rate. 1. An amount fixed by mathematical formulas or adjusted according to some standard. 2. A charge that is the same to all persons for the same service.

Rate fixing. The power of some **administrative agencies** (such as state power commissions) to set the charges a company may get for its services. This is not the same as **price fixing,** which is done by sellers of goods or services and may be illegal.

Ratification. Confirmation of a previous act done by you or by another person; for example: when the President signs a **treaty,** the Senate must *ratify* it (make it valid from the moment it was signed). Also, if a child makes a **contract,** it is probably not enforceable, but if the child *ratifies* it after becoming an adult, it becomes a binding contract.

Ratio decidendi. (Latin) The central core of a judge's **decision**; the basic point that decides a case.

Ravishment. 1. Rape (see that word). **2.** Old word for unlawfully taking away a person who is in the care of another.

Re. (Latin) "Concerning"; see "**in re.**"

Real. 1. Having to do with land and things on land. **2.** Having to do with a thing, rather than with a person; for example: a *real defense* is a defense based on the validity of a document, rather than on the circumstances surrounding it. Real defenses include **forgery,** the fact that the person signing was a **minor, alteration** of the document, etc.

Real evidence. Objects seen by the jury; for example: wounds, fingerprints, weapons used in a crime, etc.

Realized. Actual; cashed in; for example: a "*realized profit*" is a cash-in-hand gain as opposed to a "*paper profit*," which is the increase in value of property (such as a **stock**) that might be lost again if the value goes down.

Realty (or Real estate or real property). Land and things attached to land, such as buildings.

Reasonable. A broad, flexible word used to make sure that a decision is based on the facts of a particular situation, rather than on abstract legal principles. It has no exact definition, but has come to take on general meanings when combined in words such as *reasonable* "care," "certainty," "doubt," "man," "speed," "time," etc.

Rebate. A discount or deduction (usually given at the end of the transaction).

Re<u>but</u>. Dispute, defeat, or take away the effect of facts or arguments. This is called "*rebuttal*" of the opposing arguments.

Re<u>but</u>table. Disputable; for example: a *rebuttable presumption* is a conclusion that will be drawn unless facts or arguments are raised to counter it.

Recall. To put an elected official out of office by a vote of the people.

Recaption. Taking something back that has been taken away.

Receipt. 1. Written acknowledgement that something has been received or put into your hands. 2. The act of getting or receiving.

Receive evidence. **Admit evidence** (see that word).

Receiver. 1. An outside person appointed by the court to manage money and property during a lawsuit. 2. A person who gets stolen goods.

Receivership. A court putting money or property into the management of a **receiver** (see that word) in order to preserve it for the persons ultimately entitled to it. This is often done when the **creditors** of a business suspect **fraud** or **gross** mismanagement and ask the court to step in and watch over the business to protect them.

Receiving stolen goods. The criminal offense of possessing any property known to be stolen.

Recess. 1. A brief suspension of court business, usually lasting an hour or two at most. 2. A break in a legislative session, sometimes lasting many weeks.

Recidivist. A habitual criminal; a "repeater."

Reciprocal. Mutual; **bilateral** (two-sided or two-way); for example: *reciprocal wills* are **wills** made by two persons, each putting something in his or her will that the other wants because the other put something in his or hers that the first one wants.

Reciprocity. Two states (or countries) giving identical privileges to the citizens of the other state.

Recital. A formal statement in a document that explains the reasons for the document or for the transaction behind the document.

Recognition. In most cases, when a taxpayer has received some financial gain, it is *"recognized."* This means that it must be reported on tax forms and tax must be paid on it. Some gains, however, are *"non-recognized."* This means that paying taxes on them may be put off to a later year. One example of possible "non-recognition" of a gain comes when you sell a house at a profit, but within a year buy another more expensive one in which to live.

Recognizance. A formal obligation to do a certain act that is recorded in court; for example: a person accused of a crime may be allowed to go free before trial without putting up a bail bond. The person gives the court a formal written statement that failure to show up will mean payment to the court of a certain amount of money. This is called getting out on your *"own recognizance."*

Reconciliation. Renewal of a broken relationship with forgiveness on both sides.

Reconveyance. The return of title to property; for example: the return of title papers to a house when the **mortgage** is paid off.

Record. 1. A formal, written account of a case containing the complete formal history of all actions taken, papers filed, **rulings** made, **opinions** written, etc. A "*court of record*" includes all courts except for the lowest level courts in which no permanent records of proceedings are kept. 2. A "*public record*" is a document filed with, or put out by, a government agency and open to the public for inspection; for example: a *title of record* to land is an ownership interest that has been properly filed in the public land records. The official who keeps these records is usually called the "*recorder of deeds.*"

Recoupment. 1. Keeping or holding something back that you owe because there is a fair, just reason to do so. 2. Taking or getting something back (especially money lost). 3. A **counterclaim** (see that word).

Recourse. The right of a person who holds a **negotiable instrument** (see that word) to get payment on it from anyone who **endorsed** (signed) it if the person who made it out in the first place fails to pay up.

Recovery. 1. The thing received when a lawsuit is decided in your favor. 2. The amount of money given by a **judgment** in a successful lawsuit.

Recrimination. A countercharge; for example: a husband asks a court for a divorce based on his wife's **adultery,** but the husband has also committed adultery. If the court knows all the facts, the divorce will not be granted because the husband's adultery was *recrimination*.

Recusation. The process by which a judge is disqualified (or disqualifies himself or herself) from hearing a lawsuit because of **interest** or **prejudice.**

Redeem. 1. Buy back; reclaim property that has been **mortgaged** or **pledged.** 2. Turn in for cash.

Redemption. Repurchase or turn in for cash (see **redeem**).

Redress. 1. Satisfaction or payment for harm done. 2. Access to the courts to get no. 1.

Reductio ad absurdum. (Latin) "Reduce to the absurd"; disproving an argument by showing that it leads to a ridiculous conclusion.

Re-entry. Taking back possession of land by a right you kept when you left the land before.

Refer. 1. Point to; direct attention to. 2. A judge's action of turning a case or part of a case over to a person who has been appointed to sort things out by taking **testimony,** examining documents, and making decisions and recommendations. This person is often called a "*referee*."

Referee in bankruptcy. A Federal judge who runs **bankruptcy** hearings.

Reference. 1. An agreement in a contract to submit certain disputes to an **arbitrator** for decision. 2. The act of sending a case to a **referee** for a decision (see **refer**). 3. A person who will provide information for you about your character, credit, etc. 4. Mention in a book or document of another place to find information on a subject or of the place from which the information used was taken. **5.** See **incorporation by reference.**

Referendum. Putting an important law to a direct vote of the people rather than passing it through the **legislature** (or in addition to passing it through the legislature).

Referral plan (or Referral sales scheme). Pyramid sales scheme (see that word).

Reformation. A procedure in which a court will rewrite, correct, or "reform" a written agreement to conform with the original intent of the persons making the deal. The court will do this only if there was **fraud** or **mutual mistake** in writing up the original document.

Refreshing memory. A **witness** may use notes, books, or other documents to remind him or herself of details, but may not rely entirely on them.

Refunding. Refinancing a debt.

Register. **1.** A book of public facts such as births, deaths and marriages (also called a registry). **2.** The public official who keeps the book mentioned in no. 1. **3.** To place information into the book in no. 1. **4.** Other examples of public record books are the *register of patents* (a list of all patents granted) and the register of ships (kept by customs). **5.** Other examples of public record keeping officials are the register of deeds (land records) and the register of wills (clerk of probate court). They are often called "Recorder" or "Registrar."

Registered. Listed on an official record; for example: a *registered stock* can only be cashed in by

261

the person who is listed as the owner and each time ownership changes that fact is registered.

Registrar. See **register** definition no. 5.

Registration. 1. Recording (see **record**). 2. Making up a list. 3. Putting yourself on a list of eligible voters.

Registry. See **register** definition no. 1.

Regnal years. **Statutes** in England are usually dated by the name of the king or queen on the throne at the time and the year of their reign. This date is a *regnal year*.

Regressive tax. Opposite of **progressive tax** (see that word).

Regular. 1. Steady; uniform; with no unusual variations. 2. Lawful; legal; in conformity with usual practice.

Regulate. To control; a government *regulates* businesses that have a big effect on the general public (such as power companies) by writing laws on the subject and setting up government organizations called regulatory agencies (or **administrative agencies**) to write rules and **regulations** that explain what power companies can and cannot do and how they may operate. The agencies also administer and enforce the rules by giving orders, holding hearings, etc.

Regulation. A "mini-law"; a rule that is put out by a low-level branch of government, such as an **administrative agency.**

Regulatory agency. See **regulate.**

Rehabilitation. The restoring of former rights, abilities, authority, etc.; for example: *rehabilitating* a witness means restoring the witness's believability after the other side has destroyed it or put it in question, and rehabilitating a prisoner means to equip him or her for an honest productive life once released.

Reinstate. Place back in a condition that has ended or been lost; for example: to *reinstate* a case is to put it back into court after it has been **dismissed** (thrown out).

Reinsurance. A contract by which one **insurance** company insures itself with another insurance company to protect itself against all or part of the risk it took on by insuring a customer.

Relation. "Relating back" or having retroactive effect.

Relator. Person in whose name a state brings a legal action (the person who "relates" the facts on which it is based).

Release. **1.** The giving up or relinquishing of a claim or a right by the person who has it to the person who owes the claim or against whom it might have been enforced; for example: most persons demand a *release* in exchange for paying money to settle an accident claim. **2.** The piece of paper in no. 1.

Relevancy. Applicability to an issue in a lawsuit (see **relevant**).

Relevant. Having an impact on a question or issue; having to do with a disputed issue in a lawsuit. **Evidence** is *relevant* if it proves or disproves a theory or position (by one side in a lawsuit) that will influence the result of the lawsuit. Evidence must be relevant to be **admitted** (accepted) by the court.

Relict. Old word for widow or widower.

Relief. The help given by a court to a person who brings a lawsuit. The "relief asked for" might be the return of property taken by another person, the enforcement of a contract, etc.

Rem. (Latin) "Thing;" see "**in rem.**"

Remainder. **1.** An interest or **estate** in land that takes effect only when another interest in land ends; for example: if Mary's will says "I leave my house to Joe for ten years and then to Jane, Jane's interest is a *remainder*. **2.** As used in a will, "remainder" may mean "leftovers;" for example: "My house and clothing to Joe and the remainder to Jane."

Remainderman. Old name for a person who gets **trust** property after the trust is ended.

Remand. To send back; for example: a higher court may **remand** a case to a lower court for the lower court to take some action ordered by the higher; also, a prisoner is remanded if he or she is sent back to jail after a day in court.

Remedial statute. **1.** A law that is passed to correct a defect in a prior law. **2.** A law passed to provide a **remedy** (for example, creating a new **lien**) where none previously existed.

Remedy. The way a right is enforced or satisfaction for a harm done is received; the means by which a violation of rights is prevented, redressed, or compensated; for example: Ron's *remedy* against Don if Don refuses to give back Ron's book might be to take it back, to argue with Don until he gives it back, or to go to court to either get it back or make Don pay for it. (Note:

lawyers often mean "legal remedy" or "court remedy" when they say "remedy.")

Remise. **Release,** give up, or forgive.

Remission. **1. Release** (ending or forgiving) of a debt. **2.** Forgiving an offense, injury or harm done.

Remit. **1.** Send; send in or send back. **2.** Give up or pay.

Remittance. Money (or a check, etc.) sent by one person to another.

Remittitur. **1.** The power of a trial judge to decrease the amount of money awarded by a jury to a **plaintiff.** **2.** The power of an **appeals** court to deny a new trial to the **defendant** if the plaintiff agrees to take a certain amount of money less than that given in the trial. **3.** *Remittitur of record* is the return of a case from appeals court to trial court for the trial court to carry out the higher court's decision.

Removal. The movement of a person or thing from one place to another; for example: *"removal* from the state" means absence from the state long enough to be a change of residence, and "removal of a case" is the transfer of a case from one court to another (most commonly, from a state to a Federal court).

Render. **1. Pronounce,** state, or declare; for example: a judge *"renders judgment"* by giving a decision in a case in court. **2.** Give up or return. **3.** Pay or perform.

Renewal. Keeping an agreement alive by a fresh agreement.

Renounce. Reject, cast off, or give up openly and in public.

Rent strike. An organized **tenant** refusal to pay rent in order to force the **landlord** to do something.

Renunciation. Abandoning a right; giving up a right without transferring it to anyone else.

Renvoi. A legal rule by which a court uses a foreign country's rules to choose which laws should apply to a case and the foreign rules say that the law where the court is should apply.

Reorganization. A reorganization of an **insolvent** (broke) **corporation** is a court-supervised **winding up** of business and a transfer of ownership to a new corporation owned by old owners and by **creditors.**

Rep. **Reporter** or **reports.**

Reparable injury. A wrong that can be compensated by money.

Reparation. Payment for an injury; redress for a wrong done.

Repeal. The complete wiping out of an earlier **statute** by a later one.

Replevin. A lawsuit to get back **personal property** in the hands of another person.

Replevy. To give back **personal property** to a person who has brought a lawsuit for **replevin** of the goods.

Replication. Old form of pleading similar to the modern **reply** (**plaintiff's** response to a **defendant's** first **pleading**).

Reply. In **pleading**, the *reply* is the **plaintiff's** response to the **defendant's answer** or **counterclaim.**

The usual order is: complaint, answer, reply. The reply denies some or all of the facts in the answer. Sometimes, it adds new facts, but only to counter facts in the answer.

Report. An official or formal statement of facts or proceedings.

Reporter. 1. Published volumes of decisions by a court or group of courts. 2. Person who compiles **reports.** 3. The "*court reporter*" is the person who records court proceedings in court and later makes good copies of some of them. 4. A **loose-leaf** book on current developments in an area of law, such as the Poverty Law Reporter.

Reports. Published volumes of case decisions by a particular court or group of courts.

Repossession. Taking back something sold because payments have not been made.

Represent. 1. To say or to state. 2. To act for, do business for, or "stand in" for another person. 3. To act as another person's lawyer.

Representation. 1. See **represent.** 2. In the law of **contracts,** a *representation* is any statement (or any attempt to give an impression about a state of facts) that was done to convince the other person to make a contract. 3. In the law of **inheritance,** *taking by representation* is the same as taking **per stirpes** (see that word).

Representative. 1. A person who **represents** (see that word) another. 2. A public official elected to the lower **house** of a **legislature.**

Representative action. A lawsuit brought by one **stockholder** in a **corporation** to claim rights or to fix wrongs done to many or all stockholders in the company.

Reprieve. Holding off on enforcing a criminal **sentence** for a period of time after the sentence has been handed down.

Republic. A country with a government by elected officials and with ultimate power in the hands of the citizens.

Repudiation. Rejection or refusal; for example: *repudiation of a contract* is the refusal to go through with it.

Repugnancy. Inconsistency; a condition which occurs if one part of a document is true (or correct), so that another part cannot be true (or correct).

Requirements contract. A **contract** for the supply of goods in which the exact amount of goods to be bought is not set, but will be what the buyer needs for the life of the contract (so long as the needs are real and reasonable).

Requisition. A demand or a request for something to which you have a right; for example: one state governor asking another to hand over a fugitive from justice.

Res. (Latin) A thing; an object; things.

Res adjudicata. See **res judicata.**

Res gestae. (Latin) "Things done"; the entire event or transaction; everything said and done as part of a single incident or deal. Statements that are part of an occurrence that has already been shown to have existed are *res gestae.* This means that they can usually be **admitted** in **evidence** despite the fact that out-of-court statements cannot usually be used as evidence.

Res ipsa loquitur. (Latin) "The thing speaks for itself"; a **rebuttable presumption** (a conclusion that can be changed if contrary facts are brought out) that a person is **negligent** if the thing causing an accident was in his or her control only and that type of accident does not usually happen without negligence. It is often abbreviated "res ipsa" or "R.I.L."

Res judicata. (Latin) "A thing decided"; "a matter decided by judgment; " if a court decides a case, the subject of that case is firmly and finally decided between the persons involved in the suit, so no new lawsuit on the same subject may be brought by the persons involved.

Rescind. To take back, "unmake," or annul; to cancel a **contract** and wipe it out "from the beginning" as if it had never been.

Rescission. The "unmaking" of a **contract** (see **rescind**).

Reservation. **1.** A holding back of a thing or a right; for example: a **deed** to land in which the right to cross it is "*reserved*" to the person selling the land. Also, a judge may "*reserve*" decision of a legal question by putting it off until the end of the trial. **2.** Land owned by an American Indian nation as a whole for the use of its people.

Reserve. **1.** "*With reserve*" in an auction means that the thing will not be sold if the highest bid is not high enough. **2.** To "*reserve* **title**" is to keep an ownership right as **security** that the thing will be fully paid for.

Residence. A place where a person lives all or part of the time.

Residuary. The part left over; for example: a "*residuary clause*" in a will disposes of all items not specifically given away (the "leftovers").

Residuum. (Latin) Leftovers.

Resolution. A formal expression of the opinion of a public body such as a **legislature.** It is voted on like a **statute,** but does not become a law.

Resolve. A **resolution** (see that word).

Resort. A *court of last resort* is a court whose decision cannot be **appealed** within the same court system.

Respondeat superior. (Latin) "Let the master answer"; a legal rule that an employer is responsible for the actions of an employee done in the course of employment.

Respondent. **1.** The person against whom an **appeal** is taken. (This person might have been either the **plaintiff** or the **defendant** in the **lower** court.) Also called the "**appellee.**" **2.** The person against whom a **motion** is filed.

Responsive. Answering; a "*responsive pleading*" is a court paper that directly answers the points raised by the other side's **pleading.**

Rest. To "*rest a case*" is to stop putting on **evidence** and let the other side do so or let the decision be made.

Restatement of Law. Books put out by the American Law Institute that tell what the law in a general area is, how it is changing, and what direction the authors think this change should take; for example: the *Restatement of the Law of Contracts.*

Restitution. Giving something back; making good for something.

Restrain. 1. Prohibit from action; hold back. 2. Hinder or obstruct.

Restraining order. See **temporary restraining order.**

Restraint of trade. Illegal agreement or **combination** that eliminates competition, sets up a **monopoly,** or artificially raises prices.

Restrictive covenant. A **clause** in a group of **deeds** that forbids all the landowners (and all later owners) from doing certain things with their land; for example: put up outhouses. This is for the protection of the rest of the landowners.

Restrictive indorsement. Signing a **negotiable instrument** (see that word) in a way that ends its **negotiability**; for example: "Pay to Robert Smith only."

Resulting trust. If Peter gives money to Paul to be held in **trust** and the trust fails for some legal reason, Paul holds the money in a *"resulting trust"* for Peter. If Peter buys a house, but puts the **title** in Paul's name, it may be called a *"purchase money resulting trust"* in favor of Peter.

Retainer. 1. The act of a client employing a lawyer. 2. The specific agreement in no. 1. 3. The first payment in no. 1.

Retaliatory eviction. A landlord's attempt (prohibited in many places) to throw out a tenant for complaining to the health department, forming a tenants' union, etc.

Retirement. Making the final payment owed on a **bond, note,** or other **security** and ending its existence and all obligations under it.

Retirement income credit. A way to set aside income from being taxed each year and paying taxes on it upon retirement when your taxes are lower.

Retraction. Taking something back; for example: taking back a statement and admitting that it was false.

Retro. Back; backwards; behind; past; for example: a *"retrospective"* or *"retroactive"* law is one that tries to change the legal status of things already done or that tries to apply to past actions.

Return. 1. The act of a **sheriff** or other **peace officer** in delivering back to a court a brief account of whether or not (and how) he or she **served** (delivered) a court paper to a person. 2. **Yield** or profit. 3. Tax form turned in to the government.

Return day (or Return date). The day by which a defendant must **file** a **pleading** after receiving a **summons** to come to court.

Rev. 1. Review. 2. Revised.

Revenue. 1. Income. 2. **Return** on an investment. 3. Money raising or taxing act of government.

Reverse. Set aside; for example: when a higher court *reverses* a lower court on **appeal,** it sets aside the **judgment** of the lower court and either substitutes its own judgment for it or sends the case back to the lower court with instructions on what to do with it.

Reversion. Any **future interest** (see that word) kept by a person who transfers away property; for example: John rents out his land for ten years. His ownership rights during those years, his right to take back the property after ten years, and his **heirs'** right to take back the property after ten years if he dies are "*reversionary interests.*"

Review. Examination of a case by an **appeals** court.

Revised statutes. **1.** A **code** (see that word). **2.** A book of **statutes** in the order they were originally passed with temporary and **repealed** statutes removed.

Revive. Bring back to life; restore to original force or legal effect.

Revocation. **1.** The taking back of some power or authority; for example: taking back an **offer** before it is **accepted** ends the other person's power to accept. **2.** The ending or making **void** of a thing; for example: *revocation of a will* takes place when a person tears it up intentionally or makes another will.

Revoke. Wipe out the legal effect of something by taking it back, cancelling, rescinding, etc. (see **revocation**). If something can be revoked, it is "*revocable.*"

Revolving charge. Credit, often provided through credit cards or department stores, by which purchases may be charged and partially paid off month-by-month. New purchases may be made, charged, and paid off during the same period.

Rex. (Latin) The king.

Richard Roe. Common name used for a **fictitious party** or a name used along with "**John Doe**" to illustrate a legal situation.

Rider. An additional piece of paper attached at a later time to a larger document; for example: a *rider to a bill* is an addition made late in the legislative process and is usually unrelated to the subject of the **bill**, but "tacked on" anyway.

Right. 1. Morally, ethically and legally just; the underlying law of a society. 2. One person's *legal* ability to control certain actions of another person or of all other persons. Every *right* has a corresponding **duty**; for example: if a person has a right to cross a street on a green light, all ordinary drivers have a duty to avoid hitting the person with their cars. (Note: when lawyers speak of "a right," they mean a legal, not moral right.)

Right of action. A claim that can be enforced in court.

Right-to-work law. A state law prohibiting **union shop** arrangements that require a person to join a union in order to work.

Riparian. Having to do with the bank of a river or stream.

Ripe. A case is *ripe* for decision by the U.S. Supreme Court if the legal issues involved are clear enough and well enough evolved and presented so that a clear decision can come out of the case. Any court or agency that has the power to turn down cases may use "*ripeness*" as a way of deciding whether to take the case.

Robbery. The illegal taking of property from the person of another by using force or fear of force.

Rogatory letters. A request from one judge to another asking that the second judge supervise the examination of a **witness** (usually in another state and usually by written **interrogatories**).

Roll. 1. A record of official proceedings. 2. A list of **taxable** persons or property.

Roomer. A lodger; a person who rents rooms in a house, as opposed to a **tenant** (see that word).

Royalty. A payment made to an author, an inventor, an owner of oil or other mineral lands, etc. for the use of the property.

Rubric. 1. General purpose. 2. Title.

Rule. 1. To settle a legal issue or decide a **motion, objection,** etc. raised by one side in a legal dispute. 2. An established standard, principle, or guide. 3. A **regulation**; a "mini-law" made by a group or by an **administrative agency** to govern its internal workings.

Rule against accumulations. A state law that prevents a **trust** from storing up money for too long. It is similar to the Rule against perpetuities (see **perpetuities**).

Rule against perpetuities. See **perpetuities.**

Rule of Law. 1. There are many different definitions of this phrase. According to Kelso's *Programmed Introduction To The Study Of Law,* a *rule of law* is "a general statement that is intended to guide conduct, applied by government officials, and supported by an authoritative source." 2. A governmental system in which the highest authority is the law, not one person or a group of persons.

Ruling. A judge's decision on a legal question (usually minor) raised during a trial.

Run. 1. To have legal **validity**; for example: the law *runs* throughout the state. 2. To apply during a time period; for example: a **statute of limitations** *runs* when the time to bring a lawsuit of a certain type has ended or run out. 3. To be attached to another thing; for example: a **covenant** (see that word) may *run* with the land.

S

S.B.A. Small Business Administration: a U.S. agency that provides loans and advice for small businesses.

S.E. South Eastern Reporter (see **National Reporter System**).

S.E.C. Securities and Exchange Commission: a U.S. agency that **regulates** the sale and trading of **stocks, bonds,** etc.

S.R.S. Social and Rehabilitative Service: the branch of the U.S. Department of Health, Education and Welfare that runs the Federal **welfare** program.

SS. A vague and unnecessary symbol found on many **affidavits**; its meaning is not known for sure.

S.S.A. Social Security Administration: the branch of the U.S. Department of Health, Education and Welfare that runs the Federal program of old age and disability insurance.

S.W. South Western Reporter (see **National Reporter System**).

Said. An unnecessary word, used in legal writing to mean "the one mentioned before"; for example: "*said table.*" Usually "the" or "this" will do.

Sale. 1. A **contract** in which property is exchanged for money. 2. The actual exchange of property for money.

Salvage. Property recovered after an accident or other damage or destruction.

Sanction. 1. To assent to or confirm another person's actions. 2. A penalty or punishment attached to a law to make sure it is obeyed.

Sanity. Of sound mind; the opposite of **insanity** (see that word).

Satisfaction. Taking care of a debt or **obligation** by paying it.

Satisfactory. A general word for "enough," or "good enough," used when it is hard to pin down how much is enough.

Save. Hold until later; reserve; preserve.

Schedule. List.

Scienter. (Latin) Knowingly; with guilty knowledge.

Scintilla. A very little bit; usually used in the sense of "even a little bit is enough."

Scire facias. (Latin) 1. A judge's command to a person to come to court and explain why a record in that person's possession should not be wiped out. 2. Other **writs** called *scire facias* were used for various purposes, but all had to do with some public record or the record of a case.

Scope of employment. An action of the general sort a person was employed to do, even if not exactly what the employer wants.

Scott. *Scott on Trusts*; a treatise on the law of trusts.

Seal. An identification mark pressed in wax. Originally, for a document to be valid, it had to have a wax seal on it to show that it was done seriously, correctly and formally. Later, the use of the letters "*L.S.*" took the place of wax. Now, there is no need for the seal at all except for making sure that the right person actually signed (like in front of a **notary public,** who has a seal), or to formalize certain **corporate** documents with a corporate seal.

Search warrant. Written permission from a judge or **magistrate** for a police officer (or **sheriff,** etc.) to search a particular place for evidence, stolen property, etc. The police must give a good reason for needing these items and a likely reason why they might be in the place they want to search.

Seasonable. In a reasonable amount of time.

Second look statute. **Wait and see statute** (see that word).

Secondary authority. **Persuasive authority** (see that word).

Secondary boycott. A **boycott** (see that word) aimed at a business that does business with the one a union is actually having a dispute with. It is indirect pressure.

Secretary of State. **1.** In U.S. government, this is a **Cabinet** member who heads the State Department and is in charge of foreign relations. **2.** In most state governments, the official who takes care of many types of formal state business, such as the **licensing** of **corporations.**

Section. 1. A subdivision of a chapter in a book or document. 2. A subdivision of a township that is one mile on a side or 640 acres.

Secure. To give **security** (see that word); to guarantee the payment of a debt or the keeping of a promise by giving the person a **mortgage,** a **pledge,** etc. (see these words).

Secured creditor. A person who is owed money and is protected by a **lien, mortgage,** or other special **interest** in the **debtor's** property.

Securities. 1. See **security.** 2. **Stocks, bonds, notes,** or other documents that show a share in a company or a debt owed by a company.

Security. Property that has been **pledged, mortgaged,** etc. as financial backing for a loan or other obligation. A *"security interest"* is any right in property that is held to make sure money is paid or that something is done.

Sedition. Stirring up persons to armed resistance against the government.

Seisin. Full and complete present ownership and possession of land.

Seizure. The act of a public official (usually the police) taking property because of a violation of the law.

Selectman. A member of some local legislatures or town councils. When a town is too small to have a mayor, the role of mayor is taken by the "first selectman."

Self-dealing. A **trustee** who acts to help himself or herself rather than the person for whom he or she is supposed to be working.

Self-defense. The right to use physical force against a person who is threatening a **felony**, committing a felony, threatening the use of physical force, or using physical force. This is a right if the person's own family, property, or body is in danger, but only if the danger was not provoked and there is no reasonable way to escape.

Self-executing. Laws or court decisions that require no further official action to be carried out.

Self-help. Taking an action with legal consequences, whether the action is legal or not; for example: a *"self-help eviction"* may be a **landlord's** removing the **tenant's** property from an apartment and locking the door against the tenant.

Senate. The upper **house** of a state or the U.S. **legislature.**

Senior interest. An **interest** or right that takes effect or that collects ahead of others.

Sentence. The punishment, such as time in jail, given to a person **convicted** of a crime.

Separate but equal. A legal principle, now totally dead, that facilities such as schools could be segregated by race as long as they were "equal."

Separate maintenance. Money paid by one married person to the other for support if they are no longer living as husband and wife.

Separation. A husband and wife living apart by agreement. If it is by order of a court, it is a *"judicial"* or *"legal"* separation. A *"separation agreement"* is a document sometimes made up to set out who gets what and who pays what, both temporarily, and, in some cases, permanently.

Separation of powers. Each branch of the government (**executive, legislative,** and **judicial**) has a different job and each acts to keep the others from becoming too powerful. This "balancing" of jobs and strengths is called *separation of powers.*

Sequester. To isolate or hold aside; for example: to *sequester a jury* is to keep it from having any contacts with the outside world during a trial, and to *sequester property* is to have it put aside and held by an independent person during a lawsuit.

Seriatim. (Latin) One by one.

Servant. A person employed by another person and subject to that person's control as to what work is done and how it is done. An employee is a "*servant.*"

Service. 1. The delivery (or its legal equivalent, such as publication in a newspaper in some cases) of a legal paper, such as a **writ,** by an officially authorized person in a way that meets all the formal requirements. It is the way to notify a person of a **lawsuit.** 2. Regular payments on a debt.

Servient. Land subject to a **servitude** (see that word), **charge,** or **burden** is "*servient.*" (For an example of how "servient" is used, see **easement.**).

Servitude. 1. A **charge** or **burden** on land in favor of another; for example: the owner of a piece of land may be required by the **deed** to avoid building within a certain distance from the next property. The land so restricted is the "*servient estate*" and the land benefiting from the restriction is the "**dominant estate.**" 2. The condition of being a slave or servant.

Session. Either a day or a period of days in which a court, **legislature,** etc. carries on its business.

Session laws. **Statutes** printed in the order that they were passed.

Set aside. Cancel, **annul,** or **revoke** a court's **judgment.**

Set down. Put a case on the list for the court to **hear.**

Setback. A distance from a curb, other line, or structure, within which building is prohibited.

Set-off. A **defendant's** counterdemand for money against a **plaintiff** that has nothing to do with the plaintiff's lawsuit against the defendant.

Settle. 1. To come to an agreement about a debt, payment of a debt, or disposition of a lawsuit. **2.** Finish up; take care of completely. 3. Transfer property in a way that ties it up for a succession of owners. 4. Set up a **trust.**

Settlement. 1. See **settle.** 2. The meeting in which the ownership of **real property** actually transfers from seller to buyer and all payments and debts are **adjusted** and taken care of. These financial matters are put down on a "*settlement sheet,*" also known as a "**closing statement.**"

Settlor. Person who sets up a **trust** by providing the money or property for it.

Sever. Cut off; for example: to *sever* the trial of a person from others is to **try** that person's case separately and at another time. It is often called "severance."

Severable. Capable of carrying on an independent existence; for example: a *severable statute* is one that can still be valid even if one part of it is struck down as **invalid** by a court.

Several. 1. More than one. 2. Separate, individual, independent.

Severally. Distinctly; separately; each on its own.

Severalty ownership. Sole ownership; ownership by one person.

Sewer service. Telling the court that you have properly **served** (officially delivered) a court paper when it has actually been thrown away.

Sham. False or fake.

Share. 1. A portion. 2. One piece of **stock** in a **corporation.**

Shelley's case. The "*Rule in Shelley's Case*" is that when a **life estate** is given to a person, followed by a **remainder** given to **heirs,** the heirs take nothing, but the holder of the life estate gets an interest in **fee** (see these words). This rule is no longer followed; life estates and remainders are permitted.

Shelter. 1. The principle that a buyer has as good a **title** to property as the seller had. 2. A way of investing money to minimize taxes on it.

Shepardizing. Using a Shepard's **Citator** (see that word) to trace the history of a case after it is decided.

Sheriff. Chief law officer of a county, who, with the help of deputies, is in charge of **serving process,** calling **jurors,** keeping the peace, **executing judgments,** etc.

Sheriff's deed. A document giving ownership rights in property to a buyer at a *sheriff's sale* (a sale held by a **sheriff** to pay a court **judgment** against the owner of the property).

Sherman Act. The first anti-**trust** or anti-**monopoly** law; passed by the Federal government to break up "combinations in restraint of trade."

Shifting. Changing; varying; passing from one person to another.

Shop-book rule. An older, more limited version of the **business-records exception** (see that word) in **evidence** law.

Short cause (or Short calendar). A lawsuit or part of a lawsuit that must be heard by a judge, but can be scheduled early because it will not take up much time.

Short sale. A contract for the sale of **stock** the seller does not own. It is a method of profiting from the expected fall in price of a stock.

Show cause. A court **order** to a person to show up in court and explain why the court should not take a proposed action. If the person fails to show up or to give sufficient reasons why the court should take no action, the court will take the action.

Shyster. Dishonest lawyer.

Si. (Latin) If.

Sic. (Latin) Thus; so; in such a way.

Sight. "*At sight*" means **payable** when shown and requested; a **bill** or **draft** payable when shown is a "*sight bill*" or "*sight draft.*"

Signature. 1. A hand-signed name. 2. In some commercial situations, any mark that normally serves as a hand-signed name.

Silver platter. Federal officials using **evidence** that was gathered illegally by state officials.

Simple. 1. Pure, unmixed or uncomplicated. **2.** Not **aggravated.**

Simulate. Take on the appearance; imitate; fake.

Sine. (Latin) Without; for example: *sine die* means "without day" or a final ending or **adjournment** of a **session** of a court or a **legislature.**

Sine qua non. (Latin) A thing or condition that is indispensable.

Single-name paper. A **negotiable instrument** (see that word) that has only one **maker** (original signer) or, if more than one original signer, persons signing for exactly the same purpose (for example, as **partners**). This is opposed to **accommodation paper** (where one person signs as a favor to another) or a **suretyship** (where, for a fee, one person co-signs to back up another person's debt).

Single proprietorship. A business owned by one person.

Sit. 1. To hold court as a judge. **2.** To hold any session (a court, **legislature,** etc.); to be formally organized and carrying on official business.

Situs. (Latin) Site or fixed location; place.

Slander. Oral **defamation** (see that word); the speaking of false and **malicious** words that injure another person's reputation, business, or property rights.

Slating. Booking (see that word).

Slip decision (or Slip sheet or Slip opinion). A printed copy of a U.S. Supreme Court **decision** (or certain other court decisions) that is distributed immediately.

285

Slip law. A printed copy of a **bill** passed by Congress that is distributed immediately once signed by the President.

Small business. A company may be a "*small business*" if it has few employees, a low sales volume, etc. The definition differs, depending on who (Small Business Administration, workmen's compensation, etc.) defines it.

Small claims. The name for a court in many places that will handle cases under a certain money limit (often about one thousand dollars). These courts have a more streamlined procedure, faster action, and fewer formalities than regular courts. They were originally set up to help the "little person" get a day in court, but are mostly used by stores and collection companies to collect overdue bills.

Smart money. **Punitive damages** (see that word).

Smuggling. The crime of secretly bringing into a country things that are either prohibited or **taxable.**

So. Southern Reporter (see **National Reporter System**).

Sodomy. A general word for sexual intercourse involving a man's genitals and almost anything other than a woman's genitals. It is a crime in most states. Some states limit it to situations involving penetration of the anus.

Soldiers' and Sailors' Civil Relief Act. A Federal law that suspends or modifies a military person's **civil** liabilities or requires persons who want to enforce their **claims** against persons in the service to follow certain procedures.

Solicitation. 1. Asking for; enticing; strongly requesting. 2. A lawyer's drumming up business in too aggressive a way. This is prohibited by the lawyers' **Code of Professional Responsibility.**

Solicitor. An English lawyer.

Solicitor General. The second-ranking U.S. government lawyer; in charge of all **civil** suits involving the U.S.

Solvency. 1. The ability to pay debts as they come due. 2. Having more **assets** than **liabilities.**

Solvent. See **solvency.**

Sound. 1. Whole; in good condition; healthy. 2. "Of the type"; for example: a lawsuit "*sounding in damages*" is one where more than one **remedy** might be appropriate, but "**damages**" was chosen.

Sovereign immunity. The government's freedom from being sued for **damages** (money) in all but a few special situations where it consents to suit by passing **statutes** allowing it (for example: the Federal Tort Claims Act).

Special. 1. Limited; for example: a *special indorsement*" is the signing over of something to one particular person. 2. Unusual; for example: a "*special session*" is an extra meeting of a court or **legislature.**

Special appearance. Showing up in court for a limited purpose only; for example, to argue that the court has no **jurisdiction** (see that word) over you.

Special assessment. A **real estate tax** on certain landowners to pay for improvements that will, at least in theory, benefit them all; for example: a sidewalk.

Special warranty deed. A transfer of land that includes the formal, written promise to protect the buyer against all claims of ownership of the property that are based on relationships with or transfers from the seller.

Specialty. Formerly, a **contract** under **seal** (see that word).

Specific performance. See **performance.**

Speedy trial. A trial free from unreasonable delay; a trial conducted according to regular rules as to timing; not necessarily a fast trial or a trial as soon as you want one.

Spendthrift. A person who spends money wildly and whose property the state may allow a **trustee** to look after. This protection of a person's property against himself or herself is called a *"spendthrift trust."*

Spin-off. A **corporation** sets up and funds a new corporation and gives the **shares** of this new corporation to the old corporation's **stockholders.** This new corporation is a *"spin-off"* and the process is a "spin-off."

Split-off. A **corporation** sets up and funds a new corporation and gives the **shares** of this new corporation to the old corporation's **stockholders** in exchange for some of their shares in the old company. This new company is a *"split-off"* and the process is a split-off.

Split-up. A **corporation** divides into two or more separate new corporations, gives its **shareholders** the shares of these new corporations, and goes out of business. This process is a *"split-up."*

Spoliation. 1. Destruction by an outsider; for example: alteration of a check by someone who has nothing to do with it. 2. The failure by one side in a trial to come forward with **evidence** in its possession (and the inferences that the other side may draw from this failure).

Spot zoning. Changing the **zoning** of a piece of land without regard for the zoning plan for the area.

Squatter's rights. The "right" to eventual ownership of land because you have occupied it for a long time. This is different from **adverse possession** (see that word) and is not recognized as a right in most places.

Stale check. A **check** that has been held too long before attempting to cash it. This time period is often set by state law.

Stamp tax. A tax on certain legal documents, such as **deeds,** that requires that the revenue stamps be bought and put on the documents in order to make them **valid.**

Stand. 1. The place where a witness sits or stands to **testify.** 2. Remain; refuse to change.

Stand mute. A refusal by a defendant to **plead** "guilty" or "not guilty." It is usually treated as a "not guilty" plea.

Standard deduction. A fixed amount of money subtracted from a person's **taxable income.** This is subtracted by persons who do not wish to list all their possible individual deductions when they do their **income tax returns.**

Standing. A person's right to bring a lawsuit because he or she is directly affected by the issues raised.

Stare decisis. (Latin) "Let the decision stand"; a legal rule that when a court has decided a case by applying a legal principle to a set of facts, that court should stick by that principle and apply it to all later cases with clearly similar facts unless there is a good, strong reason not to. This rule helps promote fairness and reliability in judicial decision-making.

State. **1.** Say; set down; or declare. **2.** The major political subdivision of the U.S. ("*State action*" is by a state, such as New York.) **3.** A nation. ("*Act of state*" is by a country, such as France.) **4.** Condition; situation. **5.** Department of State: the U.S. Cabinet department that handles our relations with foreign countries.

State secret. Facts that the United States need not reveal to a court (or to anyone else) because they might hurt national security or another equally important national interest.

Statement of affairs. The summary financial form filled out when filing for **bankruptcy**.

State's evidence. General word for **testimony** for the **prosecution** given by a person who is involved in a crime against others involved in the crime.

Status. **1.** Basic condition; basic legal relationship of a person to the rest of the community; class. **2.** State of things; for example: "*status quo*" is the existing state of things or the way things are at a particular time.

Statute. A law passed by a **legislature**.

Statute of frauds. Various state laws, modeled after an old English law, that require many types of **contracts** (especially large or long-term ones) to be signed and in writing to be valid.

Statute of limitations. See **limitation**.

Statute of wills. Various state laws, modeled after an old English law, that require a **will** to be in writing, signed, and properly **witnessed** to be valid.

Statutes at large. A collection of all **statutes passed** by a particular legislature (such as the U.S. Congress), printed in full and in the order of their passage.

Statutory. Having to do with a **statute**; created, defined, or required by a statute; for example: *statutory rape* is the act of a man having sexual intercourse with a female under an age defined by state statute.

Stay. 1. To stop or hold off; for example: to *stay a judgment* is to hold off from allowing it to be enforced. 2. A stopping; for example: the act mentioned in no. 1 is called a "stay of judgment."

Stenographic recording. The taking down of **testimony** by a **court reporter** who uses a paper-punching device, a tape recorder, a shorthand notebook, or other device to take down testimony and court proceedings, and then types an exact copy later. *Non-stenographic* recording would be the use of a tape recorder, videotape, etc. without the court reporter to run it.

Stipulation. A formal agreement between lawyers on opposite sides of a lawsuit. It is usually in writing and usually concerns court procedure; for example: an agreement to extend the time in which a **pleading** is due.

Stirpes. See **per stirpes.**

Stock. 1. The **goods** held for sale by a merchant. 2. Shares of ownership in a **corporation.** Stock is usually divided into "**preferred**" (getting a fixed rate of income before any other stock) and **common** (the bulk of the stock).

Stock dividend. Profits of **stock** ownership paid out by a corporation in more stock rather than in money.

Stockholder's derivative suit. A lawsuit in which a **shareholder** of a corporation sues someone for the corporation because a wrong has been done to the company. The company itself is not suing.

Stop order. A customer's notice to his or her bank to tell the bank to refuse payment on a check the customer has written to another person.

Stoppage in transit. The right of a seller to stop the delivery of goods even after they have been given to a **carrier** (railroad, etc.) if, for example, the seller finds out that the buyer is **insolvent** and will not be able to pay for the goods.

Straight-line depreciation. Dividing the cost of a thing used in a business by the number of years it will be used and **deducting** that fraction of the cost each year from **taxable income.**

Stranger. Person who takes no part in a deal in any way; a **third party.**

Straw man. 1. A "front"; a person who is put up in name only to take part in a deal. 2. A man who stood around outside a court in old England and was hired by lawyers to give false **testimony.**

Strict. Exact; precise; governed by exact rules; for example: "*strict construction*" of a law means taking it literally or "what it says, it means."

Strict foreclosure. A **creditor's** right, in some circumstances, to take back property and cancel the debt. In these situations, the property acts as an exact cancellation of the debt and neither the creditor nor the **debtor** can sue the other for any additional money.

Strict liability. The legal responsibility for damage or injury even if you are not at fault or **negligent**; for example: a manufacturer may be liable for injuries caused by a defective product even if the person hurt cannot prove how the manufacturer was careless.

Strike. **1.** Employees stopping work in order to win demands from an employer. **2.** Take out; for example: to strike a word is to remove it from a document.

String citation. A series of case names and references to where they are found that is printed after an assertion or legal conclusion in order to back it up.

Strong-arm provision. A part of the Federal bankruptcy law. It says that a **bankruptcy trustee** has all the powers of the most powerful **secured creditors,** whether or not one actually exists, so he or she has the "*strong arm*" *power* to gather in all the bankrupt's property.

Struck jury. A group of persons chosen as supposedly "best qualified" to try a criminal case.

Style. Official name.

Sua sponte. (Latin) On his or her own will; voluntarily; on a judge's own **motion,** without a request from one of the **parties.**

Sub. (Latin) Under; for example: *"sub judice"* means "under **judicial** consideration" or in court and not yet decided, and *"sublet"* means to rent out something you yourself are renting.

Sub nom. (Latin) Abbreviation for *sub nomine* or "under the name of"; under the title of.

Sub silentio. (Latin) "Under silence"; in silence; without taking any notice or giving an indication.

Subcontractor. A person who contracts to do a piece of a job for another person who has a contract for the whole job.

Subdelegation. Same as **delegation** (see that word) of authority.

Submit. 1. To put into another's hands for decision. 2. Allow; yield to. 3. **Introduce** evidence.

Subordination. Signing a document that admits that your **claim** or **interest** (for example, a **lien**) is weaker than another one and can collect only after the other one collects.

Subornation of perjury. The crime of asking or forcing another person to lie under **oath.**

Subpoena. A court's **order** to a person that he or she show up in court to **testify** (give **evidence**) in a case.

Subpoena duces tecum. A **subpoena** (see that word) by which a person is commanded to bring certain documents to court.

Subrogation. The substitution of one person for another in claiming a lawful right or debt; for example: when an **insurance** company pays its customer for damage to the customer's car, the company becomes *subrogated to* (gets the right to sue on or collect) any claim the customer has against the person who hit the car.

Subscribe. 1. Sign at the end of a document (as the person who wrote it, as a **witness,** etc.). 2. Agree to purchase some initial **stock** in a **corporation.**

Subsidiary. 1. Under another's control; lesser. 2. "*Subsidiary*" is often short for "*subsidiary corporation*" or one that is run and owned by another company which is called the "*parent.*"

Substance. 1. Reality, as opposed to mere appearance. 2. The "gist" or meaning of something.

Substantial. 1. Valuable; real; worthwhile. 2. Complete enough. 3. "A lot," when it is hard to pin down just how much "a lot" really is.

Substantiate. Establish the existence of something or prove its truth; verify.

Substantive law. The basic law of **rights** and **duties** (**contract** law, criminal law, accident law, law of **wills,** etc.) as opposed to **procedural law** (law of **pleading,** law of **evidence,** law of **jurisdiction,** etc.).

Substituted service. **Service of process** (see that word) by any means other than personal delivery; for example: by mail, publication in a newspaper, etc.

Succession. The transfer of a dead person's property. *Intestate succession* is the transfer of property by law to **heirs** if the person does not leave a **will.**

Sue. To start a **civil** lawsuit.

Suffer. Allow or permit something to happen.

Suffrage. The right to vote.

Sui generis. (Latin) One of a kind.

Sui juris. (Latin) "Of his or her own right"; possessing full **civil** and **political rights** and able to manage his or her own affairs.

Suit. A lawsuit; a **civil action** in court.

Summary. Short; concise; immediate; without a full trial; for example: *summary judgment* is a win for one side in a lawsuit before the conclusion of a full trial.

Summary process. An abbreviated type of court hearing available in some situations; for example: an **eviction** where the tenant's failure to pay rent automatically ended the **lease.**

Summons. A **writ** (a notice delivered by a **sheriff** or other authorized person) informing a person of a lawsuit against him or her. It tells the person to show up in court at a certain time and place to present his or her case or risk losing the suit without being present.

Sumptuary laws. Laws controlling the sale or use of socially undesirable, wasteful, and harmful products.

Superior. Higher; having some control over.

Supersede. 1. Set aside; wipe out; make unnecessary. 2. Replace one law or document by another, later one.

Supersedeas. (Latin) A judge's order that temporarily holds up another court's proceedings.

Supervening. New; newly effective; interposing.

Supplementary proceedings. A **judgment creditor's** (see that word) in-court examination of the **debtor**

and others to find out if there is any money or property available to pay the debt.

Support. 1. The obligation to provide for your immediate family. 2. The payments made to a wife, husband, children, etc. (with or without court supervision or formal agreement) to meet the obligation in no. 1. 3. "*Lateral support*" is the obligation landowners have to avoid the collapse of adjoining land (due to digging, etc.).

Suppress. To "*suppress evidence*" is to keep it from being used in a criminal trial by showing that it was either gathered illegally or that it is irrelevant.

Sup-pro. Supplementary proceedings (see that word).

Supremacy of law. A government in which the highest authority is in law, not in persons.

Supreme Court. The highest U.S. court and the highest court of most, but not all, of the states. (For example, it is a lower court in New York.) It is abbreviated "*Sup.Ct.*"

Surcharge. 1. An extra charge on something already charged. 2. A special payment such as the personal payment a **trustee** must make to a **trust** if he or she has negligently handled the account and it has lost money.

Surety. A person or company that **insures** or **guarantees** that another person's debt will be paid by becoming **liable** (responsible) for the debt when it is made.

Surplusage. Extra, unnecessary words in a legal **pleading**.

Surprise. The situation that occurs when one side in a trial, through absolutely no fault of its own, is faced with something totally unexpected that places an unfair burden on its case. When this happens, a new trial may be requested.

Surrebutter (or Surrejoinder). Two old forms of **pleading** no longer used. Modern court practice usually stops with two or three pleadings, not the five or more it would take to reach these.

Surrender. Give back; give up; hand back or return.

Surrogate. Name for the judge of a **probate** court in some states.

Surtax. 1. An additional tax on what has already been taxed. 2. A tax on a tax; for example: if you must pay a hundred dollar tax on a one thousand dollar income (ten percent), a ten percent *surtax* would be an additional ten dollars, not an additional hundred dollars.

Survivorship. The right to property held by more than one person when the others die.

Suspended sentence. A **conviction** of a crime followed by a **sentence** that is given formally, but not actually **served.**

Suspicion. 1. Being temporarily held by the police without specific charges against you. 2. More than a guess but less than full knowledge.

Sustain. 1. Grant; when a judge *sustains an objection,* he or she agrees with it and gives it effect. 2. Carry on; bear up under. 3. Support or justify; if the evidence fully supports a verdict it is said to "*sustain*" the verdict.

Syllabus. A **headnote,** summary, or **abstract** of a case.

Symbolic delivery. Giving something by giving a valid symbol of ownership; for example: giving a key to a safety deposit box may be **evidence** of the actual gift of what is in the box.

Syndicate. A **joint adventure** (see that word).

Synopsis. A summary of a document, book, etc.

T

T. Old abbreviation for the Latin "testamentum" (**will**).

T.R.O. Temporary restraining order (see that word).

Table of cases. Alphabetical list of cases mentioned in a book with page numbers on which they are found.

Tacit. Understood without being openly said; done in silence; implied.

Taft-Hartley Act. A Federal law, passed in 1947, that added several employers' rights to the union rights in the **Wagner Act.** It established several union "unfair labor practices" (such as attempting to force an employee to join a union).

Tail. Limited; limited to only children, grandchildren, etc.

Talesman. A person taken from off the street or inside the courthouse to serve as a **juror.**

Tamper. Make changes by meddling; interfering.

Tangible. Capable of being touched; real.

Tariff. Import tax.

Tax. A required payment of money to support the government; for example: **estate taxes, income taxes, sales taxes, property taxes,** etc. (see these words).

Tax avoidance. Planning finances carefully to take advantage of all legal tax breaks, such as **deductions** and **exemptions.**

Tax deed. A proof of ownership of land given to the purchaser by the government after the land has been taken from another person by the government and sold for failure to pay taxes.

Tax evasion. Illegally paying less in taxes than the law permits; committing **fraud** in **filing** or paying taxes.

Tax rate. The percentage of **taxable income** (or of inherited money, things purchased subject to sales tax, etc.) paid in taxes. The Federal income tax has a *graduated* tax rate. This means, for example, that the first ten thousand dollars of a person's taxable income might be taxed two thousand dollars and the next one thousand to two thousand dollars at twenty-five percent. This percentage rate is what most people think of as their "*tax bracket.*"

Taxable income. Under Federal tax law, this is either the "**gross income**" of businesses or the "**adjusted gross income**" of individuals (see these words) minus **deductions** and **exemptions** (see these words). It is the income against which tax rates are applied to compute tax paid.

Taxing cost. Making one side in a lawsuit pay the other side's costs of the suit when legally required.

Technical. **1.** Having to do with an art or a profession; technical terms are often called "**words of art.**" **2.** Minor; "just" procedural.

Temporary restraining order. A judge's **order** to a person to keep from taking certain action before a **hearing** can be held on the question.

Tenancy. The condition of being a **tenant**; the interest a tenant has; the **term** (amount of time) a tenant has (see tenant).

Tenant. **1.** A person who holds land or a building by renting or **leasing.** Tenants include persons who have a lease, tenants at **will** (started out with a lease and still living there with permission), tenants at **sufferance** (started with a lease, but holding onto property against the wishes of the owner), etc. **2.** A person who holds land or a building by any legal right including ownership. For example: **joint** tenants own a whole piece of land together, tenants by the **entirety** are a husband and wife who own land together (and each owns it all if the other dies) and tenants in **common** each hold a share of land that can be passed on to **heirs** at death, etc.

Tender. **1.** An offer of money; cash on the line offered to settle a debt. **2.** An offer to buy **stock** in order to take control of a company.**3.** Any offer combined with a readiness to do what is offered.

Tender offer. An offer (usually public) to buy a certain amount of the **stock** of a company at a set price; it is often done to get control of the company.

Tenement. **1.** Any house, apartment, or place where people live. **2.** Particular kinds of living places, such as apartment houses. The word may be defined differently by different **statutes** or **regulations.**

Tenor. A vague word that can mean anything from "the exact words" to "the general meaning" or "train of thought."

Term. 1. A word or phrase (especially one that has a fixed technical meaning). 2. A fixed period; the length of time set for something to happen; for example: a *term of court* is the time period in which the court may hear cases (hold **sessions**).

Termination. Under the **Uniform Commercial Code,** "*termination*" means legally ending a **contract** without its being broken by either side.

Territorial. 1. Having to do with a particular country; for example: "*territorial waters*" are the oceans surrounding a country. These waters "belong" to the country out to a certain distance. 2. Having to do with a particular area; for example: *territorial jurisdiction* is the power of a court to take cases from within a particular geographical area.

Territorial courts. U.S. courts in each territory, such as the Virgin Islands. They serve as both Federal and state courts.

Test case. A lawsuit brought to establish an important legal principle or right.

Testacy (or Testate). Leaving a valid **will.**

Testament. A **will** (see that word).

Testamentary. Having to do with a **will;** for example: "*testamentary capacity*" is the mental ability needed to make a valid will.

Testator. Person who makes a **will.**

Testify. Give **evidence** under **oath.**

Testimony. **Evidence** given by a **witness** under oath.

Theft. Stealing of any kind.

Thereabout. A vague, overly formal word meaning "approximately there." Like all the other "there" words (thereafter, thereat, thereby, therein, thereof, thereon, thereto, theretofore, thereunder, thereupon, and therewith), it is best left out of a sentence or replaced by the exact thing referred to.

Third degree. Illegal methods of forcing a person to confess to a crime.

Third party. A person unconnected with a deal, lawsuit, or occurrence, but who may be affected by it. For example: a *third party beneficiary* is a person who is not part of a **contract,** but for whose direct benefit the contract was made.

Time draft (or Time bill or Time loan). A **draft** (or **bill** or loan) payable at a certain time.

Time is of the essence. When this phrase is in a **contract,** it means that a failure to do what is required by the time specified is a **breach** (breaking) of the contract.

Time-price doctrine. Courts may allow a higher price charged for things bought on credit than for the same things paid for in cash. This is a way for a seller to get around state **usury** (see that word) laws.

Timely. Done in time; for example: a *timely* **suit** is one that is brought to court soon enough to be valid (not barred by a **statute of limitations,** by **laches,** etc.).

Title. 1. The formal right of ownership of property. 2. A document that shows no. 1. 3. The name for a part of a **statute**; for example: "Title IV of the Juvenile Court Act."

To have and to hold. An unnecessary phrase used in many deeds. At one time, this phrase had to be used to make the transfer of land valid, but it is now just excess words.

To wit. An unnecessary phrase meaning "that is to say" or "namely." It can usually be replaced by just a colon (:).

Toll. 1. A fee to use a road, bridge, etc. 2. To *toll* a **statute of limitations** (see that word) is to do something to put off its effect to the future.

Tontine. A reverse type of life **insurance,** now illegal, in which many persons pay into a fund and only those living by a certain date split it up.

Tort. A **wrong** done to another person; a **civil** (as opposed to criminal) wrong that does not involve a **contract.** For an act to be a *tort*, there must be: a legal **duty** owed by one person to another, a **breach** (breaking) of that duty, and harm done as a direct result of the action. Examples of torts are **negligence, battery,** and **libel** (see these words).

Tortfeasor. A person who commits a **tort** (see that word); a wrongdoer.

Tortious. Wrongful (see **tort**).

Totten trust. Putting your money into a bank account in your name as **trustee** for another person. You can take it back when you want, and when you die it becomes the property of that other person.

Town. A type of local government or local area. It means different things in different states. It is important in some states, trivial in others, large in some, small in others.

Township. A division of state land having six miles on each side and varying in importance as a unit of government from state to state.

Trade. 1. Buying and selling; commerce. 2. A job or profession. 3. Barter; swapping.

Trademark. A distinctive mark, motto or sign that a company can reserve by law for its own exclusive use in identifying itself or its products.

Transaction. 1. A business deal. 2. An occurrence; something that takes place; a group of facts so interconnected that they can be referred to by one legal name, such as a "crime," a "contract," a "wrong," etc.

Transcript. A copy; especially the official typed copy of the **record** of a court proceeding.

Transfer. To change or move from person to person (sell, give, or sign something over, etc.) or place to place (court to court, etc.).

Transfer tax. A tax on large transfers of property or money which are made without something of value given in return. Often called a "gift tax."

Transitory action. A lawsuit that may be brought in any one of many places.

Trauma. 1. An injury to the body caused by an external blow. 2. Sudden psychological damage.

Traverse. An old form of **pleading** in which facts in the other side's pleading were denied.

Treason. The act of a U.S. citizen's helping a foreign government to overthrow, make war against, or seriously injure the U.S.

Treasury. Department of the Treasury: the U.S. Cabinet department that handles most national financial, monetary, and tax matters. It runs the Internal Revenue Service (taxes), the Mint (coins), the Secret Service (protection of public officials), etc.

Treasury stock (or Treasury shares). Shares of **stock** that have been rebought by the **corporation** that issued them.

Treatise. A large, comprehensive book on a legal subject.

Treaty. A formal agreement between countries on a major political subject.

Treble damages. Triple the amount of actual **damages** will be given in some lawsuits to strongly discourage certain kinds of wrongful actions. It requires a **statute** for treble damages to be given out.

Trespass. 1. A wrongful entry onto another person's property. 2. An old term for many types of civil wrongs or **torts.** For example: the "*trespass*" in no. 1 was called "*trespass quare clausum fregit*" (see that word); modern **contract** lawsuits grew out of "*trespass on the case*" and "*trespass vi et armis* (force and arms) grew into modern lawsuits for both **negligence** and **battery** (see these words).

Trial. The procedures in open court to finally decide a case (giving **evidence,** making **arguments,** deciding by a judge and **jury,** etc.).

Tribunal. Court.

Trover. An old type of lawsuit, now rarely used, in which a piece of property was claimed to be lost by you and then found by the person from whom you want it back. This got around the problem of proving the thing was taken because all you had to prove was that it was yours and that the other person had it.

True bill. An **indictment** approved and made by a **grand jury.**

Trust. 1. A group of companies that has a **monopoly** (see that word). 2. Any transfer of money or property to one person for the benefit of another. For example: a mother signs over **stocks** to a bank to manage for her daughter with instructions to give the daughter the **interest** each year until she turns thirty and then to give it all to her. In this example, the mother is the **settlor** of the **trust,** the bank is the **trustee** and the daughter is the **beneficiary.** However, a trust need not be set up explicitly by name; for example: if a father gives a son some money saying "half of this is for your brother," this may be a trust also.

Trust company. A bank that manages **trusts** (see that word) for persons and organizations.

Trust deed. See **deed of trust.**

Trust receipt. A document by which one person lends money to buy something and the borrower promises to hold the thing in **trust** for the lender until the debt is paid off.

Trustee. 1. A person who holds money or property for the benefit of another person (see **trust**). 2. A person who has a **fiduciary relationship** (see

that word) towards another person; for example:
a lawyer, an **agent**, etc.

Try. To *try* a case is to argue it in court as a
lawyer, decide it as a judge, or participate in it in
one of several ways.

Turpitude. Unjust, dishonest or immoral activity.

Tying in. A seller's refusal to sell a product unless
another product is bought with it. If a seller has
a **monopoly** on a product, *tying in* the sale of
another product may be a violation of the **anti-
trust** laws.

U

U.C.C. **Uniform Commercial Code** (see that word).

U.C.C.C. **Uniform Consumer Credit Code.** (Also
called the "*U.C.3.*") A Uniform Law, adopted by
some states to regulate the way merchants and
lending institutions give credit to consumers.

U.C.M.J. Uniform Code of Military Justice; rules
of conduct and criminal behavior for members of
the Armed Forces.

U.S.C. United States Code; the official lawbooks
where all Federal laws are collected by subject
matter.

U.S.C.A. **1.** United States Code Annotated; the
lawbooks where all Federal laws are collected by
subject and partially explained. **2.** United States
Court of Appeals.

U.S.D.A. United States Department of Agriculture: the Cabinet department that **regulates** farm
activities, sets agricultural policy, carries on agricultural research and education programs, etc.

U.S.D.C. United States District Court.

Ubi. (Latin) Where.

Ultimate facts. Facts essential to a **plaintiff's** or a **defendant's** case; basic or "core" facts.

Ultra. (Latin) Beyond; outside of; in excess of; for example: *ultra vires* actions are things a **corporation** does that are outside the scope of powers or activities permitted by its **charter** or **articles of incorporation.**

Unauthorized practice. Non-lawyers doing things that only lawyers are permitted to do. Who and what fits into this definition is constantly changing and the subject of dispute. If, however, a clear case comes up (for example, a non-lawyer pretending to be a lawyer and setting up a law office), the practice may be prohibited and the person punished under the state's criminal laws.

Unconscionability. Sales practices that are so greatly unfair that a court will not permit them. For example, the use of small print and technical language in contracts with poorly-educated persons, combined with prices that were three times higher than normal, was called "*unconscionable*" by one court.

Unconstitutional. Laws or actions that conflict with the U.S. Constitution.

Understanding. A general word for "*agreement*," whether formal or informal, legally binding or not.

Undertaking. 1. A promise. 2. A promise made in the course of a lawsuit to the judge or to the other side. 3. Bonds or other financial **securities**; the process of putting out these bonds.

Underwrite. 1. To **insure.** 2. To **guarantee** to purchase any **stock** or **bonds** that remain unsold after a public sale.

Undue. More than necessary; improper; illegal; for example: *undue influence* is pressure that takes away a person's free will to make decisions. Undue influence involves misusing a position of confidence or taking advantage of a person's weakness or distress to improperly change that person's actions or decisions.

Unethical conduct. Actions that violate professional standards such as the lawyers' **Code of Professional Responsibility.**

Unfair competition. Too closely imitating the name, product or advertising of another company in order to take away its business.

Unfair labor practice. An action by a union or by an employer that is prohibited by law or court decisions; for example: an employer's attempt to force an employee to give up union organizing activities.

Uniform. Regular; even; applying generally, equally, and even-handedly.

Uniform Acts (or Uniform Laws). Laws in various subject areas, proposed by the Commissioners on Uniform State Laws, that are often adopted, in whole or in part, by many states. Some of these are the Uniform Anatomical Gifts Act, the **Reciprocal Enforcement of Support Act,** and the **Uniform Commercial Code.**

Uniform Commercial Code. A comprehensive set of laws on every major type of business law. It has been adopted by almost every state in whole or in major part. It replaced many older **Uniform Laws,** such as the Uniform Negotiable Instruments Law and the Uniform Sales Act.

Unilateral. One-sided (for unilateral **contract,** see contract).

Union shop. A business in which all workers must join a particular union once employed.

United States Court of Appeals. These are Federal courts (one to each **"circuit,"** an area of several states) that hear **appeals** from the U.S. District Courts. They used to be called the "U.S. Circuit Courts."

Unitrust. A **trust** (see that word) in which a fixed percentage of the trust property is paid out each year to the **beneficiaries.**

Unity. **1.** An identical interest in property held **jointly** (see that word). There are the unities of *time* (the property was received at the same time), *title* (received in the same **deed** or event), *interest* (each person getting the same rights) and *possession* (each owns the whole property). **2.** *Unity of possession* also refers to the **merger** (see that word) of rights in land.

Unjust enrichment. Legal principle that when one person obtains money or property unfairly, even if legally, it should be returned. (This does not include merely driving a hard bargain or being lucky in a deal.)

Unlawful. Contrary to law; unauthorized by law; not necessarily a crime, but at least disapproved of by the law.

Unlawful detainer. Holding onto land or buildings beyond the time you have a right to them.

Unwritten law. **1.** Customary law; things people do because they are considered right, just, or usual. **2.** Any one of several non-laws that will not be enforced by a court, but which people think are laws; for example, the "law" that a husband will not be punished if he kills his wife's lover.

Usage. A general, uniform, well-known course of conduct followed in a particular area or business.

Use. An old method of transferring and holding land, similar to a **trust,** in which one person got legal ownership, but another person got the use of the land.

Use tax. Tax on some products brought into a state to avoid paying the state's sales tax.

Usufruct. Old word for the right to use something as long as it is not changed or used up.

Usurious. Involving **usury** (see that word).

Usury. Charging an illegally high rate of **interest.**

Utter. **1.** Put into circulation; issue or put out a **check.** **2.** Say. **3.** Enough so that it will be considered complete, total, or **absolute.**

Uxor. (Latin) Wife.

V

V. Abbreviation for "*versus*" or "against" in the name of a case; for example: *Doe v. Roe* means that Doe is suing Roe.

V.A. Veterans Administration: the U.S. agency that administers benefits and programs for armed services veterans. These programs include hospitals, college tuition help, etc.

Vacate. **1. Annul**; set aside: take back; for example: when a judge *vacates a judgment*, it is wiped out completely. **2.** Move out or empty.

Vagrancy. A vague, general word for "hanging around" in public with no purpose and no honest means of support.

Vague. Indefinite; uncertain; imprecise.

Valid. **1.** Binding; legal; complying with all needed formalities. **2.** Worthwhile; sufficient.

Valuable consideration. Same as **consideration** (see that word).

Value. **1.** Worth. **2.** "*For value*" means for **consideration** (see that word).

Variance. **1.** A difference between what is **alleged** (said will be proved) in **pleading** and what is actually proved in a trial. **2.** Official permission to use land or buildings in a way that would otherwise violate the **zoning** regulations for the neighborhood.

Vel non. (Latin) Or not.

Vendee. Buyer.

Vendor. Seller.

Venire facias. (Latin) A command to the **sheriff** to assemble a **jury**.

Venireman. Juror.

Venue. The local area where a case may be tried. A court system may have **jurisdiction** (power) to take a case in a wide geographic area, but the proper *venue* for the case may be one place within that area for the convenience of the parties, etc. Jurisdiction is the subject of fixed rules, but venue is often left up to the **discretion** (good judgment) of the judge.

Verba. (Latin) Words.

Verdict. The **jury's** decision. The usual verdict, one where the jury decides which side wins (and how much, sometimes), is called a *general verdict.* When the jury is asked to answer specific **questions of fact,** it is called a *special verdict.*

Verify. 1. **Swear** in writing to the truth or accuracy of a document. 2. Confirm; prove the truth of; back up; check up on.

Versus. Against.

Vertical. In a chain, such as from manufacturer to wholesaler to retailer as opposed to among various manufacturers, among various retailers, etc.

Vest. 1. Give an immediate, fixed, and full right. 2. Take immediate effect (see **vested**).

Vested. **Absolute, accrued,** complete, not subject to any **conditions** that could take away; not **contingent** on anything. For example: if a person sells you a house and gives you a **deed,** you have a *vested interest* in the property even if the sale **contract** allows the seller to stay in the house for ten years.

Veto. A refusal by the president or a governor to sign into law a bill that has been passed by a **legislature.** In the case of a Presidential veto, the bill can still become a law if two-thirds of each **House** of Congress votes to *override* the veto.

Vexatious litigation. Lawsuits brought without any just cause or good reason.

Vi et armis. (Latin) Force and arms (see **trespass**).

Vicarious liability. Indirect legal responsibility; for example: the **liability** of an employer for the acts of an employee.

Vice. **1.** Illegal (and considered immoral) activities such as gambling and prostitution. **2.** An imperfection or defect. **3.** Second in command, or substitute.

Vide. (Latin) See; for example: "*vide ante*" means "look at the words or sections that come before this one.

Virtue. **1.** "By *virtue* of" means "by the power of" or "because." **2.** Something worthwhile or good (in a practical, rather than a moral sense).

Vis. (Latin) Force or violence; for example: *vis major* is an irresistable force or a natural disaster.

Visa. Permission to travel in a country, often given by officials of that country who mark it into a person's *passport*.

Vitiate. Cause to fail; destroy (either totally or partially) the legal effect or binding force of something; for example: **fraud** *vitiates* a **contract.**

Viva voce. (Latin) "Living voice"; orally, as opposed to in writing.

Viz. An awkward term, meaning "that is to say" or "these are." Usually a colon (:) alone will do.

Void. Without legal effect; of no binding force; wiped out. For example: a *void contract* is an agreement by which no one is (or ever was) bound because something legally necessary is missing from it.

Voidable. Something that can be legally avoided or declared **void** (see that word), but is not automatically void. For example: a *voidable contract* is one that one or both sides can legally get out of, but is effective and binding if no one chooses to get out of it.

Voir dire. (French) "Look-speak." The examination of a possible **juror** by the lawyers and the judge to decide whether he or she is acceptable to decide a case.

Volstead Act. A now dead Federal law prohibiting liquor. The law was passed under the now **repealed** Eighteenth Amendment to the U.S. Constitution.

Voting trust. A deal in which **stockholders** in a company pool their shares of stock for the purpose of voting in stockholders' meetings.

Vs. Versus; see "v."

W

Wage assignment. An arrangement in which a person allows his or her wages to be paid directly to a **creditor.** It is illegal in most situations in many states.

Wage earner's plan. A type of partial **bankruptcy** in which a person keeps his or her property and pays off a court-set proportion of debt over a period of time and under court supervision.

Wager of law. A practice in old England by which a person accused of something (such as owing money) could swear that the money was not owed and could bring eleven neighbors (called *compurgators*) to swear to the person's general truthfulness.

Wagner Act. A Federal law, passed in 1935, that established most basic union rights. It prohibited several employer actions (such as attempting to force employees to stay out of a union) and labeled these actions "unfair labor practices." It also set up the National Labor Relations Board to help enforce the new labor laws.

Wait and see statute. A state law that avoids some of the problems with the **rule against perpetuities** (see that word) by allowing time to pass to find out if a **will** violates the rule.

Waive. Give up, renounce, or **disclaim** a privilege, right, or benefit with full knowledge of what you are doing.

Waiver. The voluntary giving up of a right (see **waive**). For example: *waiver of immunity* is the act of a **witness** who gives up the Constitutional right to refuse to give **evidence** against himself or herself and who proceeds to **testify.**

Waiving time. Allowing a court to take a longer time than usual to **try** you on a criminal charge.

Want. 1. Desire. 2. Lack.

Wanton. 1. Reckless, heedless, or malicious. 2. Weighing about two thousand pounds. 3. Floating in broth. 4. In need.

Ward. 1. A division of a city for elections and other purposes. 2. A person, especially a child, placed by the court under the care of a **guardian.**

Warehouse receipt. A piece of paper proving that you own something stored in a warehouse. It may be a **negotiable instrument.**

Warrant. 1. To promise, especially in a contract or in a deed (see **warranty**). 2. Permission given by a judge to a police officer (or **sheriff,** etc.) to **arrest** a person, search a house, etc. 3. **An option**

to buy **stock**.   **4.** To promise that certain facts are true.

Warranty.   1. A promise in a **deed** that the **title** to the land being sold is good and is complete.   **2.** A statement or promise, made as part of a transaction (such as an **insurance contract**), upon which the transaction depends.   (The insurance company could refuse to pay a **claim** if the statement is false or if the promise is not kept.)   **3.** A statement or other **representation** (written description, etc.) made by a seller to a buyer as part of the sale as to the type, quality, ownership, use, etc. of the goods.   **4.** Any **obligation** imposed by law on a seller to a buyer; for example: that the product is fit for use.   **5.** Any promise that certain facts are true.

Wash sale.   1. Selling something and buying something else that is basically the same thing.   **2. Recission** (see that word) is sometimes called a "wash" because all original rights, **liabilities,** and property are returned.

Waste. Abuse or destruction of property in your rightful possession, but belonging to someone else.

Weight of evidence. The most believable side should win.   "Weight" does not refer to quantity, but to how convincing is each side's **evidence.**

Welfare.   1. Public financial assistance to certain categories of poor persons.   **2.** Health, happiness, and general well-being.

Whereas. A vague word, often used to mean "because" when placed at the beginning of a legislative **bill** (in the explanation for why the bill should be passed and made law).

Whereby. A vague word, meaning "by means of," "how?" or several other things. This word, like all the other vague, formal "where" words (whereas, wherefor(e), whereof, whereon, whereunder, whereupon, etc.), is best left out of a sentence or replaced by a specific thing, place, idea, etc.

Wherefore. A vague word, often found in a **complaint** (see that word) to begin the section where the **plaintiff** spells out exactly what he or she wants from the **defendant** or wants the court to do.

Wigmore. *Wigmore on Evidence*; a treatise on the law of evidence.

Wildcat strike. A strike without the consent of the union.

Will. 1. Desire; choice; for example: a *tenant at will* is a person who is permitted to use land or a building only as long as the owner desires the tenant to stay. 2. A document in which a person tells how his or her property should be handed out after death. If all the necessary formalities have been taken care of, the law will help carry out the wishes of the person making the will. For the various types of wills (**holographic, joint, mutual, nuncupative,** etc.) see these words.

Willful. 1. Intentional; deliberate; on purpose. 2. Obstinate; headstrong; without excuse. 3. With evil purpose; with criminal intent.

Williston. *Williston on Contracts*; a treatise on the law of contracts.

Wind up. Finish current business, settle accounts, and turn property into cash in order to end a

319

corporation or a **partnership** and split up the **assets.**

Withholding tax. An employer taking money out of an employee's pay and turning it over to the government as prepayment of the employee's income tax.

Within the statute. 1. Defined by the **statute.** 2. Prohibited by the statute. 3. Allowed by the statute.

Without day. Indefinite or final.

Without recourse. Words used by an **endorser** (signer other than original **"maker"**) of a **negotiable instrument** (check, etc.) to mean that if payment is refused, he or she will not be responsible.

Witness. 1. A person who is present at an occurrence (such as an accident), an event, or the signing of a document. 2. A person who makes a statement under **oath** that can be used as evidence (in a court, **legislature, hearing,** etc.).

Words and Phrases. A large set of lawbooks that defines legal (and many non-legal) words by giving actual quotes from cases.

Words of art. Technical terms that are used in a special way by a profession.

Words of purchase. The words in a **deed** or **will** that tell who is to get the land.

Workmen's compensation laws. Laws passed in most states to pay money to workers injured on the job regardless of **negligence.** Businesses pay into a fund to support those payments.

Work-product rule. The principle that a lawyer need not show the other side in a case any facts or things gathered for the case unless the other side can convince the judge that it would be unjust for the things to remain hidden.

Writ. A judge's **order** requiring that something be done outside the courtroom or authorizing it to be done. The most common *writ* is a notice to a **defendant** that a lawsuit has been started and that if nobody comes to court to defend against it, the **plaintiff** may win automatically. If the writ cannot be **served** (delivered properly) a second one (called an *"alias writ"*) may be used. Other types of writs include **prerogative** (unusual) writs such as **habeas corpus, mandamus** and **certiorari** (see these words), writs of **attachment** (see this word) and many others. These include papers that are no longer strictly "writs," but have become part of the court's ordinary processes as **judgments** and **orders.**

Write-off. An uncollectible debt.

Wrong. A violation of a person's legal rights, especially a **tort.**

Wrongful death action. A lawsuit brought by the **dependents** of a dead person against the person who caused the death. Money **damages** will be given to the dependents if the killing was **negligent** or **willful.**

Y

Year books. Reports of old English cases.

Yellow dog contract. An employment contract in which an employer requires an employee to promise that he or she will not join a union. These are now illegal.

Yield. Profits as measured by a percentage of the money invested; for example: a ten dollar profit on a hundred dollar investment is a ten percent yield.

Z

Z. **1.** *Regulation Z* is the set of rules put out by the Federal Reserve Board under the Truth in Lending Law. It describes exactly what a lender must tell a borrower and how it must be told. **2.** "**Z**" is the mark used to fill in unused blank spaces on a legal document to keep them from being filled in later.

Zoning. The division of a city or county into areas. *Zoning* laws limit the use to which land in each area may be put, the minimum size of each lot, building types, etc.

APPENDIX A

WHERE TO GO FOR MORE INFORMATION

If you cannot find the word you want in this dictionary, if the definition given here does not fit the context in which you found the word, or if you need a more elaborate definition, there are several places to look. They are listed here in order of decreasing convenience and increasing volume of information.

1. Standard English Dictionaries

Try a regular dictionary. Often, legal documents will use an ordinary English word in its ordinary way, but because of some special emphasis or because of its use in an unfamiliar place, the word looks "legal." A regular dictionary may reassure you that the word's ordinary meaning fits perfectly. Both *Merriam-Webster* and *Random House* have helpful dictionaries. For older words or for more complete definitions try the *Oxford English Dictionary*.

2. Large Law Dictionaries

These books are especially helpful for long Latin phrases, historical words, and situations in which you need several examples of how to use the word properly. Their definitions are sometimes confusing or out of date, but they have more words and more extensive definitions than this dictionary. The two best known are *Black's* (4th ed. revised, West Publishing) and *Ballentine's* (3d ed., Lawyers' Cooperative Publishing).

3. Hornbooks

If you know the legal subject your word comes from, the best starting place is a students' summary of the law in that field. This is called a "hornbook." For example, if the word belongs in the field of torts, try the index in the back of *Prosser on Torts*, West Publishing.

APPENDIX A

4. Legislation and Cases

If the word comes from a statute, ordinance or regulation, the law itself may have a "definition section" or several definition sections scattered through it. This is always true of the "Uniform Laws" and usually true of major Federal and State legislation. For example, the most important definitions for many commercial terms are found in the definition section of the Uniform Commercial Code. (If all you have is the popular name of a statute or a case, you can find it by using *Shepard's Acts and Cases by Popular Name*, found in most law libraries.)

5. Words and Phrases

If you want to be buried by every conceivable use of a term or if the word you want has not turned up in any of the preceding sources, go to a law library and use *Words and Phrases*, a multi-volume set of books by West Publishing. It has excerpts from every judge's decision that ever explained a word. It is the best place in a law library to get a start with complicated legal language. But be careful; the excerpts are frequently from cases that have been long overruled or discarded, from cases that were decided in the opposite way from what the quote would lead you to believe, from "dicta" (words that have nothing to do with the basis for the decision) or from inaccurately quoted cases. Also, do not forget to look in the supplement inside the back cover of each book for more recent uses of the word.

6. Descriptive Word Index

If the word you want is not a legal word, but you need to know if the word ever became entangled with the law, try the *Descriptive Word Index* to West Publishing Company's *American Digest System*. For example, if you want to know whether there was ever a case about a pet skunk spraying a meter reader (because your skunk gets edgy when the reader comes into the basement,) you might try looking up "skunk," "pets," or "meter readers." If you find nothing, try more general topics such as "animals," "household liability," etc.

7. Legal Encyclopedias

If you want to get into the general legal subject that your word came from and if "hornbooks" are no help, try a legal encyclopedia. The two major ones are *Corpus Juris Secundum* by West Publishing Company and *American Jurisprudence* by the Lawyers' Cooperative Publishing Company.

8. Background Material

If you want to know more about the history of legal language or about its misuse today, read Mellinkoff's *The Language of the Law*, Little, Brown Company.

If you want a delightful attack on all legal language, try Rodell's *Woe Unto You, Lawyers*, Reynal and Hitchcock.

If you need more information on legal research for non-lawyers, start with Statsky's *Introduction to Paralegalism*, West Publishing.

APPENDIX B

PRONUNCIATION

Most words have no pronunciation given

This dictionary does not give the pronunciation for many legal words because they are often merely regular English words used in a different way. In most cases, they are pronounced just as you would expect.

Words needing only stressing

Many legal words are pronunciation problems only because it is hard to tell which syllable gets the accent. These words have their emphasized parts underlined. For example, "ad<u>duce</u>" means that the "duce" is emphasized.

Latin words

Many Latin words can be pronounced almost any way that they are read. This is because there are at least three acceptable pronunciations for them: "Classical" Latin, "Church" Latin and "English" Latin. For example, "Certiorari" may be pronounced, among other ways, "sir-sho-<u>rar</u>-ee," "sir-sho-<u>rare</u>-eye," or sir-shore-<u>air</u>-ee." Further, many Latin words may be pronounced as if they were ordinary American English. Pronunciations are not given for these words.

The problem list

Some Latin, French and English words have pronunciations that give non-lawyers trouble. The following list contains eighty of the worst:

a fortiori	a for-she-<u>o</u>-ri
a priori	a pri-<u>o</u>-ri
ab initio	ab in-<u>ish</u>-i-o
absque	<u>ab</u>-skway
affiant	a-<u>fi</u>-ant
aleatory	<u>a</u>-le-a-<u>to</u>-ri

PRONUNCIATION

aliquot	al-i-quo
amicus curiae	a-mi-kus cure-ree-eye
autre vie	oh-tr vee
bona fides	bo-na fee-dez
causa mortis	cow-sa more-tis
caveat emptor	kav-e-at em-tor
certiorari	sir-sho-rare-i
cestui que	set-i kuh
chose	shows
codicil	cod-i-sill
consortium	con-sore-she-um
cy-press	see-pray
de jure	de joo-re
debenture	de-ben-chur
del credere	del cred-er-e
detinue	det-i-new
devise	de-vize
divers	dive-ers
domicile	dom-i-sill
droit	drwah
eleemosynary	el-e-mos-i-nary
en ventre sa mere	ahn vahnt sa mare
enfeoff	en-feef
ex parte	ex par-tee
fieri facias	fie-er-e fay-she-as
feme couvert	fem cov-er
habeas corpus	hay-be-as core-pus
in pais	in pay
in re	in ray
indicia	in-dish-i-a
indictment	in-dite-ment
injuria	in-joo-ri-a
inter se	in-ter say
jeopardy	jep-er-dee
jus gentium	jus jen-shi-um
laches	latch-es
lien	leen

327

APPENDIX B

mala fides	<u>ma</u>-la <u>fee</u>-dez
mandamus	man-<u>day</u>-mus
martial	<u>mar</u>-shall
mesne	men
nisi prius	<u>ni</u>-si <u>pri</u>-us (i = eye)
nudum pactum	<u>new</u>-dum <u>pack</u>-tum
oyez (oyer)	oy-<u>yay</u>
pais	pay
parens patriae	<u>pa</u>-rens <u>pat</u>-ri-eye
pendente lite	pen-<u>den</u>-te <u>lee</u>-te
praecipe	<u>pres</u>-i-pee
prima facie	<u>pry</u>-ma <u>fay</u>-shi
pro hac vice	pro hock <u>vee</u>-chay
prochein ami	pro-<u>shen</u> ah-mee
profits a prendre	<u>prof</u>-it a <u>prahn</u>-d
quaere	<u>quee</u>-ree
quantum meruit	<u>quan</u>-tum <u>mer</u>-u-it
quare	<u>kwa</u>-ree
quasi	<u>kway</u>-si
ratio decidendi	<u>ra</u>-shi-o des-i-<u>den</u>-di
relator	re-<u>late</u>-or
renvoi	ron-<u>vwa</u>
res ipsa loquitur	rez <u>ip</u>-sa <u>lock</u>-we-tur
scienter	si-<u>en</u>-ter
seisin	<u>si</u>-zin (i = eye)
sine die	<u>si</u>-ne <u>de</u>-ay
stare decisis	<u>sta</u>-re de-<u>si</u>-sis (first i = eye)
statute	<u>stah</u>-chute
stirpes	<u>stir</u>-pees
sub judice	sub <u>joo</u>-di-se
subornation	sub-or-<u>nay</u>-shun
subpoena duces tecum	sub-<u>pee</u>-na due-ces <u>tay</u>-cum
sui generis	<u>sue</u>-i <u>jen</u>-er-is
supersedeas	sue-per-<u>see</u>-de-as
tortfeasor	<u>tort</u>-fee-zor
tortious	tor-shus
voir dire	vwah deer

APPENDIX C
LAWYER TALK

This section is written primarily for paralegals, law students and others who use legal words professionally. Its message is simple: legal words are valuable technical tools, but they can be used to excess. This smothers clear thinking, clear writing and clear speaking.

The section is also written for the "person on the street" who uses the dictionary to help with legal questions that come up in everyday life or to learn something about the law. The ability to sort out useful legal language from "Legalese" is a big advantage when dealing with public officials, salespersons and, of course, lawyers.

There are many reasons why legal language is overused and misused. Lawyers, paralegals and legal writers get carried away by legal jargon because of their training. Traditional law schools teach by the "case method." Students spend most of their time studying how appeals judges (who have never seen the actual trial or any of the persons involved in the case) decide cases. This involves applying abstract legal concepts to abstract summaries of facts. After three years of dealing with legal words and abstract ideas, law students have problems talking about the real world in clear English.

Even after working for real clients who have real problems, many lawyers and paralegals still use legal jargon either from habit or to cover up fuzzy thinking. There are several different ways that legal words are overused or misused. Some of these ways are:

1. Using TECHNICAL legal words when dealing with non-lawyers.
2. Using VAGUE legal words when clear English would be more precise.
3. Using TOO MANY legal words.
4. Using certain WORTHLESS legal words.

APPENDIX C

1. Technical Words

Even when used accurately, legal words may be out of place when speaking to or writing for non-lawyers. For example:

Lawyer talk	English
An "annulment" voids the marriage ab initio.	An "annulment" wipes the marriage off the books as if it never happened.
Plaintiff alleges Jones is the vendee.	Smith claims he sold it to Jones.
If you don't bequeath it in a codicil, it will go by intestate succession.	If you don't change your will to put it in, some cousin may get it.
I'll move for a continuance, but it may be denied as dilatory.	I'll try to put it off, but the judge will think we are stalling.
You hold the estate in fee, but if you alienate it, you activate the acceleration clause in the security interest.	You own the house, but if you sell it or give it away, the whole mortgage comes due.
You hold legal title on the face of the instrument, but extrinsic evidence shows that Smith has equitable title.	The papers are in your name, but a court would give it to Smith.

2. Vague Words

Some legal words have a "built in" vagueness. They are used when the writer or speaker does not want to be pinned down. For example, when a law talks about "*reasonable* speed" or "*due* care," it is deliberately imprecise about the meaning of the words because it wants the amount of speed allowed or care required to be decided situation-by-situation, rather than by an exact formula. Vague words, however, just as often accompany vague thoughts. A small list of vague words, drawn from many possibilities, is given below:

Sounds precise	But is it?
Above cited	Earlier on the page? In the chapter? The book?
Accident	Intentional? Negligent? Pure chance?
Adequate	For what? By what standard? Who decides?
Civil death	For all legal purposes? Just some? Permanent?
Community	The "block"? That section of town? The state?
Face	The whole document? The first page?
Facsimile	Exact copy? Close copy? How close?
Fair hearing	Fair in what way?
Final decision	Final before appeal? Final with no appeal?
Fixture	May be removed? May not be removed?
Foreign	Different country? Different State? City?
Heirs	Children? All who may inherit? One only?
Infant	Baby? Young child? Under legal age?
Reasonable person	By what standards? With hindsight?
Stranger	Not part of the deal? Knew nothing about it?
Substantial	A lot? More than a little? Above a cutoff?
Undue	A lot? Too much? By force? Illegal?

Some legal words have been in dispute in thousands of cases. Judges have decided that many of them "clearly" mean a dozen different, conflicting things. These words can rarely be avoided, but should be replaced by specific objects, facts or concepts whenever possible even if this requires using extra words. For example, lawyers almost never agree about the following words:

Consideration	Law
Conspiracy	Obscenity
Holding	Preponderance of evidence
Insanity	Proximate cause
Jurisdiction	Willful

3. Too Many Words

Doubling legal words that mean the same thing can be confusing. The best examples of legal word-doubling (and tripling) are found in pages 346 to 366 of *The Language of the Law* by Mellinkoff (1963, Little, Brown, Co.) Some of these are:

Fit and proper	Mind and memory
Force and effect	Name and style
Give, devise and bequeath	Null and void
Have and hold	Over and above
Known and distinguished as	Rest, residue and remainder
Last will and testament	Written instrument

There are a few useful doublings such as "aid and comfort" (describing treason) or "cease and desist order" (an administrative equivalent of an injunction by a court.) Most doublings, however, are just clutter.

4. Worthless Words

Many legal words are worthless. Some are useless because they are almost meaningless. Others mean exactly the same thing as a clear English word. Here are some of both types:

Aforesaid	Hitherto	Here (or There) about	inafter
Ambulatory	Issue (for "children")	after	to
And/or	Party of the first part	by	tofore
Firstly	Re (for "about")	for	upon
Forthwith	Said (as in "said table")	from	with
Four corners	To wit	in	unto
	Viz		
	Whereas		

Before using a legal word, stop and think. Even if it is precise and useful, is it too technical for the situation? Is a vague word being used to smooth over vague thinking? Would fewer words do the job? Is the word on the "worthless list"?

What can a non-lawyer do about legal jargon? First, learn to recognize it. Legal language is less imposing once the garbage is stripped away. Next, ask for a translation when something you hear is confusing. And finally, don't use it.

ABOUT THE AUTHOR

Mr. Oran is a graduate of Hamilton College and Yale Law School. He has practiced law in Connecticut and the District of Columbia. In addition, he has been Assistant Director of the National Paralegal Institute and Professor of Law at Antioch Law School. He has written professional and popular articles on paralegal education, psychiatry and law, poverty law and individual rights.

FINAL NOTE

This book was written with the needs of many different groups in mind: paralegals, law and pre-law students, legal secretaries, people in police and criminal justice work, administrators, social workers, businesspersons, foreign lawyers, lawyers who explain, rather than just practice the law and interested non-lawyers in general.

Because the dictionary covers many areas in which I have only a "reading" knowledge, I need suggestions for additional words and definitions. If you have any ideas, large or small, for the next edition, please send them to me care of West Publishing Company.

†